For Kathleen " Richard

Christmas 1989

from Mother

Merry Christmas
& good food !
Love Dad

Don't
Tell 'Em
It's Good
for 'Em

NANCY BAGGETT • RUTH GLICK
and GLORIA KAUFER GREENE

Don't Tell 'Em It's Good for 'Em

Times
BOOKS

Published by TIMES BOOKS
The New York Times Book Co., Inc.
Three Park Avenue, New York, N.Y. 10016

Published simultaneously in Canada by
Fitzhenry & Whiteside, Ltd., Toronto

Coordinating Editor: Rosalyn T. Badalamenti

Designed by Giorgetta Bell McRee/Early Birds

Library of Congress Cataloging in Publication Data

Baggett, Nancy, 1943–
    Don't tell 'em it's good for 'em.

    Includes index.
    1. Cookery, American.   2. Cookery (Natural foods)
I. Glick, Ruth, 1942–   . II. Kaufer Greene,
Gloria, 1950–   .   III. Title.
TX715.B148   1984   641.5   83-40087
ISBN 0-8129-1099-0

Manufactured in the United States of America

84 85 86 87   4 3 2 1

This book is for our spouses and children, who are the reasons we began cooking this way in the first place, and who eventually began each meal with the question, "Which Nutri-Step is this?"

Acknowledgments

While we are, of course, ultimately responsible for this book's content, it is a pleasure to acknowledge the encouragement and assistance we have received from many individuals. We would like to thank Bonnie Liebman and Michael F. Jacobson from the Center for Science in the Public Interest for their suggestions regarding nutritional information. We also received assistance from the Food and Nutrition Information Center of the USDA Agricultural Research Library, the National Cancer Institute, the National Academy of Sciences, and the American Heart Association. In addition, Geoffrey E. Greene, M.D., served as a consultant.

Norman Glick provided invaluable assistance in manuscript preparation and in solving complicated word processor problems. Charlie Baggett also gave technical assistance. We would especially like to thank Linda Hayes for her help and support from the book's conception to completion. Finally, our gratitude goes to all those friends and family members who enthusiastically tasted our recipes and offered suggestions.

Contents

Introduction

Ｉf you're reading this book, you're probably a lot like us. You're worried about the impact of your family's eating habits on their health. You've heard all those reports linking the typical American diet to a wide variety of diseases you'd rather not think about. And you'd like to improve your family's chances of living long, healthy lives—while still preparing food they enjoy.

But you grew up, as we did, in an era when nutritious cooking meant filling the family with lots of good red meat and plenty of eggs and creamy milk products. And all of us happily carried on this tradition once we had families of our own.

Of course, busier schedules did mean some adjustments in our cooking habits. Most of us were grateful for the growing number of appealing convenience foods on supermarket shelves. We didn't necessarily have to fix fresh vegetables or make our own cookies, snacks, French fries, and pot pies. We could rely on canned, frozen, and packaged versions.

If we were troubled by our diet at all, it was usually in terms of calories: how to consume less so we wouldn't gain weight. We thought the way to do that was to cut down on starchy foods, such as bread, pasta, potatoes, and beans.

But somewhere along the line, when we weren't looking, the rules began to change. Experts started questioning the typical American diet. First they said it contributed to digestive disorders, heart disease, and high blood pressure. Then they began to claim it increased the chance of getting many types of cancer. They strongly recommended that we cut back drastically on all our fatty, salty, sugary foods and increase our consumption of fresh fruits and vegetables (particularly those rich in vitamins A and C), whole grains, and legumes.

Like most Americans, we wanted to ignore the ominous rumblings. They contradicted everything we had learned at our mothers' stoves. However, there was finally just so much convincing evidence that we felt compelled to consider a change.

But how to proceed? The experts' advice sounded straightforward and logical, yet, as any family cook knows, logic plays very little part in what household members will—or will not—eat. And the only sources of information we could find were far-out health food cookbooks or those designed for people with serious medical problems. Some of these books expected us to substitute veggie-burgers, bean loaf, and tofu pie for fried chicken, sloppy joes, and cheesecake. Others cut out *all* the salt or *all* the sugar from recipes. Family reactions when we tried to implement these drastic changes should have been predictable:

"What *is* this?"

"If we're having weird stuff for dinner again, I'm going out for pizza!"

"Don't you ever cook anything we *like* anymore?"

So we took another tack. What if favorite dishes could be made lower in fat, salt, and sugar and still taste good? Could we replace some of the meat in our spaghetti sauce and sloppy joes with vitamin-rich vegetables and still produce the taste and texture our families loved? Could we reduce the fat in our salad dressings, sauces, and desserts? Could we include more whole grains and beans in our menus? Could we "cook healthy"* in such a way that nobody would even know?

Admittedly we were skeptical. But we had all been developing recipes and writing about food for years, so we decided to try.

Since we had learned from our earlier dabblings in "health food" cookery that radical dietary shifts just wouldn't be accepted, our first improvements were very modest. Cautiously, we began by decreasing sugar in quick breads, substituting extra fresh vegetables for some of the meat in stews, and using a bit of lowfat yogurt in sour cream dips.

When no one seemed to notice, and family members even applauded our tasty meals, we were encouraged to take bolder steps. Gradually, we devised other ways to increase the healthfulness of recipes while still producing dishes our families considered "regular food."

As we talked about what we were doing and compared notes, we made a surpris-

---

*Specifically, the recipes in *Don't Tell 'Em It's Good for 'Em* are based on recommendations of the National Academy of Sciences' report *Diet, Nutrition and Cancer*, as well as those of other recognized authorities such as the American Heart Association.

ing discovery: We were actually reforming our families' tastes! Once they adapted to our first round of nutritional changes, we were able to continue making additional improvements in recipes without any resistance. For example, as soon as everybody got used to less sugar, some lowfat yogurt, and a bit of whole wheat flour in the "sour cream" coffee cake, we got brave enough to substitute egg whites for whole eggs. In the same way, after they accepted the reduced salt and ground vegetables in the spaghetti sauce and sloppy joes, we took away even more of the salt (compensating with a flavorful blend of herbs and spices) and replaced even more of the meat with vitamin-rich vegetables. If we made the new substitutions slowly and paid careful attention to seasonings and texture, nobody complained.

With a real sense of accomplishment, we realized that our children and spouses had learned to enjoy healthier versions of their favorite dishes. In fact, we were even able to include some new dishes like hearty vegetarian soups and casseroles in our repertoire.

We also began to share what we'd learned with friends. Their reactions were so positive that we wanted to reach an even wider audience. That's how this book came about.

The basic recipes are designed to appeal to average families. Our major emphasis is on nutritionally superior versions of popular American fare—spaghetti sauce, pot roast, buttermilk biscuits, and chocolate chiffon pie, for example—along with a sprinkling of less familiar dishes we're sure your family will like.

Right away you'll notice that the format of *Don't Tell 'Em It's Good for 'Em* is different from other cookbooks. Each basic recipe is followed by one or two or even three further improved variations we call "Nutri-Steps." These modifications will give you an opportunity to increase the wholesomeness of your own family's diet gradually, without anyone even noticing a change.

This book includes everything from main dishes to soups, salads, breads, snacks, and desserts. We feel these latter are just as important as the other recipes, because a dessertless diet makes most families feel deprived. Our solution has been to concentrate on adaptations of favorites that taste good and still keep fat, salt, and sugar to a minimum.

Although all of our basic recipes are more healthful than versions found in standard American cookbooks, none of them involves any difficult techniques or exotic ingredients. However, you may want to use a food processor—and in some cases a blender—in dishes calling for large quantities of chopped, grated, or ground vegetables.

We'd like to assure you that cooking more healthfully won't mean astronomical grocery bills. Although many of our recipes *do* call for fresh produce (which is sometimes more expensive than canned or frozen), you will be spending considerably less on expensive meat. And the whole grains and legumes used liberally throughout the book are one of the best bargains at the grocery store.

Good and healthful recipes are not all this book has to offer. We've also provided lots of quick tips to help you reform cooking habits and make improvements in your own personal collection of dishes. And we've even included a short table of more healthful substitutions for ingredients in standard recipes.

Here, then, is a volume that represents what we've learned while revolutionizing the diets of our own families. It can serve as a blueprint for you. And the best part is that each dish will be tailored to your family's specific needs and tastes. Our own families have enjoyed all the dishes in *Don't Tell 'Em It's Good for 'Em*, and have been enthusiastic tasters as recipes went through various stages of development. We hope that you'll enjoy them, too.

Don't
Tell 'Em
It's Good
for 'Em

Chapter 1

The Sad State of the American Diet

If you're uncertain about altering family eating habits, you may be interested in a summary of the information that helped *us* decide to take this step. Admittedly, it isn't light reading (you may even find it a bit scary), but the discussion that follows should give you enough facts to make a judgment for yourself.

To put it briefly, we Americans consume far too much fat, salt, and sugar, as well as too many smoked and salt-cured foods. Many experts feel this diet contributes to our high rates of cancer, heart and blood vessel diseases, and obesity.

TOO MUCH FAT

High fat consumption is the most dangerous American dietary habit. Excessive fat—mostly from meat, creamy dairy products, fried foods, and pastries—has been linked to various major health problems, including cancer of the breast, colon, and prostate. Dietary fat also plays a major role in the development of fatty deposits in the arteries (atherosclerosis), which, in turn, often leads to heart and circulatory problems, including strokes and heart attacks. In addition, because fat contains so many calories, it is also a major factor in obesity. (Fat has 9 calories per gram—compared to 4 calories per gram for protein or carbohydrate.)

How do researchers know that fat causes so many health problems? For one thing, they have compared the diets and disease rates of people in different nations. Where fat consumption is high, there is generally a high rate of atherosclerosis and heart disease as well as the cancers mentioned above. Where fat consumption is low, the reverse is generally true. Researchers have also noted similar effects in laboratory animals consuming high- versus low-fat diets.

Until recently it was generally thought that unsaturated fat (mostly from vegetable sources) was less harmful than saturated fat. However, more recent animal studies indicate that this is not necessarily so. Diets rich in unsaturated fat have been shown to produce a high incidence of malignant tumors in laboratory animals. As a result, researchers are now recommending that dietary fat *from all sources*, not just saturated fat, should be reduced.

At present, Americans typically obtain 40 percent of their daily calories from fat. The National Academy of Sciences Committee on Diet, Nutrition and Cancer suggests that decreasing fat consumption to 30 percent of our total calories is "a moderate and practical target." (The committee emphasizes, however, that scientific data could be used to justify an even greater reduction.)

HOLD THE SALT

Another unhealthy American dietary habit is eating too much salt. Although some salt is essential to good health, many of us consume up to twenty times the amount now recommended by most health experts.

The overwhelming majority of authorities agree that too much salt can lead to hypertension (high blood pressure) and ultimately to heart disease and strokes. (The National Institutes of Health estimates that about sixty million Americans have some degree of high blood pressure.)

Americans tend to assume that hypertension is a natural consequence of aging. However, in countries where sodium consumption is low, blood pressure tends to drop as people age. And researchers say that, for many people, moderating sodium intake throughout life can lower the chance of developing hypertension.

Notice that we used the word "sodium." This is because it is really sodium, not salt per se, that causes the problems. Actually, table salt is a mineral made up of sodium and chloride. Therefore, when salt intake is high, sodium intake is also high. Table salt is the major source of dietary sodium. But sodium also occurs naturally in significant amounts in a wide variety of foods, including milk products, some vegetables, eggs, and seafood.

Because salt is a flavor enhancer, it is also added liberally to many commercial food products, such as frozen dinners, seasoning mixes, potato chips and pretzels, pickles, and condiments, such as soy sauce and prepared mustard. To give some specifics, each of the following has about ½ teaspoon of salt: a 1-cup serving of canned or dehydrated soup, 2 slices of processed cheese, and a 1-cup serving of canned beef and macaroni.

These quantities may not seem high until you consider that The National Academy of Sciences recommends a *total* daily intake of between ½ and 1½ teaspoons of salt for healthy adults. So it's prudent to cut back on salty, processed foods and minimize the use of salt during cooking and at the table.

CURED MEATS

One of the most confusing issues confronting anyone who wants to eat healthfully is the problem of nitrate, nitrite, and nitrosamines. Although the relationship among these three chemicals and cancer may be a little hard to grasp, it is important. Nitrate is a harmless compound found abundantly in the environment. Along with nitrite, nitrate has been used for hundreds of years to "cure" meat to keep it from spoiling. The problem comes when preservative action or cooking gradually changes nitrate into more chemically active nitrite. Some of the nitrite in turn can combine in food or in the stomach with other compounds called amines, forming very powerful carcinogens known as nitrosamines. Since meat and fish are naturally high in amines, all the ingredients for trouble are right there in cured meat products. Nitrosamines are among the most potent carcinogens yet discovered and, in high concentrations, cause cancer in virtually all species of animals tested so far.

There are many vegetables, such as spinach and beets, which store nitrate from the soil. However, it does not convert readily to nitrite in fresh produce. Nitrite from vegetables becomes a problem only when produce is improperly stored or when long periods elapse between harvesting and eating—because it is the process of deterioration that changes the harmless nitrate into nitrite. What's more, many of these same vegetables are high in vitamin C, which has been found to block the formation of nitrosamines in the body. (There's more on the benefits of vitamin C in the next chapter.)

The smoking of meats, both on the home charcoal grill and during commercial curing, may be another problem. When meat is "bathed" in smoke, deposits called polycyclic aromatic hydrocarbons (PAHs) are formed on the surface. PAHs have been found to be mutagenic (that is, capable of causing cell changes), and thus are considered potential carcinogens. Indeed, in populations that consume large quantities of smoked meat, there is an increased incidence of cancer of the esophagus and stomach.

HOW SWEET IT ISN'T

Sugar is the most common additive in processed foods today. If your household enjoys a typical American diet, each family member consumes almost 130 pounds of sugar—in everything from desserts to breads, breakfast cereals and salad dressings— a year. That's 26 five-pound bags of sugar per person.

Many people assume that honey, molasses, brown sugar, turbinado sugar, and maple syrup are "healthier" than refined white sugar. But nutritionally speaking, they're all about the same. Except for molasses, which does contain small amounts of iron and other minerals, these sweeteners contribute nothing significant to the diet other than calories.

There are relatively few studies that specifically examine the effects of sugar on health. However, authorities are in almost universal agreement on several points. First, sugar promotes tooth decay. Second, researchers agree that high sugar consumption contributes to obesity. In turn, there is a correlation between being overweight and increased risk of developing a wide range of ailments—from high blood pressure and gallbladder disease to diabetes and even uterine cancer.

What's more, it's hard to get the nutrients your body requires if many of your calories are coming from sugar. It can quickly put you over the top of your daily calorie quota while leaving the body undersupplied with vitamins, minerals, protein, and fiber.

As you can see, current nutritional research paints a fairly grim picture of the American diet. However, understanding the problems is the first step in changing the situation. And there really is a positive side to all this. Unlike the generations before us, modern Americans have abundant food resources and the chance to *choose* what we want to eat. In short, we have the wonderful opportunity to avoid unhealthful foods and eat more of those that help keep us well.

To find out what you should be eating, turn to the next chapter.

Chapter 2

On the Road to Eating Right

Considering all the current criticism of the American diet, it might seem as if it's going to take a radical change in eating habits to make any real contributions to your family's health.

Fortunately, this is not the case. Most of us are already eating and enjoying the foods that experts say are especially beneficial. It's just that the emphasis in our diet should be altered a bit. We should be consuming more fresh vegetables—particularly certain varieties—and fruits. We should be obtaining more of our protein from low-fat sources, such as whole grains, legumes, chicken, and fish. And we should be consuming more fiber from a wide variety of plant sources. In a way, eating more healthfully is simply a matter of making the diet more balanced instead of relying too heavily on certain food groups (as many of us have done in the past).

There are a number of reasons why experts are now recommending this shift in emphasis. Here's a summary of their findings and of the positive dietary steps you can take to protect your family's health.

"EAT YOUR VEGETABLES—
THEY'RE GOOD FOR YOU"

Everybody has known for years that fresh vegetables and fruits provide vitamins, minerals, and roughage (fiber). But this isn't the only reason nutritionists have decided we should eat more of them. There are strong indications that certain varieties actually help prevent some of our most feared diseases.

The Carotenes

Fruits and vegetables that are rich in carotene (a pre-vitamin which the body converts to vitamin A), appear to have some wonderful health-promoting properties. In this category are many of the bright green and yellow-orange fruits and vegetables, such as carrots, spinach, cantaloupe, apricots, squash, broccoli, and peaches. (For a more complete list of carotene-rich varieties, see the end of this section.)

A growing number of both population studies and animal experiments have indicated that consuming plants high in carotene helps protect the body against certain types of cancer. Approximately twenty separate studies done on populations as diverse as Norwegian men, Chinese women in Singapore, and middle-aged male Chicago factory workers all revealed a lower incidence of lung cancer in those individuals who consumed large amounts of carotene-rich foods. In the Chicago survey, protective effects seemed to extend even to men who had been smoking most of their adult lives. There is also evidence, both from animal and population studies, that carotene may protect against cancers of the breast, bladder, and skin.

Researchers note that rather than taking vitamin A tablets, it's best to rely on natural sources of carotene—fruits and vegetables—and let the body convert it to vitamin A as needed.

Some Good Sources of Carotene

apricots
broccoli
Brussels sprouts
carrots
cherries
chives
collard greens
endive
garden cress
grapefruit
green onions (tops only)
mustard greens
kale

parsley
peaches
peppers (green, red bell, hot, pimiento)
pumpkin
rutabaga
spinach
sweet potato (sometimes called yams)
Swiss chard
tomatoes
watercress
winter squash (acorn, hubbard, butternut, etc.)

Vitamin C-Rich Fruits and Vegetables

Fruits and vegetables rich in vitamin C (ascorbic acid) also have special health-promoting qualities. Nearly everyone knows that citrus fruits, particularly oranges, are high in this vitamin, but it may come as a surprise to learn that sweet (bell) peppers are actually one of the very best sources. (A list of vitamin C-rich fruits, vegetables, and herbs appears at the end of this section.)

Most of us were taught the importance of ascorbic acid in maintaining healthy body tissues and in preventing the deficiency disease scurvy. However, there is another equally important reason for making sure you get enough of this vitamin. Population studies and animal experiments have suggested that vitamin C also helps prevent cancer of the stomach and esophagus by blocking the formation of nitrosamines, highly carcinogenic chemicals which are present in some foods and are also produced during digestion.

Because of ascorbic acid's remarkable blocking action, some researchers are now saying that it's a good idea to consume a vitamin C-rich fruit or vegetable at every meal. This is especially important when cured meats are eaten, because the ingredients for producing nitrosamines—amines and nitrite—are present in large amounts. (Chapter 1 has a more complete discussion of the nitrosamine problem.)

Some Good Sources of Vitamin C

bean sprouts	lemons
broccoli	limes
Brussels sprouts	okra
cabbage	oranges
cantaloupe	parsley
cauliflower	peppers (green, red bell, hot,
chives	pimiento)
collard greens	plums
garden cress	spinach
grapefruit	strawberries
green onions (tops only)	Swiss chard
kale	watercress

The Cruciferous Vegetables

The cabbage, or cruciferous, family of vegetables (which includes kale, Brussels sprouts, broccoli, cauliflower, collard greens, garden cress, watercress, kohlrabi, rutabaga, turnip, and cabbage itself) likewise seems to have special cancer-preventing properties. Laboratory animals fed a diet high in cabbage, cauliflower, or Brussels sprouts, for example, exhibit lowered cancer rates, even when exposed to carcinogenic substances. Although the way these vegetables provide protection is not yet well understood, research suggests that they stimulate the production of an anti-cancer enzyme.

There is evidence that cabbage and its relatives may help prevent cancer in humans as well. A number of population studies have indicated that people who eat large amounts of cruciferous vegetables have a lower risk of cancer, especially of the gastrointestinal tract.

GRAINS—NOT JUST FOR THE BIRDS

In the past, whole grains were a much more important part of the American diet than they are today, and authorities are advising that we once again take advantage of the full range of varieties available—including wheat, barley, oats, rye, rice, millet, and corn. Fortunately, increasing consumption is easy for most families because nearly everyone loves hearty, full-flavored breads and side dishes featuring grains. Moreover, they are relatively inexpensive.

One of the reasons experts recommend these foodstuffs is that they're very satisfying without contributing a lot of fat to the diet. Despite what many people think, grains are not particularly high in calories. (Remember, *all* carbohydrates contain only 4 calories per gram, compared to 9 calories per gram for fats.)

The reason for the misconception may be that grain products are often combined with other, very fattening, ingredients. For example, it's not the dark bread you have at lunch that will put on the pounds. It's the ham, cheese, and mayonnaise tucked in between the slices! Nor is it the whole wheat flour in your piece of coffee cake; it's the shortening, sugar, sour cream, and nuts. (In *our* recipes for baked goods, these ingredients are kept to a minimum.)

Notice that when we talk about increased grain consumption, we stress whole grains—those containing the bran and germ as well as the other parts of the kernel. These are good sources of the B vitamins and fiber as well as protein and iron. In highly refined grain products (which omit the bran and germ), many of the beneficial nutrients are removed. To compensate, food manufacturers often replace a few of the missing elements artificially and then label the resulting products "enriched." However, most of what was removed is not put back—particularly fiber and certain trace minerals. This means that when it comes to grains, less refining is more.

LEGUMES—PROTEIN IN SMALL PACKAGES

It's no coincidence that we're discussing grains and legumes (dried beans and peas) one right after the other. Together they make a powerful nutritional team. When eaten at the same time, they "complement" one another and provide protein that is every bit as good as that from meats and dairy products. Not only that, but plant protein sources are generally much lower in fat than animal sources.

Grains and beans are referred to as being "complementary" because each has certain important nutritional elements the other lacks. Actually, legumes—which include peanuts, split peas, soybeans, kidney beans, lentils, black-eyed peas, and many other varieties—are the richest sources of vegetable protein. But they are low in some of the essential amino acids (building blocks of protein) necessary to sustain life. Grains happen to contain abundant amounts of the amino acids in which legumes are deficient.

The concept of relying on grain and bean dishes rather than on large quantities of meat for high-quality protein isn't as startling as it may seem. In much of the world, people depend on such combinations for most of their protein. Consider the following duos: Mexican tortillas (corn) and beans, Italian white beans and pasta (wheat), or Chinese tofu (soybeans) and rice.

Experts are now recommending that Americans, too, make beans, along with grains, a larger part of our diet. Besides being lower in fat than animal protein sources, these foods are abundantly available and are relatively inexpensive. Moreover, they are excellent sources of fiber.

Nutritionists do stress, however, that dried beans should always be thoroughly cooked before they are eaten. Unlike most leafy vegetables, legumes become more appetizing during long cooking and are far easier for the body to digest. (Although bean sprouts are, of course, grown from dry beans, it's perfectly all right to eat them raw. In fact, due to the chemical changes that occur during germination, bean sprouts are most nutritious when eaten raw or only lightly cooked.)

FIBER—BACK TO BULK

In our discussions of leafy vegetables, fruits, grains, and beans, we've mentioned that these are all good sources of fiber—what folks used to call "roughage." Fiber comes only from plant sources, not from foods of animal origin.

It may sound surprising, but fiber has no actual nutritional value, because it consists of the plant parts which are *not* digested or absorbed into the human body. Nevertheless, there is ample evidence that fiber plays an important role in good health.

Plants provide two basic types of fiber: soluble and insoluble. The body makes use of both, so it's important to eat foods containing both kinds on a daily basis.

Soluble fibers, which are especially plentiful in legumes, oats, corn, and fruit, are thought to help keep blood sugar from rising steeply. A number of studies have suggested that a diet high in soluble fiber also lowers blood cholesterol levels and thus may reduce risk of heart disease.

Insoluble fiber, such as that from wheat bran, helps keep the lower digestive tract in good working order. Moreover, some researchers believe it may provide protection against cancer of the large intestine either by diluting or by "binding up" and carrying away carcinogenic chemicals.

Fiber has another important benefit. While contributing almost no usable calories to the human body, it has a lot of volume and also must be chewed well. Thus, high fiber foods do a good job of filling you up without filling you out!

As you can see, eating more healthfully doesn't mean clearing out the pantry and the refrigerator and starting all over again. But it does mean de-emphasizing some foods and making a point of serving some others much more often. (Our recipes are, of course, designed with this in mind.) For some specific tips on how to put these general guidelines into practice in your own kitchen, turn to the next chapter.

Chapter 3

Easy Tips for Cooking More Healthfully

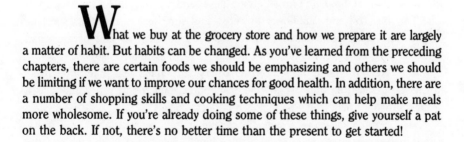

What we buy at the grocery store and how we prepare it are largely a matter of habit. But habits can be changed. As you've learned from the preceding chapters, there are certain foods we should be emphasizing and others we should be limiting if we want to improve our chances for good health. In addition, there are a number of shopping skills and cooking techniques which can help make meals more wholesome. If you're already doing some of these things, give yourself a pat on the back. If not, there's no better time than the present to get started!

TIPS FOR EATING MORE FRUITS AND VEGETABLES

● Take care not to bruise fresh produce. Bruising not only speeds deterioration, but it can also cause a loss of vitamins A and C.

● Prepare more stews, soups, casseroles, and similar meat-and-vegetable

13

combinations. Gradually increase the variety and quantity of vegetables in these dishes and reduce the amount of meat.

● Be careful not to overcook vegetables. They taste better when served "crisp-tender," and more of their nutrients are preserved.

● Most vegetables can be cooked by "steaming" in a small amount of water (an inch deep or less) or by using a special steamer insert in your saucepan (or a full-fledged steamer). Use leftover cooking water in homemade broths to add nutrients and flavor.

● "Sneak" additional healthful vegetables into the family diet by chopping or grating them very finely, and mixing them into sauces, casseroles, stews, and soups. This will not only boost the nutritional score of recipes, but will enrich the flavor as well.

● Use a small amount of ground, finely chopped, or grated vegetables to stretch ground meat for chili, meatloaves, meat sauces, etc. You'll save money, cut down on fat, and get the nutritional benefits of the vegetables.

● Slip some finely chopped, grated, or puréed carotene-rich vegetables, such as carrot, pumpkin, and winter squash, into baked goods. These vegetables can really improve the taste and texture of quick breads and desserts. (For example, see our recipes for Pumpkin Bread and Spicy Carrot Cake.)

● Make a habit of grinding up and using the parts of some vegetables that are ordinarily discarded, like broccoli stems and leaves, cauliflower and cabbage cores, peels from well-scrubbed potatoes (but NOT green-tinged areas or sprouted eyes) and carrots, beet leaves, celery leaves, and green onion (scallion) tops. These not only contain many vitamins and minerals, they are also very flavorful.

● For appetizers and snacks, frequently serve an attractive assortment of raw vegetables, such as carrots, green and/or red bell peppers, celery, broccoli and cauliflower flowerets, string beans, cucumber, cherry tomatoes, and zucchini, along with a tasty lowfat dip. Don't forget about these same raw vegetables for tossed salads. Tiny broccoli and cauliflower flowerets and shredded carrots are especially tasty in the salad bowl. Also, include shredded cabbage as one of the salad "greens." Red cabbage, in particular, makes a festive addition.

● Keep trimmed, washed carrots, celery, and similar vegetable "munchies" in the refrigerator, so they are available whenever someone in your family has a "snack attack." Fresh fruit also makes a perfect snack.

● Stretch meals with side dishes that emphasize vegetables and fruits, rather than serving large amounts of highly-refined white bread and butter, or fatty, sugar-laden desserts.

● For dessert, make fresh fruit tempting and "special" by slicing and attractively arranging it on a fancy serving tray. Or, dress it up with a dollop of lowfat vanilla yogurt or a small scoop of refreshing sherbet (see the Index for recipes). Don't ever say, "We're not having dessert—just fruit."

● Nutritionally, frozen vegetables and fruits are the best substitute when fresh produce is unavailable. Frozen fruits and vegetables will best maintain their nutritive value (and fresh taste) if stored at 0 degrees Fahrenheit or colder. If kept warmer than this, they may lose up to three fourths of their vitamins in one year of freezer storage.

● Use chopped vegetables and fruits along with or instead of bread cubes as poultry stuffing.

● Use puréed vegetables to make soups thick and creamy tasting, as well as flavorful. (See the Soups chapter for examples.)

● Brighten dinner platters with a slice or section of fresh fruit, especially one that is high in Vitamin C and carotene. Be creative and make garnishes especially appealing and appetizing. For instance, use toothpicks or wooden skewers to make "mini-kebabs" from peeled citrus sections, or cut a melon into thin slices and set one perfect grape or fresh cherry on top of each slice.

TIPS FOR EATING MORE WHOLE GRAIN FOODS AND LEGUMES

● Use whole grain and sprouted-grain sandwich loaves for brown-bag lunches and other meals. If family members are new to whole grain bread, you might "break them in" with milder-flavored cracked wheat or part whole wheat bread. Also, try whole wheat English muffins, pita bread, and rolls, as well as some of the muffins and quick breads in this book. (When looking for whole wheat commercial products, don't be misled by the terms "wheat flour" or "wheat bread" on a label, as these may not mean *whole* wheat flour or bread.)

● Serve whole grain side dishes as a nice change from pasta or potatoes. (Our chapter on Grain and Legume Side Dishes will give you some ideas.)

● Substitute brown rice for white rice at some meals. To help your family adjust to the difference in taste, cook brown rice in well-seasoned broth; stir in some sautéed onions and a few raisins; then call it "pilaf." Bulgur wheat, buckwheat groats, and whole millet, which make great alternatives to rice, can also be cooked in the same way. Like white rice, these three take only about 20 minutes each to cook. (See our recipes using these grains.)

● Don't overlook the many whole grain crackers now available. These include a variety of Scandinavian-style 100-percent rye crackers, whole wheat crackers, corn chips, and others. Use the labels as a guide in choosing those brands with the least amount of salt and fat.

● When choosing breakfast cereals, emphasize unsweetened, whole grain ones, such as bran flakes and shredded wheat. For hot cereals, cook rolled or steel-cut oats, un-degerminated cornmeal, bulgur wheat, millet, buckwheat, rye flakes, and other whole grains with extra water to turn them into a delicious, satisfying breakfast "mush" like the kind the pioneers enjoyed. Try combining a variety of grains for new flavors and textures. Also, mix some whole grain flours into pancake batters.

● Use small amounts of wheat germ and bran along with whole wheat bread crumbs as toppings on casseroles and as a filler in meatloaves and patties. Bread crumbs are easy to make in a food processor or blender. Extras keep well in an airtight container in the freezer, and can even be used frozen. When "dry" bread crumbs are needed, make them from slightly stale or crisply toasted bread.

● Make your own whole wheat croutons by cutting slices of whole wheat bread into ½-inch cubes. Spread the cubes on a baking sheet, and toast them in a 300-degree oven until they are dry. Cool croutons completely; then store in an airtight container.

● Try substituting whole wheat flour for some of the white flour in baking. A little whole wheat flour will hardly be noticed, especially in spicy cakes. (Very light sponge cakes, angel food cakes, and white layer cakes may be exceptions.) In fact, the flavor and texture of some muffins and coffee cakes may actually be improved with some whole wheat flour. [Note: The all-purpose whole wheat flour now stocked in most supermarkets is quite satisfactory for just about all baking. However, if you have access to a health food store, you may wish to try whole wheat pastry flour and whole wheat bread flour. Whole wheat *pastry* flour (a "soft," low-gluten flour) can be used for all non-yeast baking—including cakes, muffins, cookies, pancakes and waffles—to produce results almost as light as with all-white flour. Whole wheat *bread* flour (a high-gluten flour), on the other hand, helps yeast-raised breads, rolls and pastries rise higher and be lighter. Graham flour, the kind originally used to make graham crackers, is basically the same thing as all-purpose whole wheat flour.]

● Try whole wheat pasta (which is available at some supermarkets and most health food stores) in family meals. At first, incorporate it into spicy, saucy dishes where it will be accepted easily, or mix it with some regular pasta for an interesting contrast in taste and texture.

TIPS FOR DECREASING THE FAT IN YOUR DIET

● Include more chicken and fish in your menus, as these are generally lower in fat than red meat. When buying beef, pork, and veal, choose only lean cuts, and trim all visible fat before cooking. (Remember that USDA "prime" meat is the fattiest, followed by "choice" and then "good." Some stores also carry very lean grass-fed beef, which may be labeled "lean.")

● Get in the habit of broiling, baking, steaming, poaching, or "oven-frying" foods instead of pan-frying or deep-frying in large amounts of fat. (See our "oven-fried" chicken and fish recipes.)

● Roast meat on a rack so that the fat drips off and can be discarded. Set shish kebab skewers on the edges of a roasting pan so that the fat from the marinade and meat can drain into the pan. (See the recipe for Shish Kebabs.)

● Cut way down on the fat needed for sautéing and browning by using nonstick skillets with well-bonded coatings (such as Silverstone). You can also cook eggs and pancakes in this sort of skillet with little or no fat.

● If oil must be used to cook patties or pancakes, use only a teaspoon or two and spread it all over the skillet with a paper towel. Reserve the greased paper towel and simply rub it over the skillet again if a little more oil is needed.

● Ground meat can almost always be browned without adding the extra fat called for in some recipes, even if a nonstick skillet is not available. Simply begin cooking over medium heat until the meat releases some fat; then raise the heat to medium high.

● When browning meat (especially ground meat), spoon off or drain away all excess fat released into the skillet or pot. Also, "blot" cooked meat patties, strips, or chops on a double thickness of paper towels before serving.

● When sautéing onions with ground meat, do not use extra oil or butter; simply cook the onions in the fat from the meat. Then, spoon off or drain away any excess fat.

● Try substituting nonstick vegetable sprays for grease on baking pans and in casseroles. These sprays (most of which are made from a natural substance called lecithin) spread farther than ordinary fat and often do a better job of preventing sticking, so you can use much less. Look for the pump-style bottle, as this lets you control the direction and amount of spray and avoids the problem of inhaling an aerosol.

● Since most chicken fat is in and under the skin, get in the habit of removing and discarding the skin (and any surface fat) before cooking chicken. This not only lowers fat content and calories quite a bit, but it also allows the meat to absorb the flavorings and spices better.

● When buying tuna, sardines, and other canned fish, look for those packed in water, tomato sauce, mustard, and other non-oil dressings. If you must use oil-packed fish, drain it well.

● Before making gravy, refrigerate meat drippings so that the chilled and hardened fat can be lifted off the top and discarded. Use the same technique for removing fat from soups and stews.

● If onions stick to the pan or begin to burn during sautéing, add a tablespoon or two of water (or broth) and cook until all the liquid evaporates. This lets you use a minimal amount of fat, and still avoid sticking problems.

● Cut back on fat-laden salad dressings, gravies, and sauces. Rather than let family members "overdress" foods, serve dishes already sauced.

● Often, no one will notice that the total amount of dressing on tossed salad has been reduced if you make the salad itself more interesting. Include some "unusual" vegetables, such as snow peas, red cabbage, or fresh bean sprouts, and sprinkle fresh herbs on top. Add homemade croutons prepared by cubing and toasting leftover bread.

● To cut fat in salad dressings, make your own using lowfat yogurt, buttermilk, and flavored vinegars (see our herb vinegar recipes). Cut way down on the classic proportion of 3 parts oil to 1 part vinegar by trying a mixture of half oil and half vinegar, or use even a smaller proportion of oil.

● "Cut" mayonnaise in salad dressings with some plain yogurt. Begin with 1 part yogurt for every 3 parts mayonnaise, and gradually increase the ratio of yogurt to mayonnaise each time you use the mixture in a particular recipe.

● When selecting dairy products, emphasize milk, cottage cheese, and yogurt labeled "lowfat" or "skimmed," as well as commercial buttermilk (which is actually cultured skim milk), part-skim ricotta cheese, and ice milk. Some supermarkets and specialty cheese shops now carry lowfat or part-skim hard and semi-soft cheeses, including part-skim mozzarella, Longhorn, and Jarlsburg. (Check labels carefully to be sure these cheeses are actually lower in fat than "regular" versions.)

● In baking, substitute lowfat or regular plain yogurt for part or all of the sour cream. Cakes will be lower in fat and calories, and the yogurt will give them a good flavor.

● Well-chilled evaporated milk (regular, lowfat, and skimmed) can actually be whipped just like cream, and used to make delicious lowfat desserts. (One of our recipes which uses this technique is Frozen Lemon Mousse.)

● If you have a family of ice cream and other frozen dessert lovers, try making some of your own lowfat sherbets.

● Remember that although nuts and seeds (and nut butters) contain many useful nutrients, they are also very high in fat and calories. (There is more fat in 1/2 cup of most nuts than in a 3-ounce package of cream cheese!) If you do use nuts, purchase them raw or dry-roasted, and preferably unsalted. (Keep in mind that peanuts are actually legumes and should not be eaten raw.)

● Since virtually all the fat of whole eggs is in the yolk, omit some yolks in cooking and baking and use extra whites instead. In recipes that use eggs primarily as a binder (such as meatloaves or meatballs), as well as many recipes for cakes and other baked goods, try substituting 2 large egg whites for 1 whole large egg, or 3 egg whites for 2 whole eggs. (When separating eggs for these sorts of substitutions, the whites don't have to be completely free of yolk, unless they are to be beaten to peaks as part of the recipe.)

● Use unsweetened plain cocoa powder instead of baking chocolate whenever possible. Cocoa powder provides the same rich taste as chocolate but is much less fatty, because most of the cocoa butter has been removed. To cut fat still further, use "dark" carob powder in recipes calling for plain cocoa powder. Although it doesn't taste exactly like cocoa, carob powder (particularly the dark-roasted style) has a similar look and flavor, and is much lower in fat and calories. Also, unlike cocoa, carob does not contain caffeine.

TIPS FOR DECREASING THE SALT IN YOUR DIET

● Substitute other natural seasonings for salt. Experiment with lemon juice, flavored vinegars, aromatic bitters, wine, onion, garlic, horseradish, dry mustard, hot pepper sauce, ground black pepper, herbs (such as basil, parsley, chives, thyme, oregano, marjoram, sage, rosemary, dill, mint, chervil, bay leaf, etc.), and spice blends, such as curry powder and chili powder. For convenience, mix up some of your own herb/spice blends (see our recipe suggestion), and use them at the table as well as in cooking. If your family objects to bits of herb leaves in food, process the herbs in a blender or food processor until very finely ground. Don't hesitate to double or even triple the amount of herbs called for in conventional recipes.

● Do not put salt shakers on the table. If diners insist on having something to "shake" on their food, offer them black pepper or, perhaps, a finely ground herb blend. Encourage everyone to taste food before adding seasonings.

● If you like the convenience of using onion salt or garlic salt for flavoring, substitute onion or garlic *powder* or *flakes* which have no added salt.

● Soy sauce and Worcestershire sauce, as well as many other commercial seasonings and condiments, contain a lot of salt. Use these products in moderation.

● Read labels very carefully. Look out not only for the ingredient "salt," but also for the word "sodium" or its scientific abbreviation, "Na." Also, watch out for monosodium glutamate (MSG), a high-sodium flavor enhancer used in many processed foods.

● Look for the unsalted canned vegetables that many supermarkets now stock on regular (not dietetic) shelves. Although we generally prefer fresh or frozen produce, these unsalted canned vegetables may be substituted in a pinch.

● Note that seltzer, club soda, and soda water often contain salt. Choose those brands labeled "no salt added."

● Decrease or eliminate the salt used in non-yeast baking. It's quite unlikely you will miss it at all, especially if the baked product includes salted butter or margarine. (In yeast-raised breads, salt plays a role in the reaction of the yeast; however, salt can still usually be decreased by at least one-third or more without any noticeable difference.) Remember that both baking soda and, in smaller proportion, baking powder contain sodium.

● When cooking pasta, don't add salt to the water. If you wish, add a few drops of lemon juice instead. Grains can be cooked in lightly salted broth seasoned with herbs and spices. Vegetables taste best when steamed and then seasoned with herbs or a light sauce.

● Before using canned fish packed in salted liquid, drain well; then rinse the fish off by filling the can with tap water and draining again. Or, simply take the extra salt into consideration when preparing the fish.

● To improve the flavor of salt-free homemade stocks, cook them down with some puréed vegetables and herbs until the flavor is concentrated. (If desired, strain the stocks before using.)

● Use fewer processed foods, as these are often very high in salt. Some examples of high-sodium products are commercial sauces and gravies, canned soups, most canned vegetables, pickles and relishes, olives, cured meats, processed cheese, quick-cooking cereals, self-rising flours and biscuit mixes, and prepared heat-and-eat foods, such as frozen dinners and fish sticks.

● Try to avoid salt-coated snacks, such as potato chips, corn chips, pretzels, crackers, and nuts. (Many of these are also high in fat.) Instead, emphasize fresh fruit and raw vegetables.

TIPS FOR DECREASING THE SUGAR IN YOUR DIET

● Recipes in many traditional cookbooks (especially older ones) often call for far greater amounts of sugar and other sweeteners than are actually needed for good taste and texture. Try using only two thirds to three fourths of the sugar suggested. (In our recipes, we've already made these adjustments for you.)

● Try to avoid sugar-laden soft drinks. Instead, substitute unsweetened fruit juice mixed with seltzer or club soda. Be wary of fruity beverages called "-ade" or "drink," as these contain very little real fruit juice and are mostly water, sugar, and artificial flavoring or coloring.

● To cut down on sugar in coffee and tea, try flavoring them with spices that give the "illusion" of sweetness. For instance, mix ground cinnamon or cardamom into ground coffee before brewing, or stir tea with cinnamon sticks. You may also want to try some of the unsweetened flavored teas now available.

● Pancakes, waffles, French toast, muffins, and quick breads may also seem sweeter when seasoned with spices, such as cinnamon, cardamom, nutmeg, and ginger, as well as extracts like vanilla, almond, orange, and maple.

● Fresh fruit purées (especially ripe banana, pineapple, and apple) and bits of chopped dried fruit add natural sweetness and give good flavor to baked goods, pancakes, etc., so less sugar is needed.

● Avoid overly sweetened snacks and heavily sugared cereals. (Be aware that some so-called natural snacks and granolas may contain a lot of sugar. After all, sugar is "natural.") Instead, provide cut-up raw vegetables, fresh fruit, or unbuttered, unsalted (or lightly salted) popcorn for snacks. Don't pack sugar-laden desserts, such as commercial cookies, cakes, and candies, in brown-bag lunches.

● Avoid using boxed gelatin mixes and puddings. These highly processed foods are loaded with sugar, not to mention artificial colorings and flavorings.

● Mix plain, lowfat yogurt with pure, frozen fruit juice concentrates, unsweetened puréed fruit, or jars of unsweetened strained "baby" fruit, as an alternative to the pre-flavored yogurts, which are typically laden with jams and corn syrup.

• Make your own frozen "pops" for summer treats. For clear "ice pops," just freeze pure fruit juice (one kind or a mixture—orange juice is especially good) in plastic pop molds, or use paper cups and insert sticks when the juice is partially frozen. For "yogurt pops," flavor yogurt as suggested in the previous tip, and freeze. Or, try our Orange Yogurt Pops (page 285).

• Plain, frozen bananas make wonderful, naturally-sweet snacks that taste almost as rich as ice cream. Peel ripe (but not overripe) bananas and cut them in half crosswise. If desired, insert a popsicle stick (available at craft or toy stores) into each cut end. Tightly wrap each banana half in plastic, or freeze several in an *airtight* freezer container. They will not darken if kept tightly wrapped and eaten within a week or two. Enjoy banana "pops" right out of the freezer. [*Note:* Frozen (and thawed) bananas can also be used in baking. They darken as they thaw, but this doesn't affect the finished baked goods. Be sure to peel the bananas before freezing, and wrap them airtight.]

• Try substituting unsweetened or very lightly sweetened apple butter or apple spread (available at health food stores, some supermarkets, and farmers' markets) for the jam in peanut butter sandwiches or as a spread on toast. (Also, see our recipes for Apple Butter or Pear Butter.)

• When buying frozen fruit, choose fresh-frozen (or "dry-pack") without added sugar. And, choose canned fruit packed in water or fruit juice instead of in light or heavy syrup.

• Try unsweetened canned or bottled applesauce (now stocked by most supermarkets) or make your own. Instead of using tart apples, as many recipes recommend, try naturally sweet ones, such as McIntosh or Golden Delicious, and cook them in a little cider or apple juice. If unsweetened applesauce needs some "zip," mix in a dash of cinnamon, nutmeg, and/or allspice.

• Dark-roasted carob powder (available in health-food stores and some supermarkets) looks and tastes similar to cocoa, but it's naturally sweeter, and needs less sugar. Try replacing some cocoa with carob powder in baked goods, puddings, etc., and cut down the sugar about one fourth.

• Dilute commercial pancake syrup with a little water so that it goes further, and less is used. (*Real* maple syrup actually *is* thinner than "maple-flavored" pancake syrup. It seems nature has the right idea!)

• As a nice ending to a company meal, try the European custom of serving seasonal fresh fruit and very thin slices of special cheeses, rather than a rich dessert.

• Don't use sweets as a reward for good behavior for your children or yourself. There are so many other ways to show your love and appreciation for a job well done—such as going on a special family outing, playing a game, reading a story together, or buying a new book.

Chapter 4

How to Use These Recipes

You've probably already noticed that the recipes in *Don't Tell 'Em It's Good for 'Em* are presented in a new format. Here are some tips on how to use them to best advantage. Each recipe appears in complete basic form, followed by one or more Nutri-Steps. If there's only one Nutri-Step, the recipe is already so healthful that there is little need for further improvement. Other recipes that lend themselves more readily to nutritional revision are followed by one, two, or, sometimes, even three Nutri-Steps.

We recommend starting with the basic recipes, since they've been carefully designed to have wide appeal. Once your family becomes accustomed to the basic dish, you can move on to Nutri-Step 1.

We've found it's best not to advance through the Nutri-Steps too quickly. Give your family's tastes time to change. If you discover a more nutritious variation is less well accepted, just back up to the previous version.

Also, it isn't necessary to try every single Nutri-Step given. Sometimes you'll be so satisfied with a particular variation that you won't want to move on any further.

The recipes in *Don't Tell 'Em It's Good for 'Em* are designed to be as easy as possible to use. For example, here's a recipe for Zippy Coleslaw. Although the basic dish tastes remarkably like "regular" coleslaw, it is actually lower in fat and salt because it replaces some of the usual mayonnaise with lowfat yogurt and some of the salt with a flavorful herb and spice blend.

ZIPPY COLESLAW

¼	cup mayonnaise ●■
3	tablespoons plain lowfat yogurt ●■
1	tablespoon red wine vinegar or apple cider vinegar
1	tablespoon chopped fresh chives, or 1½ teaspoons dried chives
1	tablespoon chopped fresh parsley leaves
½	teaspoon sugar
⅛	teaspoon celery seed
⅛	teaspoon dried dillweed
⅛	teaspoon dry mustard
⅛	teaspoon salt ■
⅛	teaspoon black pepper, or to taste, preferably freshly ground
5½	cups shredded or grated cabbage
½	cup shredded or grated carrots
1	tablespoon finely chopped celery

Stir the mayonnaise and yogurt together in a small bowl. Add all the remaining seasonings and stir until well mixed.

Combine the vegetables and dressing in a serving bowl, tossing to mix. Serve immediately or cover and refrigerate until needed.

Yields 4 to 6 servings.

NUTRI-STEP 1

- Decrease the mayonnaise to 3 tablespoons.
- Increase the lowfat yogurt to ¼ cup.

NUTRI-STEP 2

- Decrease the mayonnaise to 3 tablespoons.
- Increase the lowfat yogurt to ¼ cup.
- Decrease the salt to a pinch or omit. ***And add*** a pinch of garlic powder.

To use the basic recipe, proceed exactly as you would with any recipe in a standard cookbook, ignoring the symbols after some ingredients. These symbols key you in to changes in the Nutri-Steps. The symbol ● indicates that the amount of an ingredient changes in Nutri-Step 1. The symbol ■ indicates the proportion changes in Nutri-Step 2. When there is a Nutri-Step 3, the ▲ symbol is used. (In one of the Nutri-Steps, notice that the words *"And add"* also appear. This will tell you that a new ingredient, not included in the basic recipe, has been *added*.)

There's one more point to keep in mind. The changes in each Nutri-Step are interdependent, since adjustments in one ingredient often affect others. For example, if you're asked to decrease the mayonnaise in a salad dressing, it's very likely that you'll be asked to increase something else. Therefore, always use each Nutri-Step as a unit.

A WORD ABOUT INGREDIENTS

A lot of thought has gone into the choice of ingredients in our recipes. Above all, we wanted to use food and seasonings that were healthful, but we also wanted to make sure the ones we called for would be readily available to the average cook.

As a result, we made a point of depending almost exclusively on typical American grocery stores for our cooking supplies. And, in nearly every case, you can use this book with products that come right off supermarket shelves.

Still, it's important to read labels and shop carefully. As you look through the chapters, you will notice that we're often very specific about ingredients. This is to control the amount of fat, salt, and sugar in recipes and at the same time increase the proportion of healthful ingredients.

For example, since one of the main goals of this book is to lower fat consumption, recipes frequently call for reduced-fat milk products, such as lowfat yogurt, lowfat milk, and nonfat dry milk. Higher-fat dairy products are used only in minimum quantities needed for good taste and texture, or when they offer a nutritional advantage. (For instance, in some recipes, sour cream replaces part of the mayonnaise that would normally be used. Sour cream is, of course, not low in fat, but it contains less than half the fat of commercial mayonnaise.)

As another fat-reducing measure, most of the basic recipes that use eggs give you the option of replacing whole eggs with all whites or with a higher proportion of whites than yolks. This is because it is the yolks that contain virtually all the fat and cholesterol, and these can often be removed without affecting taste or texture. As recipes grow progressively more healthful in the Nutri-Steps, egg yolks are usually decreased or omitted.

In a few of the baked goods, soy flour, which is high in protein, is used to boost nutrition. However, most soy flour is higher in fat than white or whole wheat flour. If you wish to avoid this additional fat, simply substitute an equal amount of whole wheat or white flour in recipes or Nutri-Steps that call for soy flour.

We've likewise made a point of cutting back on salt. For one thing, we never call for cooking vegetables, rice, or pasta in salted water. And when a recipe includes cooked rice or another grain product, we assume that it has also been prepared without salt.

In addition, a number of our recipes use tomato paste and tomato purée (which are often salt-free) instead of tomato sauce, which can be fairly salty. When tomato sauce is called for, we limit additional salt. In the same way, if a dish just won't taste right without a salty product like soy sauce, prepared mustard, ketchup, or bouillon, we restrict the amount and add no other salt—or very little—to the dish.

But that doesn't mean our food is bland. We've compensated for lowered salt by taking advantage of a wealth of herbs and spices and other seasonings, too, to make food taste delicious.

We've also been careful to reduce sugar in our recipes. In desserts and other dishes, we've relied as much as possible on the natural sweetness of fresh and dried fruits and fruit juices. But even in dishes without fruit, we've found we could use far less sugar than called for in traditional recipes—without significantly affecting good taste and texture. And there was no need to replace sugar with artificial sweeteners. In fact, our recipes almost never call for products with artificial colorings, flavorings, or flavor enhancers.

There are other types of foods we have also chosen to omit. For example, you'll notice that none of our recipes calls for cured, smoked, or pickled meats. This is because we wish to avoid the fat and salt in these products as well as nitrite and polycyclic aromatic hydrocarbons. (See Chapter 2 for a discussion of these.)

On the other hand, you may be struck by the fact that *Don't Tell 'Em It's Good for 'Em* includes an abundance of vegetables—and some interesting and innovative ways to use them. We've frequently slipped grated or ground vegetables into sauces, soups, and main dishes. And we've even used parts of vegetables—such as broccoli stems—which are usually discarded. Though this may seem a bit strange at first, we *assure* you that when used as called for, the camouflaged vegetables will actually help add rich flavor and texture.

Finally, we've provided a chapter with some "convenience foods" that can be quickly and easily prepared in your own kitchen. With homemade versions of familiar products you can control just how much fat, salt, and sugar goes into them.

Chapter 5

Soups

There are so many good things to say about soups that it's hard to know where to begin. We like them because it's possible to pack so much nutrition and flavor into a soup stock, because they make an easy and satisfying main dish, and because they're perfect for using up leftovers. We like soup so much that we'll often start a large pot in the morning, enjoy it for lunch, and then serve it to our families for supper.

Many of the recipes in this chapter rely on a flavorful combination of ground or grated vegetables simmered with the broth. In fact, we save broccoli and cauliflower stems, cabbage cores, and other "tough" vegetable parts especially for our stocks. These not only add extra vitamins and fiber, but they also enhance the flavor of the finished product.

Because there's such a rich blend of other ingredients, our meat soups need very little meat for flavor and are thus quite economical to serve. But even relatively small amounts of meat do add some fat. So we recommend that you "degrease" meat-based soups carefully before serving. The easiest method of doing this is to chill the soup until the fat solidifies on the surface. This solid layer can then be lifted off with a large spoon and discarded. If you are in a hurry and want to skip the chilling process, simply skim across the surface of the hot broth repeatedly with a large spoon until most of the fat has been "scooped up." Tipping the pot slightly to one side may make this easier.

A word about our creamy soups: They don't contain any cream! Most are made with lowfat milk products and grated or ground vegetables. These, along with careful seasonings, produce rich and satisfying flavors which your family will enjoy.

VEGETABLE–BEEF SOUP

4½	pounds beef soup bones (with little or no meat)
8	cups water
¼	cup dry navy beans, sorted and rinsed •
¼	cup dry baby lima beans, sorted and rinsed
3	cups coarsely chopped fresh cauliflower flowerets
2	cups coarsely chopped cabbage
3	medium-sized onions, coarsely chopped
1	large turnip, peeled and coarsely chopped
1	medium-sized rutabaga, peeled and coarsely chopped
½	cup chopped fresh parsley leaves
1	teaspoon Worcestershire sauce
½	teaspoon paprika
¼	teaspoon celery salt
⅛	teaspoon dried thyme leaves
¼	teaspoon black pepper, preferably freshly ground
1½	teaspoons salt •
1¼	pounds well-trimmed, boneless beef chuck arm, shank, or other lean stew beef, cut into ½-inch cubes •
4	medium-sized carrots, coarsely sliced
1	16-ounce can tomatoes, including juice, broken up with a spoon
2	large celery stalks, coarsely sliced
1	cup frozen corn kernels •

Combine the soup bones, water, dried beans, cauliflower, cabbage, onions, turnip, rutabaga, and all the herbs and seasonings in a large soup kettle or pot. Bring to a boil over medium-low heat. Reduce the heat, cover the pot, and simmer gently for 1 hour. Add the stew beef to the pot and continue simmering, covered, for 45 minutes longer. Add all the remaining ingredients and cook for 45 to 55 minutes longer, or until the vegetables and meat are tender. Remove the beef bones from the pot and discard them.

Makes about 3½ quarts of soup, or 8 to 9 servings.

Note: The soup may be served immediately or refrigerated for later use. If serving immediately, skim off and discard all the fat from the surface of the soup with a large spoon; tipping the pot slightly to one side may make this easier. If refrigerating first, lift off and discard the hardened layer of fat on top of the chilled soup before reheating. (While reheating, add a bit more water if the soup seems too thick.) Vegetable–Beef Soup also freezes well.

NUTRI-STEP 1

- Increase the dry navy beans to ⅓ cup.
- Decrease the salt to 1¼ teaspoons.
- Decrease the beef cubes to 1 pound.
- Increase the corn kernels to 1½ cups.

LAMB, BEAN, AND BARLEY SOUP

This soup will have a richer flavor if you ask your butcher to crack the shank bones.

4	lamb shanks (about 3 pounds)•
8	cups water
¼	cup uncooked pearl barley
¾	cup dry navy beans, washed and sorted
¾	cup peeled and finely chopped or shredded turnip •
1	large carrot, grated or shredded
1	celery stalk, including leaves, shredded
1	large onion, grated or shredded
1	clove garlic, peeled and minced
3	large bay leaves
½	teaspoon black pepper, preferably freshly ground
¼	teaspoon ground thyme
1¼	teaspoons salt •
½	teaspoon celery seed
¼	cup coarsely chopped fresh parsley leaves, or 2 tablespoons dried parsley flakes
2 to 3	drops hot pepper sauce
¼	teaspoon dry mustard
½	teaspoon ground marjoram
2	cups fresh string beans, trimmed and snapped

Combine all the ingredients except string beans in a large, heavy pot over high heat. Bring to a boil, lower the heat, and simmer, covered, for 2 hours, stirring occasionally. Add the string beans during the last 30 to 40 minutes of cooking.

When the soup is done, remove the lamb shanks. Cut the meat from the bones, carefully trimming off and discarding all fat and the bones. Return the trimmed meat to the pot. With a large spoon, skim off and discard the fat from the top of the soup. (Or refrigerate so that the fat can be easily lifted off.)

Makes 6 to 7 main-dish servings.

NUTRI-STEP 1

- Decrease the lamb shanks to three (about 2 to 2¼ pounds).
- Increase the turnip to 1 cup.
- Decrease the salt to a scant 1 teaspoon.

CURRIED TURKEY SOUP

Although loaded with healthful vegetables, this soup is so good even so-called vegetable haters usually like it. The secret is in the rich, savory curry flavor and in the fact that the vegetables are puréed (so nobody even knows they are there)!

1	tablespoon butter or margarine ●
1	large onion, coarsely chopped
1	large celery stalk, including leaves, coarsely chopped
¼	cup coarsely chopped red bell pepper, or substitute chopped green pepper if red is unavailable
2	large carrots, coarsely chopped
1	large turnip, peeled and coarsely chopped
1	cup coarsely shredded or chopped cabbage
½	cup coarsely chopped, unpeeled yellow or white (pattypan) squash
1	large unpeeled tart apple, cored and chopped
2	tablespoons raisins
6	cups water
1½	tablespoons curry powder
½	teaspoon mild chili powder
¼	teaspoon black pepper, preferably freshly ground
1⅛	teaspoons salt ●
2½ to 3	pounds turkey wings
1	cup canned garbanzo beans (chick-peas), well drained
1½	cups lowfat milk

In a 4-quart or larger soup pot or Dutch oven, melt the butter over medium-high heat. Add the onion, celery, and sweet pepper and cook, stirring, for 3 to 4 minutes, or until the vegetables are limp. Stir in all the remaining vegetables, apple, raisins, water, all spices, and salt. Add the turkey wings and bring to a boil. Lower the heat, cover, and simmer, stirring occasionally, for 1 hour and 35 to 45 minutes, or until the turkey is tender.

Remove the turkey wings from the pot and set aside to cool. Tip the pot slightly to one side; then, skim off and discard any fat floating on the surface of the soup with a large spoon. Purée the soup in batches, in a blender or food processor, until completely smooth. Return the puréed mixture to the pot. Purée the garbanzo beans with the milk in two batches, until completely smooth; then stir into the soup.

Remove all the meat from the turkey wings, and cut it into bite-sized pieces; discard the bones and skin. Stir the turkey meat into the soup. Reheat the soup over low heat, stirring occasionally, until piping hot but not boiling.

Makes about 2½ quarts of soup, or 6 to 8 servings.

NUTRI-STEP 1

- Omit the butter or margarine. Omit the sautéing of onion, celery, and sweet pepper. Instead, add all the vegetables to the pot at once, along with the apple, raisins, water, spices, and salt. Then add the turkey wings and proceed as directed.
- Decrease the salt to 1 teaspoon. *And add* a generous pinch of cayenne pepper along with the other spices.

CHUNKY CHICKEN AND VEGETABLES SOUP

This recipe features only simple, economical, and healthful ingredients. Yet, the finished soup is full-flavored and satisfying.

A considerable amount of fat may collect on the surface of the broth during cooking, so be sure to "degrease" the soup as directed in the recipe.

3   pounds bony chicken pieces (backs, wings, etc.), all visible fat removed
8   cups water
⅓   cup dry navy beans, picked over and rinsed
¼   cup uncooked pearl barley
1   large onion, chopped
2   tablespoons chopped fresh parsley leaves, or 1 tablespoon dried parsley flakes

3	tablespoons chopped fresh chives, or 1½ tablespoons dried chopped chives
¼	teaspoon dried marjoram leaves
¼	teaspoon dried basil leaves
1¼	teaspoons salt ●
	Generous ¼ teaspoon black pepper, preferably freshly ground ●
3	large carrots, coarsely sliced
2	large celery stalks, including leaves, coarsely chopped
1	cup frozen green peas
1	cup frozen corn kernels
¼	cup uncooked small elbow macaroni (or similar pasta)
1	16-ounce can tomatoes, including juice

In a large soup kettle or pot combine the chicken, water, and navy beans. Bring to a boil over medium-high heat. Cover, lower the heat, and simmer for 1½ hours. Remove the chicken from the pot and set it aside to cool. Degrease the soup by refrigerating it until the broth is cold and the fat solidifies on the surface; then lift off the layer of fat with a large spoon and discard it. (Alternately, omit the chilling process, and degrease the soup by skimming off all the fat from the surface of the broth using a large spoon.)

Add the barley, onion, parsley, chives, dried herbs, salt, pepper, carrots, and celery to the pot. Bring to a simmer and cook, covered, for 30 minutes. Stir the peas, corn, and macaroni into the pot. Simmer, covered, for 15 minutes longer.

Meanwhile, remove the chicken meat from the bones and cut the meat into bite-sized pieces; discard the skin and bones. Return the chicken meat to the pot; then add the tomatoes, breaking them up with a spoon. Simmer, covered, for 15 minutes longer and serve. The soup may also be refrigerated or frozen for later use.

Makes 3 quarts of soup, or about 8 servings.

NUTRI-STEP 1

- Decrease the salt to 1 teaspoon.
- Increase the black pepper to a scant ½ teaspoon. *And add* 1 cup shredded cabbage to the pot along with the peas, corn, and macaroni.

MANHATTAN-STYLE FISH CHOWDER

1	medium-sized onion, coarsely chopped
2	celery stalks, including leaves, finely chopped
2	tablespoons butter or margarine ●■
12 to 16	ounces fresh or frozen (thawed) flounder or halibut fillets, cut into large chunks
1	1-quart, 14-ounce can tomato juice
1	cup carrots, very thinly sliced
¾	cup fresh or frozen corn kernels
2	large bay leaves
¼	teaspoon dry mustard
½	teaspoon dried thyme leaves
2	medium-sized potatoes, peeled and cut into ¾-inch cubes
¾	teaspoon salt ●■
	Black pepper to taste, preferably freshly ground

In a large heavy saucepan or Dutch oven, over medium-high heat, cook the onion and celery in the butter until the onion is soft. Add all the remaining ingredients except the salt and pepper. Simmer, covered, for 30 to 35 minutes, stirring occasionally, or until the potatoes and carrots are tender. Add the salt and pepper and serve.

Makes 3 to 4 main-dish servings.

NUTRI-STEP 1

- Decrease the butter or margarine to 1 tablespoon.
- Decrease the salt to ½ teaspoon.

NUTRI-STEP 2

■ Decrease the butter or margarine to 1 tablespoon. ***And add*** 1 cup fresh broccoli flowerets or 1 cup fresh broccoli stems, peeled and cut in thin slices, along with the other vegetables.

■ Decrease the salt to ¼ teaspoon.

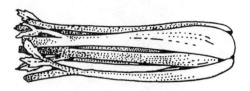

NEW ENGLAND-STYLE FISH CHOWDER

2½ cups water
1   pound fresh or frozen (and thawed) skinless lean white fish fillets, such
    as cod, haddock, turbot or flounder
2½ tablespoons butter or margarine •
2   medium-sized onions, finely chopped
1   clove garlic, peeled and finely minced
2   pounds potatoes, peeled and cut into ⅜-inch cubes (about 7 cups) •
1½ cups instant nonfat dry milk powder
1   cup cool water
2   cups frozen green peas
¼   teaspoon salt •
⅛   teaspoon black or white pepper, preferably freshly ground

Bring the water to a boil in a large skillet. Add the fish (in one layer, if possible), lower the heat, and simmer gently until done, about 10 to 15 minutes, depending on the thickness of the fillets. Remove the fish with a slotted spoon. Reserve 2 cups of the poaching liquid for the chowder broth. When the fish is cool enough to handle, flake it into large pieces and set aside.

Melt the butter in a 3- to 4-quart Dutch oven, saucepan, or soup pot. Add the onion and garlic, and cook, stirring often, until tender but not browned. Add the potatoes and mix in well. Then add the 2 cups of reserved fish poaching liquid. Bring to a boil, lower the heat, and simmer until the potatoes are soft, about 15 to 20 minutes. Remove from the heat.

Ladle about a third of the potatoes and liquid into a blender or food processor, and process until smooth. (Or mash with a fork.) Return the potato purée to the pot.

In a small bowl, mix the nonfat dry milk with the water until the milk powder is completely dissolved. Add this to the mixture in the pot, and stir well. Then add the reserved pieces of fish and the peas. Heat, stirring often, until the peas are tender and the chowder is hot. Season with salt and pepper.

Makes 6 to 8 servings.

NUTRI-STEP 1

- Decrease the butter or margarine to 2 tablespoons.
- Leave the potatoes unpeeled. Try to choose thin-skinned new potatoes and scrub them well before cutting in cubes.
- Decrease the salt to ⅛ teaspoon or omit.

LENTIL–RICE SOUP

1	cup dry lentils, sorted and rinsed
4	cups water, divided
½	cup uncooked white rice •
2	tablespoons butter or margarine •
1	medium-sized onion, finely chopped
2	cloves garlic, peeled and finely minced
1	medium-sized green pepper, seeded and finely chopped
2	celery stalks, including leaves, thinly sliced or diced •
3	cups chicken, beef, or vegetable broth or bouillon
1	teaspoon dried thyme leaves
1	teaspoon dried marjoram leaves
½	teaspoon salt •
¼	teaspoon black pepper, preferably freshly ground
2 to 4	tablespoons dry sherry (optional)

Put the lentils in a medium-sized saucepan with 3 cups of the water. Bring to a boil, lower the heat, and simmer for 20 minutes. Stir the rice into the lentils, and cook for 20 to 25 minutes longer, or until the lentils and rice are just tender. Mash the mixture slightly with a fork, then set it aside. (Do not drain off any of the excess liquid.)

Melt the butter in a Dutch oven or soup pot. Add the onion and garlic and sauté until tender but not browned. Add the green pepper and celery and sauté for a minute longer. Stir in the broth, the remaining 1 cup water, thyme, marjoram, salt, and pepper. Then add the lentil–rice mixture. Bring to a boil, lower the heat, and simmer for about 20 minutes, stirring occasionally. Stir in sherry, if desired.

Makes about 6 servings.

NUTRI-STEP 1

- Omit the uncooked white rice and SUBSTITUTE ½ cup uncooked brown rice. Add the uncooked brown rice to the lentils at the beginning of the cooking period, and cook them together for about 40 to 45 minutes.
- Decrease the butter or margarine to 1 tablespoon. Stir the onions and garlic often to make sure they don't stick.
- Increase the celery to 3 stalks.
- Decrease the salt to a generous ¼ teaspoon.

BEAN, SPLIT PEA, AND BARLEY SOUP

To avoid nitrite and extra salt, this soup is made with fresh pork. If you wish, add imitation bacon bits to give it the typical smoky flavor of ham.

12	cups water
1	small fresh boneless pork shoulder, 2½ to 3 pounds •
1	beef bouillon cube
1	medium-sized onion, chopped
2	celery stalks, including leaves, coarsely chopped
2	carrots, coarsely sliced
1¼	cups dry split peas, sorted and rinsed
1¼	cups dry Great Northern (or navy) beans, sorted and rinsed
½	cup uncooked pearl barley
1	teaspoon salt •
¼	teaspoon black pepper, preferably freshly ground
¼	teaspoon garlic powder
2	large bay leaves
1½	cups chopped cabbage •
2	tablespoons imitation bacon bits (optional)

Combine all the ingredients except the cabbage and imitation bacon bits in a soup kettle or very large, heavy pot. Bring to a boil over high heat. Cover, lower the heat, and simmer for about 2 hours, stirring occasionally to prevent sticking. Add additional pepper to taste, if desired.

Remove the pork, and cut the meat into bite-sized pieces, discarding the fat. Return the meat to the pot along with the cabbage and imitation bacon bits, if desired. Cook for 15 minutes longer.

Refrigerate the soup for several hours so that the fat solidifies on the surface. Remove and discard the fat. (Alternately, skim the fat from the surface of the hot soup.) Reheat the soup to piping hot before serving.

Makes 5 to 6 main-dish servings.

NUTRI-STEP 1

- Omit the pork; decrease the cooking time to 1½ hours. (There will be no fat to skim from the soup surface.)
- Decrease the salt to ¾ teaspoon.
- Increase the chopped cabbage to 3 cups.

CAULIFLOWER–CHEESE SOUP

1	large head fresh cauliflower
1	small onion, finely chopped
1	clove garlic, peeled and minced
1	tablespoon butter or margarine ●■
6	cups water ■
1½	cups grated or shredded potato
½	teaspoon dry mustard
¼	teaspoon celery salt
3 to 4	drops hot pepper sauce
¼	teaspoon salt ■
½	teaspoon black pepper, preferably freshly ground
2	cups whole milk ●■
1¾	cups instant nonfat dry milk powder ■
1¾	cups shredded Cheddar cheese ●■

Cut 2 to 3 cups of small flowerets from the cauliflower. Cut them into 1-inch pieces and reserve. Grind the remaining cauliflower, including the stem but not the leaves, in batches in a food processor fitted with a chopping blade. (Or chop very finely by hand.) Set aside.

In a large heavy pot over medium heat, cook the onion and garlic in the butter until the vegetables are soft. Add the water, ground cauliflower and flowerets, potato, dry mustard, celery salt, hot pepper sauce, salt, and pepper. Stir and bring to a boil. Cover, lower the heat, and simmer for 20 minutes, stirring frequently to prevent sticking.

Stir in the milk. Then slowly add the dry milk powder, stirring constantly to prevent lumping. Turn the heat very low and cook for 10 minutes, stirring occasionally, but DO NOT boil. Stir in the cheese, and cook just until it melts. Turn off the heat and allow the soup to sit for a few minutes to allow flavors to blend.

Makes 8 to 9 servings.

NUTRI-STEP 1

- Decrease the butter or margarine to 2 teaspoons. Stir the onion and garlic carefully to prevent them from sticking.
- Substitute lowfat milk for the whole milk.
- Decrease the Cheddar cheese to 1½ cups.

NUTRI-STEP 2

- Decrease the butter or margarine to 2 teaspoons. Stir the onion and garlic carefully to prevent them from sticking.
- Increase the water to 8 cups.
- Decrease the salt to ⅛ teaspoon.
- Omit the whole milk.
- Increase the nonfat dry milk powder to 2½ cups.
- Decrease the Cheddar cheese to 1½ cups.

SAVORY CORN CHOWDER

Although low in fat, this is a very well-flavored, satisfying soup. It's also one of our "sneaky" recipes; some chopped cauliflower is slipped into the mixture for enriched taste and nutrition, but nobody ever realizes it's there.

2	tablespoons butter or margarine •
2	large onions, finely chopped
1	large celery stalk, finely chopped
1½	cups finely chopped fresh cauliflower
3	cups water
1	cup instant nonfat dry milk powder
2	medium-sized potatoes, peeled and cut into ¼-inch cubes
1	pound (about 4 cups) frozen yellow corn kernels
1	teaspoon salt •
	Scant ¼ teaspoon black pepper, preferably freshly ground •

Melt the butter in a 3-quart or larger saucepan or pot over medium-high heat. Add the onions, celery, and cauliflower and cook, stirring, for 4 to 5 minutes, or until vegetables are limp. Stir in the water. Gradually add the dry milk powder, stirring until it is completely dissolved. Then stir in all the remaining ingredients. Bring the mixture to a boil, stirring occasionally. Lower the heat and simmer the soup, uncovered, for 10 minutes. Stir occasionally to prevent the potatoes from sticking to the bottom of the pan. In batches, scoop up 4½ cups of vegetables and liquid from the pan, and purée in a blender or food processor until smooth. Return the puréed mixture to the pan and simmer for 8 to 10 minutes longer. Serve piping hot. Corn chowder is also good reheated.

Makes about 1½ quarts of soup, or about 4 to 5 servings.

NUTRI-STEP 1

- Decrease the butter or margarine to 1 tablespoon. Stir the vegetables constantly and watch carefully to prevent sticking.
- Decrease the salt to a generous ¾ teaspoon.
- Increase the black pepper to a generous ¼ teaspoon.

CREAMY POTATO–CARROT SOUP

8 medium-sized potatoes, peeled and cut into ¾-inch cubes
1 teaspoon dried basil leaves
3 cups water
2 chicken bouillon cubes
3 cups lowfat milk •
3 medium-sized carrots, peeled and thinly sliced
1 tablespoon butter or margarine •
½ teaspoon salt •
¼ teaspoon black pepper, preferably freshly ground

In a large, heavy pot, combine the potatoes, basil, water, bouillon cubes, and milk. Cover and bring to a boil over medium-high heat. Lower the heat and simmer, stirring occasionally, until potatoes are tender, about 10 to 12 minutes.

Meanwhile, in a separate medium-sized saucepan, cook the carrots in boiling water until tender, about 15 minutes.

When the potatoes are tender, use an electric mixer or potato masher to blend them into the cooking liquid. If desired, make the soup almost smooth, or leave some pieces of potato to add texture.

When the carrots are cooked, drain off the water and mash the carrots with a fork or potato masher to break them up slightly. Add the carrots to the potato mixture. Stir in the butter, salt, and pepper. Add additional basil, if desired.

Makes 4 to 5 main-dish servings.

NUTRI-STEP 1

- Omit the lowfat milk and SUBSTITUTE 1 cup nonfat dry milk powder mixed with a scant 3 cups water.
- Decrease the butter or margarine to 2 teaspoons.
- Decrease the salt to a generous ¼ teaspoon.

PARSLEY–POTATO SOUP

If you're accustomed to thinking of parsley primarily as a garnish, you may be surprised at how good this vitamin A- and C-rich herb tastes featured in a soup. Fresh parsley is required for this recipe.

2	tablespoons butter or margarine •
1¼	cups chopped fresh parsley leaves
1	medium-sized onion, finely chopped
2	tablespoons finely chopped celery
3	tablespoons enriched all-purpose or unbleached white flour
2½	cups rich chicken stock or broth, preferably homemade
2	medium-sized potatoes, peeled and diced
1	teaspoon salt (decrease to ½ teaspoon if commercial chicken broth is used) •
⅛	teaspoon black pepper, preferably freshly ground
2	cups whole milk •
½	teaspoon lemon juice •

In a 2-quart saucepan or pot, melt the butter over medium-high heat. Add the parsley, onion, and celery and cook, stirring, for 4 to 5 minutes, or until the onion is limp. Add the flour and cook, stirring, for 2 minutes longer, or until thoroughly incorporated and smooth. Lower the heat to medium and slowly add the chicken broth, stirring until the mixture is smooth. Cover and simmer, stirring occasionally, for 15 minutes. Stir in potatoes, salt, and pepper. Cover the pan, lower the heat, and simmer mixture very gently, stirring frequently to prevent sticking, for 15 minutes longer, or until the parsley and potatoes are tender. Stir in the milk and lemon juice. Reheat the soup to piping hot, but not boiling, over medium heat, stirring occasionally.

Makes about 1½ quarts of soup, or 4 to 5 servings.

NUTRI-STEP 1

- Decrease the butter or margarine to 1½ tablespoons.
- Decrease the salt to ¾ teaspoon. (If commercial chicken broth is used, decrease the salt to ¼ teaspoon.)
- Omit the whole milk and SUBSTITUTE 2 cups lowfat milk.
- Increase the lemon juice to ¾ teaspoon.

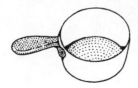

DILLY WINTER VEGETABLE SOUP

Try this one—it is good!

2	medium-sized onions, coarsely chopped
1	small turnip, peeled and coarsely chopped
2	tablespoons chopped fresh parsley leaves, or 1 tablespoon dried parsley flakes
1½	tablespoons butter or margarine •
2½	tablespoons enriched all-purpose or unbleached white flour
5	cups strong chicken broth or bouillon, preferably homemade
2	tablespoons dried dillweed, or ¼ cup finely chopped fresh dillweed, stems removed
¾	teaspoon salt (omit if commercial broth or bouillon is used) •
⅛	teaspoon black pepper, preferably freshly ground
1	large potato, peeled and cubed
1	cup coarsely chopped fresh cauliflower flowerets
½	cup plain lowfat yogurt

Combine the onions, turnip, and parsley with butter in a 2½-quart or larger soup kettle or pot. Cook over medium heat, stirring, for 4 minutes, or until the onion is transparent. Add the flour and cook, stirring, for several minutes longer. Gradually stir in the chicken broth, then the dillweed, salt, and pepper. Cover and simmer for 5 minutes.

Add the potatoes and cauliflower and simmer for about 12 minutes longer, or until the vegetables are tender. In a small bowl, stir ⅓ cup of the soup broth into the yogurt. Return the mixture to the pot. Reheat the soup to hot, but *not* boiling, and serve.

Makes about 1½ quarts of soup, or about 4 servings.

NUTRI-STEP 1

- Decrease the butter or margarine to 2 teaspoons.
- Decrease the salt to ½ teaspoon (omit if commercial broth or bouillon is used).

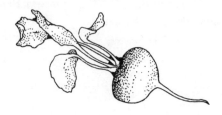

MIXED VEGETABLE SOUP

The amount of each vegetable in this recipe does not have to be exact. You can use a little more or less, if that's what you happen to have on hand.

2	tablespoons butter or margarine •
1	large onion, finely chopped
2	cloves garlic, peeled and finely minced
2½	cups shredded cabbage
4	cups chicken broth or bouillon
1	cup water
1	16-ounce can tomatoes, including juice, coarsely chopped
2	medium-sized potatoes, peeled and cut into ½-inch cubes •
1½	cups fresh cauliflower flowerets
1 to 1½	cups frozen green peas
5 or 6	water-packed artichoke hearts, quartered (optional)
½	cup chopped fresh parsley leaves
¼	teaspoon salt •
	Generous ⅛ teaspoon black pepper, preferably freshly ground •

Melt the butter in a 4-quart saucepan, Dutch oven, or soup pot. Add the onion and garlic, and cook until tender but not browned. Add the cabbage, and cook for 2 minutes longer, stirring.

Stir the broth, water, tomatoes and their juice, potatoes, and cauliflower into the pan. Bring the mixture to a boil, lower the heat, and simmer for about 20 minutes, or until the potatoes are almost tender. Stir in the peas, artichoke hearts, parsley, salt, and pepper. Simmer for 5 minutes, or until all the vegetables are tender.

Makes about 6 servings.

NUTRI-STEP 1

- Decrease the butter or margarine to 1 tablespoon. Stir the onion and garlic often to make sure they don't stick.
- Leave the potatoes unpeeled, and scrub them well before cutting into cubes. Use thin-skinned new potatoes, if available.
- Decrease the salt to ⅛ teaspoon.
- Increase the pepper to a scant ¼ teaspoon.

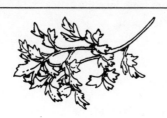

VEGETARIAN VEGETABLE SOUP

2	teaspoons butter or margarine •
1	onion, coarsely chopped
2	cloves garlic, peeled and minced
10	cups water
½	cup dry lima beans, rinsed and sorted
¼	cup uncooked pearl barley
2	packets vegetable bouillon, or amount used to make 2 cups
1	large carrot, grated or shredded
2	celery stalks, including leaves, finely chopped
1	small turnip, peeled and cut into ½-inch cubes
¼	teaspoon dry mustard
3 to 4	drops hot pepper sauce
1	teaspoon sugar
¾	teaspoon salt •
¼	teaspoon black pepper, preferably freshly ground
2	bay leaves
1	teaspoon dried basil leaves
¼	teaspoon ground thyme
¾	cup coarsely chopped fresh parsley leaves
1	large carrot, thinly sliced
1	celery stalk, coarsely sliced
3½	cups thinly sliced cabbage
1	16-ounce can tomatoes, including juice, chopped

In a large, heavy pot over medium heat, melt the butter. Add the onion and garlic and cook until the onion is limp. Add the water, lima beans, barley, vegetable bouillon, grated or shredded carrot, finely chopped celery, turnip, dry mustard, hot pepper sauce, sugar, salt, pepper, bay leaves, basil, thyme, and parsley. Reduce heat. Simmer for 1 hour and 20 minutes. Add the sliced carrot, celery, and cabbage. Cook for 20 minutes. Add the tomatoes to the pot along with their juice. Cook for 20 minutes longer.

Makes 4 to 6 main-dish servings.

NUTRI-STEP 1

- Decrease the butter or margarine to 1 teaspoon. Stir the onion and garlic carefully to prevent them from burning.
- Decrease the salt to ½ teaspoon.

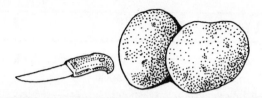

VICHYSSOISE

This cold and creamy, delicately flavored soup (pronounced "veeshy-swahz") usually calls for gobs of heavy cream. Our version is much lower in fat, but it still tastes rich and velvety.

1 **bunch fresh leeks (about 4 medium)**
3 **tablespoons butter or margarine ●■**
1 **small onion, finely chopped**
3 **cups chicken broth**
2 **cups peeled and cubed potatoes (about 1 pound)**
½ **teaspoon salt ●■**
⅛ **teaspoon white pepper ●■**
1 **cup whole milk ●■**
1 **13-ounce can evaporated milk ■**
   Chopped fresh chives or parsley for garnish

Clean the leeks carefully to remove any sand inside them. (To do this, cut off and discard the root and all the green except for about 1 inch. Then cut the leeks in half lengthwise, and separate the "layers." Rinse the layers well under cold running water; then drain on paper towels.) Chop the cleaned leeks finely. This should yield about 2 cups (but the exact amount is not critical).

Melt the butter in a large saucepan, and add the leeks and onion. Cook until tender but not browned, stirring often, about 8 to 10 minutes. If the leeks start to brown, add a little water to the saucepan.

When leeks and onions are tender, add the chicken broth, potatoes, salt, and pepper to the saucepan. Bring to a boil, lower the heat, and simmer, covered, for about 35 to 45 minutes, or until the potatoes are soft. Remove the saucepan from the heat, and purée the vegetables and broth in a blender, food processor, or food mill (in two or three batches, if necessary).

Return the purée to the saucepan, and add the whole milk and evaporated milk. Heat just until boiling, stirring constantly. Cool, cover, and refrigerate until very cold. If the soup is too thick when chilled, stir in a little additional milk. If desired, season with additional white pepper. Serve the soup cold, with some chopped chives or parsley sprinkled on top.

Makes 8 to 10 servings.

Note: Although it is traditionally served cold, this soup is also quite tasty when hot.

NUTRI-STEP 1

- Decrease the butter or margarine to 2 tablespoons. Stir the leeks and onion constantly to make sure they don't stick.
- Decrease the salt to a generous ¼ teaspoon.
- Increase the pepper to a scant ¼ teaspoon.
- Omit the whole milk and SUBSTITUTE 1 cup lowfat milk.

NUTRI-STEP 2

- Decrease the butter or margarine to 2 tablespoons. Stir the leeks and onion constantly to make sure they don't stick.
- Decrease the salt to ¼ teaspoon.
- Increase the pepper to ¼ teaspoon.
- Omit the whole milk and SUBSTITUTE 1 cup skim milk.
- Omit the evaporated milk and SUBSTITUTE 1 13-ounce can evaporated skimmed milk.

COLD AND TANGY CUCUMBER SOUP

Here's an easy soup which is not only very refreshing on a hot summer's day, it's also nutritious and low in calories. It is usually served in small portions.

1	medium-sized cucumber, peeled
2	cups plain lowfat yogurt
1 to 2	teaspoons white vinegar, or to taste
1	tablespoon good-quality olive oil •
1	small clove garlic, very finely minced or puréed in a garlic press (optional)
2	tablespoons chopped fresh mint leaves, or 1 tablespoon dried mint leaves
1	tablespoon chopped fresh dillweed, or 1½ teaspoons dried dillweed
½	teaspoon salt •
2	tablespoons finely chopped walnuts (optional) •
	Chopped fresh mint or dillweed for garnish (optional)

Cut the cucumber in half lengthwise, and scoop out and discard the seeds. Coarsely grate the cucumber halves, and place in a serving bowl. Add the yogurt and stir until combined. Then mix in the vinegar, oil, garlic, mint, dillweed, salt, and walnuts. Refrigerate for about 2 hours or longer to give the flavors a chance to mingle. If too thick, stir in 1 to 2 tablespoons of water. Serve very cold, with a sprinkling of additional herbs on top, if desired.

Makes 4 to 6 small servings.

NUTRI-STEP 1

- Decrease the oil to 2 teaspoons.
- Decrease the salt to a generous ¼ teaspoon.
- Omit the walnuts.

GAZPACHO

Cold and refreshing, Gazpacho has been aptly described as the "salad you eat with a spoon." It is a wonderful way to enjoy the produce of a summer garden. The olive oil in this recipe gives Gazpacho a delicious, distinctive flavor.

Soup

3	medium-sized vine-ripened tomatoes, cored
1	large cucumber, peeled
1	large onion, peeled
1	large green pepper, seeded
1 or 2	cloves garlic, peeled
2½	cups tomato juice, or a little more to taste
¼	teaspoon hot red pepper sauce
3	tablespoons good-quality olive oil •
3	tablespoons red wine vinegar •
¾	teaspoon salt •
¼	teaspoon freshly ground black pepper •

Garnishes

½	cup cored and diced tomatoes
½	cup seeded and diced green pepper
½	cup peeled and diced cucumber •
1	cup homemade or packaged croutons •

To make the soup, coarsely chop the tomatoes, cucumber, onion, green pepper, and garlic. Put in a blender or food processor with about 1 cup of the tomato juice, the hot pepper sauce, oil, and vinegar. Process until almost puréed, but not perfectly smooth. (Do this in two batches, if necessary.)

Pour the processed vegetable mixture into a serving bowl, and stir in the remaining tomato juice, salt, and pepper. Mix very well; then stir in the chopped vegetable garnishes. (Some of the garnishes may be reserved, and served later along with the soup for diners to add themselves.) Cover and refrigerate the soup until very cold. Just before serving, top each bowl of soup with a few croutons.

Makes about 6 servings.

NUTRI-STEP 1

- Decrease the olive oil to 2 tablespoons.
- Decrease the vinegar to 2 tablespoons (or to taste).
- Decrease the salt to ½ teaspoon.
- Increase the ground black pepper to ½ teaspoon.

Garnish
- If cucumber peel is thin and unwaxed, leave it on the cucumber used in the garnish.
- Omit the packaged croutons and USE whole wheat croutons made by cutting whole wheat bread into ½-inch cubes, and drying the cubes in a low oven.

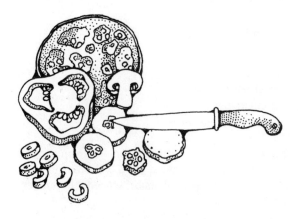

Chapter 6

Salads and Salad Dressings

Attractive, well-prepared salads—especially those featuring crisp greens or assorted fruits—are welcome on almost every table. How nice that they're also among our most healthful fare!

Because most salads are rich in vitamins, minerals, and fiber, it makes sense to serve them often and in abundance. In fact, for families who resist cooked vegetable side dishes, salads may be the best way to increase consumption of leafy green, bright orange, and cruciferous vegetables.

Remember, though, that adding even a few extra dollops of mayonnaise, sour cream, or oil-laden dressings to a salad can contribute hundreds of unnecessary calories and huge quantities of fat to a meal.

We've kept this firmly in mind in developing the recipes for this chapter. Throughout, we've concentrated on making our dressings both tasty *and* lowfat. And in many cases, salad and dressing recipes are presented as a unit, so that the right amount—but no extra—dressing gets used. Finally, our salads are designed to be appetizing and interesting in their own right; they don't need to be drowned to taste good!

47

CURRIED CHICKEN SALAD

If you like, cooked turkey white meat can be substituted for chicken in this recipe.

2   tablespoons plain lowfat yogurt •
¼   cup mayonnaise •
    Generous ¼ teaspoon salt •
1   teaspoon mild curry powder, or to taste
1   1-pound, 4-ounce can juice-packed pineapple chunks, well drained
1   8-ounce can sliced water chestnuts, well drained
2   celery stalks, including leaves, finely chopped
1   green onion (scallion), including top, finely chopped
⅓   cup blanched almond slivers •
2   cups cooked chicken (meat from about 3 breast halves)

Combine yogurt, mayonnaise, salt, and curry powder in a medium-sized bowl. Mix well. Add all remaining ingredients except the chicken and mix well. Fold in the chicken and stir until it is well coated with the dressing. Cover and refrigerate for several hours before serving to allow the flavors to blend.
    Makes 4 to 5 servings.

NUTRI-STEP 1

- Increase the plain lowfat yogurt to 3 tablespoons.
- Decrease the mayonnaise to 3 tablespoons.
- Decrease the salt to a generous ⅛ teaspoon.
- Decrease the almonds to 3 tablespoons.

TURKEY AND SPROUT SALAD

Fresh sprouts are not only loaded with vitamin C, but also have a very high ratio of protein to calories. We recommend bean sprouts for the following recipe; however, if they are unavailable, you can substitute another kind of fresh sprout, such as alfalfa. Fresh sprouts can now be found in the produce section of many supermarkets.

2   cups diced, cooked turkey meat
1   cup fresh bean sprouts
1   medium-sized apple, peeled, cored, and diced •

1   celery stalk, diced
¼   cup raisins or dried currants
3   tablespoons chopped walnuts •
¼   cup mayonnaise •
2   tablespoons plain regular or lowfat yogurt •
2   tablespoons orange juice
1   teaspoon grated orange peel (colored part only)
     Lettuce or other greens for garnish

Put the turkey, sprouts, apple, celery, raisins, and nuts in a medium-sized bowl, and mix lightly.

In a small bowl, blend mayonnaise, yogurt, orange juice, and orange peel. Toss with the turkey mixture until completely incorporated. Serve on a bed of greens.

Makes 3 to 4 servings.

NUTRI-STEP 1

- Leave the apple unpeeled.
- Decrease the nuts to 2 tablespoons, or omit.
- Decrease the mayonnaise to 3 tablespoons.
- Omit the regular yogurt and USE lowfat yogurt. Increase the amount to 3 tablespoons.

PASTA–BROCCOLI SALAD WITH TUNA

8   ounces (about 2 cups) uncooked tiny shells, spirals, or similar pasta ■
3   medium-sized stalks fresh broccoli, including stems
3   medium-sized ripe tomatoes, cored and cubed
3   green onions (scallions) including tops, thinly sliced
1   6½-ounce can water-packed tuna, drained and coarsely flaked
2   teaspoons dried basil leaves, or 2 tablespoons chopped fresh basil
1   teaspoon dried oregano leaves, or 1 tablespoon chopped fresh oregano
¼   cup red wine vinegar •■
¼   cup good-quality olive oil •■
½   teaspoon salt •■
     Freshly ground black pepper, to taste

Cook the pasta according to the package directions, but omit the salt. Drain and rinse under cold water until cool. Drain again.

Cut the broccoli tops into small flowerets. Trim and discard the bottom ½ inch of the stems. Peel the woody covering from the thick part of the stem and discard. Cut the stems into small slices. Steam flowerets and stem slices over (or in) a small amount of boiling water just until they are crisp-tender and brightly colored, about 5 to 8 minutes. Drain and rinse very briefly under cold water to stop the cooking process and retain the color. Drain again.

In a large bowl, gently toss together the cooked pasta, broccoli, tomatoes, green onions, and tuna.

Put the herbs, vinegar, oil, salt, and pepper in a small jar. Cover and shake well. Pour over the salad, and toss until the salad is coated with the dressing. Refrigerate for several hours, stirring occasionally, until the salad is chilled and the flavors are mingled.

Makes 8 to 10 servings.

NUTRI-STEP 1

- Decrease the vinegar to 3 tablespoons.
- Decrease the oil to 3 tablespoons.
- Decrease the salt to ¼ teaspoon.

NUTRI-STEP 2

- Omit the regular pasta and SUBSTITUTE 8 ounces whole wheat or soy-enriched pasta.
- Decrease the vinegar to 3 tablespoons.
- Decrease the oil to 3 tablespoons.
- Decrease the salt to ⅛ teaspoon.

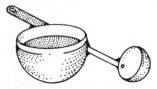

RICE SALAD SUPREME

⅓ cup raisins or dried currants
3½ cups cooked and cooled white or brown rice ●■
1 cup cooked green peas
1 cup diced unpeeled raw zucchini or broccoli flowerets
¼ cup chopped walnuts or almonds ●■
½ cup thinly sliced green onions (scallions), including tops
1 medium-sized vine-ripened tomato, cored and diced

Dressing
- ¼ cup apple cider vinegar
- 3 tablespoons vegetable oil ●■
- ¼ teaspoon ground cloves
- ¼ teaspoon ground cardamom
- 2 teaspoons dried spearmint leaves, or 2 tablespoons chopped fresh spearmint (optional)
- 3 tablespoons mayonnaise ●■
- 3 tablespoons plain lowfat yogurt ●■

Cover the raisins with warm water, and let stand until soft and plumped. Drain well. Mix the plumped fruit with the rice, peas, zucchini or broccoli, nuts, green onions, and tomato.

For the dressing, mix together the vinegar, oil, cloves, cardamom, and mint in a small bowl or jar. Toss gently with the rice mixture.

Mix together the mayonnaise and yogurt, and stir into the rice mixture. If the salad seems very dry, stir in a little more yogurt. Cover and refrigerate the salad for several hours, or until it is chilled and the flavors have mingled.

Makes about 8 servings.

NUTRI-STEP 1

- Omit the cooked and cooled white rice, and USE cooked and cooled brown rice.
- Decrease the nuts to 3 tablespoons.

Dressing
- Decrease the oil to 2 tablespoons.
- Decrease the mayonnaise to 2 tablespoons.
- Increase the yogurt to ¼ cup.

NUTRI-STEP 2

- Omit the cooked and cooled white rice, and USE cooked and cooled brown rice.
- Decrease the nuts to 2 tablespoons.

Dressing
- Decrease the oil to 2 tablespoons.
- Omit the mayonnaise.
- Increase the yogurt to ⅓ cup or a little more.

THREE-BEAN SALAD

Beans
1   15-ounce can kidney beans, drained
1   16-ounce can garbanzo beans (chick-peas), drained
1   15-ounce can string beans, drained

Dressing
¼   cup vegetable oil •
3   tablespoons apple cider vinegar
1   teaspoon sugar
½   teaspoon instant minced onions
¼   teaspoon dry mustard
⅛   teaspoon celery seed
1 to 2   drops hot pepper sauce
⅛   teaspoon salt •
     Pinch of black pepper, preferably freshly ground

In a colander, rinse all the beans thoroughly under cold running water. Set aside to drain.

To make the dressing, combine all ingredients in a medium-sized glass, plastic, or ceramic serving bowl. Stir vigorously until well mixed. Add the beans to the dressing and stir to coat the beans. Cover and refrigerate for several hours, or overnight, before serving, stirring occasionally, to give the flavors time to mingle.

Makes 6 to 7 servings.

> ## NUTRI-STEP 1
>
> ### Dressing
> • Decrease the oil to 3 tablespoons.
> • Omit the salt.

WHITE BEAN SALAD

2   cups dry navy beans, rinsed and sorted
9   cups water
1   bay leaf
1   clove garlic, peeled and minced
1   teaspoon instant minced onions
¼   cup vegetable oil •

¼   cup apple cider vinegar
½   teaspoon dried marjoram leaves
½   teaspoon dried basil leaves
¼   teaspoon dried thyme leaves
⅛   teaspoon black pepper, preferably freshly ground
½   teaspoon salt •
1   large celery stalk, coarsely chopped

Combine the beans, water, bay leaf, and garlic in a large saucepan over high heat. Cover and bring to a boil. Lower the heat and simmer until the beans are just tender, about 1½ hours. Drain the cooked beans in a colander. Discard bay leaf.

In a medium-sized bowl, combine all remaining ingredients except the celery. Stir until well mixed. Add the celery and cooked beans. Stir gently to coat the beans with the dressing. Cover and refrigerate for several hours, stirring occasionally, before serving so that flavors can blend.

Makes 6 to 8 servings.

NUTRI-STEP 1

- Decrease the vegetable oil to 3 tablespoons.
- Decrease the salt to a generous ¼ teaspoon.

SWEET AND SPICY CARROT SALAD

This unusual, colorful salad has an intriguing flavor that wins praise from everyone. It would be equally suitable served at a festive dinner or a picnic.

Carrots
⅓   cup water
1   tablespoon honey •
1   pound carrots, thinly sliced or diced

Dressing
2   tablespoons lemon juice
2   tablespoons honey •
¼   teaspoon ground cinnamon
¼   teaspoon paprika
⅛ to ¼   teaspoon ground cumin
1   small clove garlic, peeled and finely minced
¼   cup chopped fresh parsley leaves

To cook the carrots, put the water and honey in a medium-sized saucepan. Bring to a boil, add the carrots, and stir so they are all moistened. Lower the heat and simmer, covered, until the carrots are just tender, about 10 minutes. (Do not overcook, or the carrots will get mushy.)

Meanwhile, combine the dressing ingredients in a medium-sized bowl. Drain the cooked carrots well and add them to the dressing mixture. Mix well, cover, and chill at least 1 to 2 hours to give the flavors time to mingle. Stir occasionally to coat the carrots with the dressing. Serve chilled or at room temperature.

Makes about 4 servings.

NUTRI-STEP 1

Carrots
- Decrease the honey in the cooking water to 2 teaspoons.

Dressing
- Decrease the honey to 1½ tablespoons.

RED CABBAGE–APPLE SLAW

For another slaw recipe, see Zippy Coleslaw on page 23.

1 small head red cabbage (about 1¼ pounds), cored
4 large unpeeled apples, cored
2 tablespoons sugar ■
¼ cup apple cider vinegar or red wine vinegar, or more to taste
   Scant ½ cup mayonnaise (lowfat, if available) ●■
2½ tablespoons plain regular or lowfat yogurt ●●■
   Pinch of ground cloves, or to taste ■

Use a grater or food processor to finely shred the cabbage and apples. Put the cabbage and apple shreds in a large bowl, and stir in the sugar, vinegar, mayonnaise, yogurt, and cloves until well combined. Refrigerate for several hours, stirring occasionally, to give the flavors time to mingle.

Makes 8 to 10 servings.

NUTRI-STEP 1

- Decrease the mayonnaise to ⅓ cup.
- Increase the yogurt to ¼ cup.

NUTRI-STEP 2

- Decrease the sugar to 1½ tablespoons.
- Decrease the mayonnaise to ¼ cup.
- Increase the yogurt to ⅓ cup.
- Increase the cloves to ⅛ teaspoon.

MANDARIN SALAD WITH SWEET–SOUR DRESSING

Some of the ingredients in this recipe aren't typically included in a "tossed" salad. Yet, the combination of flavors is very appealing, and the colors—green, orange, purple, and white—are quite striking. The amounts of the vegetables may be altered to taste.

Salad
| | |
About 10 large leaves romaine lettuce, rinsed and dried
½   pound fresh spinach leaves, trimmed, rinsed, and dried
½   cup peeled and sliced white or red radish
½   cup peeled and thinly sliced Jerusalem artichokes or "sunchokes" (optional)
1   cup cleaned and sliced fresh mushrooms
3 to 4   green onions (scallions), thinly sliced
1   11-ounce can mandarin orange sections, well drained
2   cups coarsely shredded red cabbage
½   cup thinly sliced canned water chestnuts, drained
2   tablespoons slivered or sliced almonds (optional) •

Dressing
½   cup vegetable oil •
¼   cup white wine vinegar or apple cider vinegar
1   tablespoon honey
½   teaspoon dried tarragon leaves, finely crumbled
¼   teaspoon salt •
⅛   teaspoon black pepper, preferably freshly ground

Place all the salad ingredients in a large serving bowl, and toss gently. (This may be done several hours before serving time. Cover loosely and refrigerate the salad.)

For the dressing, place all the ingredients in a small jar, cover, and shake vigorously until completely combined. Refrigerate for at least 30 minutes (or longer) to blend the flavors. Just before serving the salad, shake the dressing again; then immediately pour it over the salad, and toss gently.

Makes 8 to 10 servings.

NUTRI-STEP 1

Salad
- Omit the almonds.

Dressing
- Decrease the vegetable oil to ⅓ cup.
- Decrease the salt to ⅛ teaspoon.

HOT POTATO SALAD

This delicious side dish is seasoned with a flavorful combination of herbs and spices—rather than the hard-boiled eggs and bacon found in most hot potato salads.

Vegetables
4½ cups potatoes, peeled and cut into 1-inch cubes ●
1 bay leaf
1 celery stalk, coarsely chopped
1 small carrot, finely chopped

Dressing
3 tablespoons mayonnaise
3 tablespoons commercial buttermilk or lowfat yogurt
⅛ teaspoon garlic powder
⅛ teaspoon onion powder
Generous ⅛ teaspoon dry mustard
Pinch of black pepper, preferably freshly ground
Scant ¼ teaspoon salt ●
½ teaspoon dried marjoram leaves
⅛ teaspoon ground thyme

In a medium-sized saucepan, cover the potatoes with water. Add the bay leaf. Cover the pan and bring to a boil. Lower the heat and simmer for 8 or 9 minutes, or until the potatoes are just tender.

While the potatoes cook, prepare the other vegetables.

Then combine all the dressing ingredients in a small bowl, and stir until blended.

When the potatoes are done, drain them well in a colander and discard the bay leaf. Transfer the potatoes to a serving dish. Stir in the celery and carrot. Pour the dressing over all, and toss lightly with a spoon to coat the potatoes. Serve at once. *Makes 4 servings.*

NUTRI-STEP 1

Vegetables
- Increase the potatoes to 5½ cups and leave unpeeled. Scrub well. *And add* 1 fresh broccoli stem, peeled and coarsely chopped, along with the carrot and celery. (Reserve the flowerets for another use.)

Dressing
- Decrease the salt to ⅛ teaspoon.

POTATO SALAD

6 cups potatoes, peeled and cut into 1-inch cubes (or unpeeled new potatoes) ●■
¼ cup mayonnaise ●■
¼ cup commercial sour cream ●■
¼ teaspoon celery seed
1 teaspoon dried basil leaves
¼ teaspoon dried oregano leaves
   Pinch of garlic powder
½ teaspoon salt ●■
1 teaspoon instant minced onions
¼ teaspoon dry mustard
2 celery stalks, coarsely chopped
⅛ teaspoon black pepper, preferably freshly ground

In a large saucepan, cover the potatoes with unsalted water. Bring to a boil over medium-high heat. Lower the heat and cook, covered, until just barely tender, about 7 to 9 minutes. (Do not overcook as very soft potatoes will need more dressing.) Drain the potatoes and cool to lukewarm.

While the potatoes are cooling, stir together all the remaining ingredients. Gently fold into the cooled potatoes. Cover and refrigerate for several hours before serving to allow flavors to blend.
Makes 4 to 5 servings.

NUTRI-STEP 1

- Leave the potatoes unpeeled and scrub them well.
- Decrease the mayonnaise to 2 tablespoons.
- Decrease the sour cream to 2 tablespoons. *And add* ¼ cup plain lowfat yogurt. If you like, add ¼ teaspoon sugar with the yogurt, as it produces a tarter dressing.
- Decrease the salt to ¼ teaspoon. *And add* 1 medium carrot, shredded or finely chopped.

NUTRI-STEP 2

- Leave the potatoes unpeeled and scrub them well.
- Decrease the mayonnaise to 2 tablespoons.
- Omit the sour cream. *And add* ⅓ cup plain lowfat yogurt. If you like, add ¼ teaspoon sugar with the yogurt, as it produces a tarter dressing.
- Decrease the salt to ⅛ teaspoon or omit. *And add* 1 medium carrot, shredded or finely chopped.

MARINATED VEGETABLE SALAD

Serve this salad by itself or tossed with lettuce and other greens.

Salad
1   large celery stalk
1   large carrot, thinly sliced
2   cups fresh broccoli flowerets
2   cups fresh cauliflower flowerets

Dressing
3   tablespoons apple cider vinegar
½   teaspoon dry mustard
1   tablespoon honey •
1   drop hot pepper sauce
⅛   teaspoon salt •
    Pinch of black pepper, preferably freshly ground
¼   cup vegetable oil •

Coarsely chop the celery and set it aside.
   Put the carrots in one layer in the bottom of a large saucepan. Cover with 1 inch

of water. Lay the broccoli and cauliflower flowerets over the carrots. Cover and bring to a boil over high heat. Lower the heat and simmer for 5 minutes. Drain the vegetables well in a colander. Then briefly rinse the vegetables under cold running water to stop the cooking process and set the color. Drain again.

In a medium-sized glass or ceramic serving bowl, combine all dressing ingredients. Stir vigorously until well mixed. Add the parboiled vegetables and celery, and stir until they are coated with the dressing. Cover and refrigerate for several hours, stirring occasionally, before serving.

Makes 4 servings.

NUTRI-STEP 1

Dressing
- Decrease the honey to 2 teaspoons.
- Omit the salt.
- Decrease the vegetable oil to 3 tablespoons.

WINTER VEGETABLE SALAD COMBO

Dressing
⅓ cup commercial buttermilk
3 tablespoons part-skim ricotta cheese (if unavailable, substitute regular ricotta) ●■
¼ cup mayonnaise ●■
Generous ¼ teaspoon dry mustard
¼ teaspoon salt ■
1½ teaspoons instant minced onions
1 teaspoon dried parsley flakes
½ teaspoon dried dillweed
⅛ teaspoon black pepper, preferably freshly ground

Vegetables
2½ cups small, fresh cauliflower flowerets
2¼ cups small, fresh broccoli flowerets
¼ cup thinly sliced water chestnuts (optional)
1 large tomato, cored and cut into wedges for garnish

Combine the buttermilk and ricotta in a blender container. Blend on medium speed for 30 seconds. Scrape down the sides of the container with a spatula and blend on high speed for 30 seconds longer, or until mixture is completely smooth. Add the mayonnaise, mustard, and salt and blend on medium speed for 15 seconds longer, or until ingredients are just mixed. Stir the remaining seasonings into the blended mixture. Cover and refrigerate the dressing for at least 10 minutes, but preferably ½ hour, so flavors can blend.

Combine cauliflower, broccoli, and water chestnuts (if used) in a serving bowl. Pour the dressing over the vegetables and toss to coat thoroughly. Refrigerate, covered, until the vegetables are chilled, at least 15 to 20 minutes. The salad can be held up to 24 hours before serving. Toss well at serving time. Garnish the salad with tomato wedges.

Makes 4 to 6 servings.

NUTRI-STEP 1

Dressing
- Increase the ricotta cheese to ¼ cup.
- Decrease the mayonnaise to 3 tablespoons.

NUTRI-STEP 2

Dressing
- Increase the ricotta cheese to ¼ cup.
- Decrease the mayonnaise to 2 tablespoons.
- Decrease the salt to ⅛ teaspoon.

CREAMY PINEAPPLE–CARROT GELATIN SALAD

⅓ cup boiling water
1 teaspoon lemon juice
1 packet unflavored gelatin
1 8-ounce carton orange-flavored lowfat yogurt
½ cup lowfat cottage cheese
⅓ cup orange juice
2½ tablespoons sugar •
1 1-pound, 4-ounce can juice-packed crushed pineapple, well drained
1 cup shredded or grated carrots
½ cup diced celery or green pepper (optional)

Combine the water, lemon juice, and gelatin in a blender container. Blend on medium speed 20 seconds, or until the gelatin dissolves and the mixture is frothy. Add the yogurt, cottage cheese, orange juice, sugar, and 1 cup of the crushed pineapple to the blender container. Blend on medium speed for 1 minute, or until the mixture is completely puréed.

Combine the puréed mixture with the remaining crushed pineapple, grated carrots, and diced celery, stirring until well blended.

Turn the mixture into a flat 8- or 9-inch square (or similar) pan or into a 1-quart ring mold. Cover and refrigerate for 2 hours, or until set.

To serve, cut the gelatin into squares in the pan and transfer to individual salad plates garnished with lettuce leaves. Or unmold the ring on a serving platter garnished with lettuce and serve whole.

Makes about 6 servings.

NUTRI-STEP 1

- Decrease the sugar to 1½ tablespoons.

WINTER FRUIT SALAD

¼ cup frozen orange juice concentrate, thawed
2 tablespoons cream sherry or fruit-flavored liqueur (optional)
1 tablespoon lemon juice
1 8-ounce can juice-packed pineapple chunks, including juice
2 bananas, sliced
2 apples, peeled, cored, and cubed •
2 pears, peeled, cored, and cubed •
2 tangerines, peeled, sectioned, and seeded

Combine the orange juice concentrate, sherry, and lemon juice in a large serving bowl. Stir to mix. Add the pineapple chunks with their juice and the remaining fruit. Stir carefully to coat all fruit with juice. Cover and refrigerate for several hours, stirring occasionally, before serving. If desired, top each serving with a dollop of lowfat vanilla yogurt.

Makes 6 servings.

NUTRI-STEP 1

- Leave the apples unpeeled.
- Leave the pears unpeeled.

RAINBOW FRUIT MEDLEY

Appealing and colorful, this simple salad is high in vitamin C. The cantaloupe is also an excellent source of vitamin A.

2 cups fresh watermelon balls or cubes
1 cup fresh hulled and sliced strawberries
1 cup fresh cantaloupe balls or cubes
1 cup juice-packed canned pineapple chunks, drained
½ cup fresh seedless grapes
½ cup fresh blueberries
1 10-ounce package syrup-packed frozen raspberries, thawed and drained •

Combine all the ingredients in a large serving bowl. Stir carefully to mix. Cover and refrigerate for several hours before serving.
Makes 5 to 6 servings.

NUTRI-STEP 1

• Omit the syrup-packed frozen raspberries, and SUBSTITUTE 1½ cups fresh raspberries, "dry-pack" unsweetened frozen raspberries, or other fruit, such as peaches or plums.

WALDORF SALAD

4 cups diced tart unpeeled red apples
1 cup finely chopped celery
¼ cup raisins
⅓ cup mayonnaise •■
¼ cup plain lowfat yogurt
2 teaspoons lemon juice
⅛ teaspoon celery seed
    Pinch of ground cinnamon
2½ tablespoons chopped walnuts •■

Combine all ingredients in a medium-sized bowl, stirring until well mixed. Cover and refrigerate for at least 15 minutes, or preferably 30 minutes, to allow the flavors to blend. Stir again before serving.
Makes 4 to 5 servings.

NUTRI-STEP 1

- Decrease the mayonnaise to ¼ cup.
- Decrease the walnuts to 2 tablespoons.

NUTRI-STEP 2

And add ½ cup finely diced cabbage to the salad along with the celery.
- Decrease the mayonnaise to ¼ cup.
- Decrease the walnuts to 1 tablespoon.

LIGHT BASIL DRESSING

3 tablespoons red wine vinegar ■
2 tablespoons vegetable oil ●■
1 teaspoon grated Parmesan cheese ●■
¾ teaspoon sugar
2 teaspoons dried basil leaves
1 tablespoon finely chopped green onion (scallions)
1 sliver fresh garlic, minced
   Scant ½ teaspoon celery salt ●■
   Freshly ground black pepper to taste

Combine all the ingredients in a cruet or jar and shake well until blended. Toss well with 8 cups of mixed greens and assorted chopped raw vegetables.
   Makes 5 to 6 servings.

NUTRI-STEP 1

- Decrease the oil to 1½ tablespoons.
- Omit the Parmesan cheese.
- Decrease the celery salt to ¼ teaspoon.

NUTRI-STEP 2

- Decrease the red wine vinegar to 2½ tablespoons.
- Decrease the oil to 1 tablespoon.
- Omit the Parmesan cheese.
- Decrease the celery salt to ⅛ teaspoon. *And add* ⅛ teaspoon celery seed.

TANGY THOUSAND ISLAND DRESSING

Part of the mayonnaise in this recipe is replaced with sour cream, which is much lower in fat.

3	tablespoons mayonnaise ●■
3	tablespoons commercial sour cream ●■
¼ to ½	teaspoon dry mustard
½	teaspoon onion powder
⅛	teaspoon garlic powder
⅛	teaspoon cayenne pepper
1	tablespoon plus 1 teaspoon sugar ■
⅛	teaspoon ground cloves
1	8-ounce can tomato sauce
1	tablespoon ketchup
1	tablespoon plus 1 teaspoon apple cider vinegar
1	teaspoon lemon juice

Combine the mayonnaise and sour cream in a small bowl. Stir in the dry mustard, onion powder, garlic powder, cayenne pepper, sugar, and cloves. Add all remaining ingredients to mayonnaise mixture, and stir vigorously with a fork or wire whisk until blended. Cover and refrigerate for several hours before using to give the flavors time to mingle. If the dairy ingredients are fresh, the dressing may be kept in the refrigerator for up to a week.

Makes 1½ cups.

NUTRI-STEP 1

- Decrease the mayonnaise to 2 tablespoons.
- Increase the sour cream to 4 tablespoons.

NUTRI-STEP 2

■ Decrease the mayonnaise to 2 tablespoons.
■ Decrease the sour cream to 2 tablespoons. ***And add*** 2 tablespoons plain lowfat yogurt.
■ Decrease the sugar to 1 tablespoon.

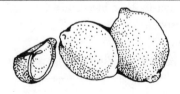

CREAMY BLUE CHEESE DRESSING

2   tablespoons plain lowfat yogurt •
¼   cup lowfat cottage cheese
¼   cup mayonnaise •
1   tablespoon plus 1 teaspoon crumbled blue cheese
2   teaspoons lowfat milk
2   teaspoons lemon juice
⅛   teaspoon black pepper, preferably freshly ground

Place all the ingredients in a blender container. Turn the blender on and off several times to mix the ingredients. Then blend on medium speed to combine well. Transfer to a jar or bowl, cover, and refrigerate for several hours before serving so the flavors can mingle.
Makes 1 cup.

NUTRI-STEP 1

- Increase the lowfat yogurt to ¼ cup.
- Decrease the mayonnaise to 2 tablespoons.

RANCH DRESSING

1   cup commercial buttermilk
⅓   cup mayonnaise •■
     Pinch of garlic powder
¼   teaspoon onion powder
⅛   teaspoon black pepper, preferably freshly ground
½   teaspoon dried basil leaves
⅛   teaspoon celery salt
¼   teaspoon salt •■
⅛   teaspoon ground thyme
⅛   teaspoon sugar ■

Combine all the ingredients in a small bowl, and mix well with a wire whisk. (Or process in a blender until thoroughly mixed.) Cover and refrigerate for several hours before serving to allow the flavors to blend. Serve the dressing over a mixed greens salad or assorted chopped raw vegetables, such as celery, carrots, broccoli flowerets, and cucumbers.
Makes about 1⅛ cups.

NUTRI-STEP 1

- Decrease the mayonnaise to ¼ cup.
- Decrease the salt to ⅛ teaspoon.

NUTRI-STEP 2

- Decrease the mayonnaise to 3 tablespoons.
- Omit the salt.
- Omit the sugar.

CRAN–APPLE–PEAR RELISH

This is a very nice side dish, especially for festive holidays like Thanksgiving. It has the zippy taste of cranberries mingled with the subtle flavors of other fall fruits.

3   cups (12 ounces) fresh or fresh-frozen ("dry pack") unsweetened cranberries
2   medium-sized apples, peeled, cored, and diced •
2   medium-sized pears, peeled, cored, and diced •
½   cup orange juice
1   teaspoon freshly grated orange peel (colored part only)
½   teaspoon ground cinnamon
¼   teaspoon ground nutmeg
¾   cup sugar •
½   cup water

Combine all the ingredients in a large saucepan. Bring to a boil. Then lower the heat, and simmer, uncovered, stirring often, until the relish has thickened and the fruit is soft (about 30 minutes). Remove from the heat and cool. Cover and chill completely in the refrigerator. (The relish will thicken even more as it chills.) Serve cold or at room temperature. This relish keeps well for several days in the refrigerator.
   Makes about 3½ to 4 cups.

NUTRI-STEP 1

- Leave the apples unpeeled.
- Leave the pears unpeeled.
- Decrease the sugar to ⅔ cup.

Chapter 7

Vegetable Side Dishes

Vegetables should have a starring role in the kitchen of every health-conscious cook. Not only are they packed with vitamins, minerals, and fiber that help keep us well, but they add welcome color, texture, and variety to menus without piling on unwanted calories or fat.

Probably the best way to make sure these "healthy" foods are popular at the family table is simply to give them a fair chance! Prepare vegetables with the same care and imagination as the other elements of a meal. Few cooks would expect plain, boiled, unseasoned meat, bean, or grain dishes to be greeted enthusiastically, yet vegetables are routinely served up that way.

In this chapter, we've provided an assortment of recipes to help you make vegetables look and taste good without depending on a lot of fat, salt, or sugar. In some recipes, we highlight the crispness, bright color, and good taste of fresh produce by cooking the ingredients briefly in a minimum of water. (Excess cooking water tends to wash away flavor, not to mention vital nutrients.) In others, we've teamed vegetables with compatible fruits, herbs, and spices to produce remarkably savory and wholesome combinations.

You'll notice that some vegetables are featured more frequently than others in the chapter. This is because certain varieties—such as the vitamin A- and vitamin C-rich and cruciferous plants—are extra-healthful, and we ought to be eating them more often. (Incidentally, corn and lima beans are missing from the chapter—with good reason. Although often served in place of the leafy green and orange vegetables, nutritionally corn and lima beans belong with grains and legumes, and that's where they are.)

BEETS WITH ORANGE SAUCE

1	bunch fresh red beets (about 4 medium)
¾	cup water
¼	cup orange juice •
2	tablespoons lemon juice •
1	tablespoon cornstarch
1½	tablespoons sugar •
1	teaspoon grated orange peel
⅛	teaspoon salt •
1	tablespoon butter or margarine •

Trim the tops and roots from the beets, and thinly peel them. Then cut the beets into julienne strips, or dice into ½-inch cubes. Put the beets and water in a medium-sized saucepan. Cover and bring to a boil. Lower the heat and simmer for about 20 minutes, or until the beets are tender. Remove the cooked beets with a slotted spoon, and set aside. Reserve the cooking liquid.

Boil down the beet liquid to ¼ cup.

Meanwhile, mix together the orange juice, lemon juice, cornstarch, sugar, orange peel, and salt in a small bowl. Stir this mixture into the hot beet liquid and cook, stirring constantly, until thick and clear, about 3 to 5 minutes. Remove from the heat, and stir in the butter until it melts. Then gently stir in the cooked beets and, if necessary, warm over low heat until heated through.

Makes 4 to 6 servings.

NUTRI-STEP 1

- Increase the orange juice to ⅓ cup.
- Decrease the lemon juice to 1 tablespoon.
- Decrease the sugar to 1 tablespoon.
- Omit the salt.
- Decrease the butter or margarine to 1 teaspoon.

ORIENTAL BROCCOLI

     2   teaspoons packed light or dark brown sugar •
     2   tablespoons dry sherry
     1   tablespoon soy sauce
2 to 3   drops hot pepper sauce
     2   large fresh broccoli stalks, including flowerets and stems
    1½   tablespoons vegetable oil •
     ¾   cup coarsely sliced green onions (scallions), including green tops
     1   clove garlic, minced

Combine the brown sugar, sherry, soy sauce, and hot pepper sauce in a small bowl. Set aside.

Cut the broccoli flowerets from the stems and divide each "head" into 2- or 3-inch pieces. Peel the broccoli stems and discard the peel. Slice the stems into thin pieces.

In a large heavy skillet, heat the vegetable oil over medium heat. Add the broccoli, green onion, and garlic and stir-fry (stir constantly while gently tossing) for 2 minutes. Add the sauce mixture to the pan and cook, stirring, for 3 to 4 minutes, or until the broccoli is just tender but still bright green. Serve immediately.

Makes 4 to 5 servings.

NUTRI-STEP 1

- Decrease the brown sugar to 1 teaspoon.
- Decrease the vegetable oil to 1 tablespoon, and stir the vegetables carefully to prevent them from sticking and burning.

SAUCED CARROTS AND CELERY

     ¾   cup beef broth or bouillon
     ¼   cup water
     ½   teaspoon lemon juice
     ⅛   teaspoon freshly ground black pepper
     1   tablespoon butter or margarine •
     1   tablespoon sugar •
     1   tablespoon enriched all-purpose or unbleached white flour
     5   large carrots, peeled, quartered lengthwise, then cut into 1½-inch-long pieces
     4   large celery stalks, halved lengthwise, then cut into 1½-inch-long pieces

Combine the beef broth, water, lemon juice, and black pepper in a small bowl or cup. Set aside.

Melt the butter in a large, heavy saucepan or medium-sized skillet over high heat. Add the sugar and cook, stirring constantly and watching carefully, until the sugar begins to melt and to turn a light caramel color. Immediately remove the pan from the heat, stirring. Continue to stir off the heat while adding the flour to the pan. Stir until the ingredients are well blended. Then gradually stir in the reserved broth mixture. The ingredients will suddenly mass and form hard bits (caramelize) on the pan bottom; this is normal. Return the pan to the heat and, stirring and scraping the bits from the bottom of the pan, bring the mixture to a boil over medium heat.

Add the carrots to the pan and lower the heat. Cover and simmer the carrots for 10 to 12 minutes, stirring occasionally to prevent sticking. Add the celery to the pan, replace the lid, and simmer, stirring occasionally, for about 12 minutes longer, or until vegetables are almost tender. Remove the pan lid, raise the heat to medium, and cook for about 3 minutes longer, or until the carrots are tender (celery will still be slightly crisp) and most of the excess liquid has evaporated from the pan. Serve the vegetables along with the sauce remaining in the pan.

Makes 4 to 5 servings.

NUTRI-STEP 1

- Decrease the butter or margarine to 1½ teaspoons.
- Decrease the sugar to 2½ teaspoons.

SAUCY CABBAGE WEDGES

Colorful and delicious, this dish is exceptionally rich in vitamin C (from the cabbage and pimiento).

1	large tomato, peeled, cored, and cut in eighths
¼	cup chopped canned pimiento, drained
¼	cup water
½	teaspoon sugar
½	teaspoon paprika
¼	teaspoon salt ●
	Pinch of black pepper, preferably freshly ground ●
1	tablespoon butter or margarine ●
1	small onion, finely chopped
1	small clove garlic, peeled and minced
4 to 5	cabbage wedges (cut from a medium-sized head), each about 2 inches thick at the widest part

Combine the tomato, pimiento, water, sugar, paprika, salt, and pepper in a blender container. Blend on medium speed for 30 seconds, or until thoroughly puréed. Set aside.

In a deep-sided, medium-sized skillet, melt the butter over medium-high heat. Add the onion and garlic and cook, stirring, for 4 to 5 minutes or until the vegetables are limp. Stir the reserved puréed tomato–pimiento sauce into the skillet and bring to a boil. Place the cabbage wedges in the skillet, spooning some of the sauce over each. Cover the skillet, lower the heat, and simmer the cabbage wedges for about 13 to 14 minutes, or until they are just tender. Baste occasionally with the sauce. Serve the cabbage wedges immediately, spooning some of the sauce over each.

Makes 4 to 5 servings.

NUTRI-STEP 1

- Decrease the salt to a generous ⅛ teaspoon.
- Increase the pepper to a scant ⅛ teaspoon.
- Decrease the butter or margarine to ½ tablespoon.

SWEET AND SOUR RED CABBAGE WITH APPLE

Sauce
1½ tablespoons packed light brown sugar
1½ teaspoons cornstarch
1½ tablespoons red wine vinegar or apple cider vinegar
¼ cup water
1 teaspoon ketchup
¼ teaspoon prepared horseradish, or more to taste
¾ teaspoon dry mustard
⅛ teaspoon salt •
⅛ teaspoon ground cinnamon
    Pinch of ground cloves

Cabbage Mixture
2 teaspoons butter or margarine •
1 medium-sized onion, finely chopped
1 medium-sized unpeeled tart red apple, cored and coarsely chopped
1 small head red cabbage (about 1½ pounds), cored, trimmed of tough outer leaves and coarsely shredded
¼ cup raisins
⅔ cup water

For the sauce, stir together the brown sugar and cornstarch in a small bowl. Add the vinegar and water, stirring until well blended and smooth. Stir in all the remaining sauce ingredients and set the mixture aside.

Melt the butter in a large heavy skillet over medium-high heat. Add the onion and cook, stirring, for about 4 minutes, or until the onion is limp. Add the chopped apple, cabbage, raisins, and water to the skillet and raise the heat to high. Bring the mixture to a boil and cook, stirring occasionally, for 5 minutes, or until the excess liquid has evaporated and the cabbage is slightly limp. Lower the heat to medium and add the reserved sauce, stirring constantly. Cook, stirring, for 6 to 7 minutes longer, or until the sauce is clear and the cabbage is just tender.

Makes 5 to 6 servings.

NUTRI-STEP 1

Sauce
- Omit the salt.

Cabbage Mixture
- Decrease the butter or margarine to 1 teaspoon. Stir the onion constantly and watch carefully to prevent it from burning.

STIR-FRIED CAULIFLOWER

Sauce

⅓   cup water
1½   teaspoons cornstarch
1½   tablespoons soy sauce •
2½   tablespoons chicken broth or bouillon
1   tablespoon dry white table wine or dry sherry
3 to 4   dashes hot pepper sauce

Vegetables

1½   tablespoons peanut or corn oil •
1   medium-sized head fresh cauliflower, trimmed and cut into flowerets
1   large onion, coarsely chopped
1   large celery stalk, cut into ¼-inch-thick diagonal slices
¼   teaspoon fresh gingerroot, peeled and finely chopped, or ⅛ teaspoon ground ginger

To prepare the sauce, stir together the water and cornstarch in a small bowl or cup until completely smooth. Stir in the soy sauce, chicken broth, wine, and hot pepper sauce. Set aside.

Heat the oil in a large skillet over medium-high heat, until very hot but not smoking. Add all the vegetables and ginger to the skillet, stirring constantly. Cook, stirring, until the vegetables are heated on all sides but are not brown, about 2 minutes. Stir the reserved sauce and add it to the skillet. Stirring constantly, cook the mixture for 2½ to 3 minutes longer, or until the sauce is clear and smooth and the cauliflower is just barely tender. Serve immediately.

Makes 4 to 6 servings.

NUTRI-STEP 1

Sauce
- Decrease the soy sauce to 1 tablespoon.

Vegetables
- Decrease the oil to 1 tablespoon.

GREEN BEANS ITALIENNE

No one will ever know that turnips are the secret ingredient in the delicious sauce for these beans.

1   pound flat, Italian-style green beans or regular string beans trimmed and snapped in thirds

Sauce
1   small onion, finely chopped
1   small turnip, peeled and grated or shredded
1   16-ounce can tomatoes, including juice, puréed
¼   teaspoon instant minced onions
¼   teaspoon dried oregano leaves
½   teaspoon dried basil leaves
1   bay leaf
½   teaspoon sugar •
⅛   teaspoon black pepper, preferably freshly ground
¼   teaspoon salt •

Put about an inch of water into a large saucepan. Add the green beans. Cover and bring to a boil over high heat. Lower the heat but keep the water simmering. Cook the beans for about 25 to 30 minutes, or until they are tender. Drain well in a colander and return to the pan.

While beans cook, combine all the remaining ingredients in a small saucepan. Cover and bring to a boil. Lower the heat and simmer the sauce for 25 minutes. Pour the sauce over the beans and simmer, uncovered, for 10 to 15 minutes so that the beans can absorb the flavor and the sauce can thicken slightly.

Makes 6 servings.

NUTRI-STEP 1

Sauce
- Omit the sugar.
- Decrease the salt to ⅛ teaspoon or omit.

GREEN PEAS AND PIMIENTO

The cabbage in this dish simply provides a flavorful (and nutritious) "background" for the peas.

2	teaspoons butter or margarine •
1	small onion, finely chopped
1½	cups finely chopped cabbage
2	tablespoons finely chopped celery
2½	cups frozen green peas
¼	cup water (approximate)
1	teaspoon lemon juice
⅛	teaspoon salt •
	Pinch of black pepper, or to taste, preferably freshly ground
⅓	cup coarsely chopped canned pimiento, drained

Melt the butter in a medium-sized saucepan over medium-high heat. Add the onion and cabbage and cook, stirring, for about 5 minutes, or until the vegetables are limp. Stir all the remaining ingredients except the pimiento into the pan. Cover, lower the heat, and simmer for 8 to 10 minutes, or until the peas are tender. (If the pan begins to boil dry, add an extra tablespoon of water.) Add the pimiento and stir until the ingredients are well mixed.

Makes about 5 servings.

NUTRI-STEP 1

- Decrease the butter or margarine to 1 teaspoon. Stir the onion and cabbage constantly, and watch carefully to prevent them from sticking.
- Decrease the salt to a pinch or omit.

POTATO PANCAKES

Most potato pancakes are quite high in fat because they're fried in butter or oil. In our version, however, the pancakes are only lightly browned in a very small amount of oil and then baked to complete the cooking.

3   cups grated or shredded peeled potatoes •
1   large egg plus 2 large egg whites •
3   tablespoons enriched all-purpose or unbleached white flour
1   medium-sized onion, grated
½   teaspoon salt •
¼   teaspoon black pepper, preferably freshly ground
2   tablespoons vegetable oil, divided

To Serve
1   16-ounce can or jar unsweetened or regular applesauce (optional)

Put the grated or shredded potatoes in a colander to drain for about 5 minutes.

Meanwhile, in a medium bowl, beat the egg and egg whites together with a fork. Add the flour, onion, salt, pepper, and drained potatoes. Stir with a fork to mix well.

Put 1 tablespoon of the oil into a large skillet (or on a griddle) and turn the heat to medium-high. When the oil is hot but not smoking, transfer about ¼ cup of the potato mixture to the skillet (or griddle) and shape with a large spoon into a flat pancake. In the same manner, form several more pancakes in the pan and brown well on both sides, using about half of the potato mixture. Transfer to a lightly oiled or nonstick spray-coated baking sheet and set aside.

Add the remaining oil to the skillet and heat. Form the remaining potato mixture into pancakes, and brown on both sides. When the second batch is ready, transfer them to the baking sheet. Bake pancakes in a preheated 350-degree oven for 20 to 22 minutes, or until cooked through. Turn once during baking. If desired, serve the potato pancakes with applesauce.

Makes 4 to 5 servings.

- Leave the potatoes unpeeled and scrub well. (The peel is really unnoticeable in the pancakes.)
- Omit the large egg plus 2 large egg whites and SUBSTITUTE 3 large egg whites.
- Decrease the salt to a generous ¼ teaspoon.

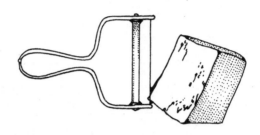

QUICK AU GRATIN POTATOES

8   cups ¼-inch-thick potato slices (4 medium baking potatoes) ■
2   tablespoons cornstarch
2   cups lowfat milk ●■
½   teaspoon onion powder
⅛   teaspoon garlic powder
⅛   teaspoon dry mustard
      Pinch of black pepper, preferably freshly ground
¼   teaspoon salt ●■
1   cup (about 4 ounces) grated Cheddar cheese ●■

Put the potatoes in a medium-sized saucepan and cover with water. Cover and bring to a boil over high heat. Lower the heat and simmer for about 9 minutes, or until the potatoes are tender. Drain the potatoes in a colander.

In a small bowl, combine the cornstarch and ¼ cup of the milk, stirring until a smooth paste is formed. Pour the cornstarch mixture into the pan used to cook the potatoes. Stir in the remaining milk. Cook over medium-high heat, stirring frequently, until the mixture begins to thicken. Lower the heat to medium and continue cooking until the sauce is smooth and thick. Turn the heat to very low and add the onion powder, garlic powder, dry mustard, pepper, and salt. Return the potatoes to the pan and heat, without boiling, for 4 or 5 minutes, stirring occasionally. Stir carefully so as not to break up the potatoes. Fold in the cheese, and cook until it melts, stirring carefully to avoid breaking up the potatoes.

Makes 6 side-dish servings.

Note: This is also hearty enough to serve as a vegetarian main dish.

NUTRI-STEP 1

- Omit the lowfat milk and SUBSTITUTE ⅔ cup nonfat dry milk powder mixed with a scant 2 cups water.
- Decrease the salt to a scant ¼ teaspoon.
- Decrease the grated Cheddar cheese to ¾ cup (3 ounces). If desired, part-skim Longhorn cheese can be substituted for the Cheddar. However, since this cheese is too soft to grate, it must be cut into very small cubes.

NUTRI-STEP 2

- Leave the potatoes unpeeled and scrub them well.
- Omit the lowfat milk and SUBSTITUTE ⅔ cup nonfat dry milk powder mixed with a scant 2 cups of water.
- Decrease the salt to ⅛ teaspoon or omit.
- Decrease the grated Cheddar cheese to ¾ cup. If desired, part-skim Longhorn cheese can be substituted for the Cheddar. However, since this cheese is too soft to grate, it must be cut into very small cubes.

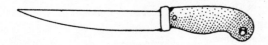

SWEET POTATO–PEAR CASSEROLE

This is great for a holiday celebration, such as Thanksgiving. It brings out the naturally sweet flavors of ripe pears and carotene-rich sweet potatoes. (By the way, sweet potatoes are also called "yams" in some parts of the country.)

5	cups peeled and thickly sliced (about ⅜ inch thick) sweet potatoes or "yams" (about 2½ pounds)
¼	cup finely chopped walnuts or pecans (optional) •
2	tablespoons dark brown sugar •
2½	tablespoons enriched all-purpose or unbleached white flour
½	teaspoon ground cinnamon •
¼	teaspoon ground nutmeg
⅛	teaspoon ground ginger •
2	tablespoons butter or margarine •
3	cups peeled and thinly-sliced ripe pears (about 3 medium) •

Put the sweet potato slices in a saucepan with about 1 inch of water. Cover tightly and bring to a boil. Then steam the sweet potatoes for about 20 minutes, or until just fork tender but not mushy. Remove from heat, and drain well.

Meanwhile, mix together the nuts, brown sugar, flour, and spices. Cut in the butter with a pastry blender, fork, or your fingertips until the nut mixture resembles coarse crumbs.

In the bottom of a greased or nonstick spray-coated 2-quart casserole, layer one third of the partially-cooked sweet potatoes. Top with one third of the pears; then sprinkle the pears with one third of the nut mixture. Repeat the layers twice more, ending with the nut mixture.

Bake the casserole, covered, in a preheated 350-degree oven for about 40 minutes, or until the pears are tender. Serve warm or at room temperature.

Makes about 6 servings.

NUTRI-STEP 1

- Decrease the nuts to 3 tablespoons.
- Decrease the dark brown sugar to 1½ tablespoons.
- Increase the cinnamon to a generous ½ teaspoon.
- Increase the ginger to ¼ teaspoon.
- Decrease the butter or margarine to 1½ tablespoons.
- Leave the pears unpeeled.

SWEET POTATO–PINEAPPLE BAKE

Here is a delicious, low-fat recipe featuring carotene-rich sweet potatoes.

3   large or 6 small sweet potatoes or "yams"
3   tablespoons butter, cut into small pieces •
½   cup orange juice
1   cup juice-packed crushed pineapple, well drained
½   cup raisins
¼   cup chopped walnuts
¼   teaspoon salt •
1   tablespoon packed light or dark brown sugar •

Bake the sweet potatoes in a preheated 375-degree oven for about 1½ hours, or until soft. Cool slightly and scoop out the pulp. Mash the pulp with a fork. You should have about 3 cups of pulp. Stir in butter until it is melted. Mix in the orange juice, pineapple, raisins, nuts, and salt. Spoon the mixture into a 1½-quart baking dish. Sprinkle the top with the brown sugar. Bake, covered, in a 375-degree oven for about 25 minutes, or until heated through.

Makes 4 servings.

NUTRI-STEP 1

- Decrease the butter to 2 tablespoons.
- Omit the salt.
- Omit the brown sugar topping.

SQUASH AND APPLE CASSEROLE

A good source of carotene, this tasty dish can be assembled in advance and then baked just before serving. It is perfect for a festive holiday dinner.

2	medium-sized acorn squash (about 1¼ pounds each)
2½	tablespoons maple syrup or packed light or dark brown sugar •
½	teaspoon ground cinnamon
¼	teaspoon ground nutmeg
1	large sweet apple, peeled, cored, and diced •
¼	cup finely chopped walnuts, divided •
¼	cup raisins or dried currants (optional)
2	teaspoons butter or margarine, cut into tiny pieces •

Cut the squash in half with a sharp heavy knife. Scoop out the seeds and fibers. Put the halves, cut side down, in a foil-lined baking pan containing about ¼ inch of water. Bake in a preheated 375-degree oven about 45 minutes to 1 hour, or until the squash flesh is quite tender when pierced with a fork.

Cool the squash slightly; then scoop the flesh into a bowl. Mix in the maple syrup, cinnamon, and nutmeg. Then stir in the apple, 2 tablespoons of the chopped nuts, and raisins.

Turn out the mixture into a lightly greased or nonstick spray-coated 1-quart casserole, and sprinkle the top with the remaining 2 tablespoons of nuts. Dab the butter pieces all over the top of the casserole. Bake, covered, in a preheated 350-degree oven for about 35 minutes, or until the apples are tender. Let the casserole stand for about 5 minutes before serving.

Makes about 4 to 6 servings.

Note: The same basic baking technique described above can be used to prepare plain, baked acorn squash, which are naturally very sweet and flavorful. After baking the squash, serve each person one hot, seeded, unpeeled squash half. If desired, each half may be drizzled with a teaspoon or two of maple syrup or topped with a teaspoon of butter or margarine at serving time.

NUTRI-STEP 1

- Decrease the syrup or brown sugar to 2 tablespoons.
- Leave the apple unpeeled.
- Decrease the walnuts to 2 tablespoons. Use ALL of the nuts as a topping on the casserole.
- Decrease the butter or margarine to 1½ teaspoons.

SUMMER SQUASH SAUTÉ

2   tablespoons vegetable oil ●■▲
1   medium-sized onion, finely chopped
1   clove garlic, peeled and finely minced
1   celery stalk, trimmed and diced
1   green pepper, seeded and diced
1   ripe, red bell pepper, seeded and diced (optional)
2   large or 4 small yellow summer squash, unpeeled and cut into ½-inch cubes
1   medium-sized tomato, cored and cut into ½-inch cubes
½   teaspoon salt ●■▲
⅛   teaspoon freshly ground black pepper

Heat the oil in a large skillet. Add the onion and garlic, and sauté for about 1 minute. Then add the celery, green pepper, red pepper, and squash. Cook, stirring constantly, for about 5 to 8 minutes, or until the vegetables are crisp-tender. Add the tomato, salt, and pepper and cook for 1 to 2 minutes longer to heat through.
    Makes about 6 servings.

NUTRI-STEP 1

- Decrease the oil to 1½ tablespoons. Stir the onion and garlic often to make sure they don't stick.
- Decrease the salt to ¼ teaspoon.

- Decrease the oil to 1½ tablespoons. Stir the onion and garlic often to make sure they don't stick.
- Decrease the salt to ⅛ teaspoon. *And add* ¼ teaspoon EACH dried basil leaves and dried thyme leaves to the vegetable mixture.

NUTRI-STEP 3

▲ Decrease the oil to 1 tablespoon. Stir the onion and garlic often to make sure they don't stick.

▲ Decrease the salt to a pinch or omit. *And add* ½ teaspoon EACH dried basil leaves and dried thyme leaves to the vegetable mixture.

STUFFED TOMATOES

These look quite elegant and are perfect for a company dinner or a special luncheon. In fact, they can even serve as the main course for a light meal which also includes some hearty soup and fresh bread.

4 or 5   **large tomatoes, preferably vine-ripened**

Stuffing

1   **10-ounce package frozen chopped spinach, thawed and very well drained**

¾   **cup part-skim ricotta cheese (if unavailable, substitute regular ricotta)**

3   **tablespoons grated Parmesan cheese ●**

1   **large egg (or 2 large egg whites) ●**

⅛   **teaspoon ground nutmeg**

2   **tablespoons fresh white or whole wheat bread crumbs ●**

¼   **teaspoon salt ●**

⅛   **teaspoon freshly ground black pepper**

Topping

1   **tablespoon fresh white or whole wheat bread crumbs ●**

1   **tablespoon grated Parmesan cheese ●**

Cut a thin, round slice from the stem end of each tomato, and discard. Carefully scoop out the pulp and seeds, and use for another purpose or discard (or eat!). Invert the tomato shells onto paper towels, and let them drain for 15 to 20 minutes.

Meanwhile, prepare the stuffing. Squeeze out any remaining water from the spinach and put the spinach in a medium-sized bowl. Add the ricotta cheese, Parmesan cheese, egg, nutmeg, bread crumbs, salt, and pepper and mix well to combine.

Place the tomato shells upright in a greased or nonstick spray-coated baking dish or in individual custard cups. Divide the stuffing evenly among the shells. Mix together the crumbs and cheese for the topping, and sprinkle on top of the stuffing. Bake the tomatoes in a preheated 350-degree oven for about 30 minutes. Serve hot, warm, or at room temperature.

Makes 4 to 5 servings.

NUTRI-STEP 1

Stuffing
- Omit the Parmesan cheese and SUBSTITUTE 3 tablespoons grated or finely chopped lowfat or part-skim cheese, such as mozzarella or your choice.
- Omit the large egg and USE 2 large egg whites.
- Omit the white bread crumbs and USE whole wheat bread crumbs.
- Decrease the salt to a generous ⅛ teaspoon. *And add* ⅛ teaspoon dried thyme and ¼ teaspoon dried basil.

Topping
- Omit the white bread crumbs and USE whole wheat bread crumbs.
- Omit the Parmesan cheese and SUBSTITUTE 1 tablespoon grated or finely chopped lowfat or part-skim cheese, such as mozzarella or your choice.

SCALLOPED TOMATOES AND CABBAGE

They'll never suspect this one is good for them; it tastes too buttery and delicious!

1½   tablespoons butter or margarine •
1   cup fresh white or whole wheat bread crumbs (made in a blender or food processor) •
1   small head cabbage (about 1 pound), cored and coarsely shredded
1   tablespoon instant minced onions
    Generous ¼ teaspoon celery seed
⅛   teaspoon celery salt
⅛   teaspoon black pepper, preferably freshly ground

⅛ teaspoon salt •
1 2-pound, 3-ounce can imported Italian tomatoes, including some juice, broken up with a spoon

Melt the butter in a medium-sized skillet over medium-high heat. Add the bread crumbs and stir until well mixed with the butter. Cook the crumbs, stirring constantly, for 6 to 7 minutes, or until they are slightly crisp and golden brown. Remove the skillet from the heat and set aside.

Lay half the shredded cabbage in the bottom of a lightly greased 1½-quart (or similar) ovenproof casserole. Press the cabbage down with your hands to form a compact layer.

In a cup or small bowl, stir together the instant onions, celery seed, celery salt, pepper, and salt. Sprinkle a generous quarter of the seasonings mixture over the cabbage.

Remove half the canned tomatoes from their juice with a slotted spoon, and place them over the cabbage layer. Sprinkle the tomato layer with a scant quarter of the seasonings and salt mixture. Spoon 2 tablespoons of tomato juice from the can over the casserole. Top the layers with half the browned bread crumbs. Lay the remaining half of the shredded cabbage over the crumbs, and press down lightly. Season with another generous quarter of the seasonings mixture; then top with the remaining tomatoes, remaining seasonings mixture, and 2 more tablespoons of juice from the canned tomatoes. (Discard the remaining juice or reserve for another use.) Sprinkle the remaining crumbs over the casserole and cover it tightly.

Bake in a preheated 375-degree oven for 35 to 45 minutes, or until the casserole is bubbly hot and the cabbage is just tender. This dish is very good reheated.
Makes about 6 servings.

NUTRI-STEP 1

- Decrease the butter or margarine to 1 tablespoon.
- Omit the white bread crumbs and USE 1 cup fresh whole wheat bread crumbs.
- Omit the salt.

SUMMER VEGETABLE MEDLEY

     1   tablespoon vegetable oil •
     1   large onion, coarsely chopped
     1   large celery stalk, cut into ¼-inch slices
     ½   cup chopped fresh parsley leaves
     1   medium yellow squash, cut into ½-inch cubes
     1   small white (pattypan) squash, cut into ½-inch cubes
     1   small eggplant, peeled and cut into ½-inch cubes
     3   large vine-ripened tomatoes, peeled, cored, and chopped
     ¾   teaspoon salt •
     ⅛   teaspoon black pepper, preferably freshly ground •
  3 to 4 drops hot pepper sauce

Put the oil in a large heavy saucepan over medium-high heat. Add the onion and celery and cook for 3 to 4 minutes, or until the vegetables are limp. Stir in the parsley and cook for 1 minute longer. Add all the remaining ingredients, stirring well. Cover and lower the heat. Stirring occasionally, simmer the vegetables for 20 to 25 minutes longer, or until they are tender.

Makes 4 to 6 servings.

NUTRI-STEP 1

- Decrease the vegetable oil to 1 teaspoon. Stir vegetables constantly and watch carefully to prevent them from sticking and burning.
- Decrease the salt to a generous ½ teaspoon.
- Increase the black pepper to a scant ¼ teaspoon.

RATATOUILLE

This French provincial vegetable "stew" (pronounced "rah-tah-too'-ee") makes a very nice side dish when served hot, and a great appetizer when chilled. It will keep for several days in the refrigerator. Olive oil gives this dish a wonderful "Mediterranean" flavor; however, you may substitute vegetable oil if you wish.

Note: The exact amounts of the following vegetables and herbs are not critical. Use what you have available, and adjust the herbs to your own taste.

     2½   tablespoons good-quality olive oil ••■
     2   large onions, thinly sliced
     3   cloves garlic, peeled and minced
     2   medium-sized green peppers, seeded and coarsely chopped

2	16-ounce cans regular tomatoes or imported Italian tomatoes, including juice, coarsely chopped ●■
1	medium-sized eggplant, peeled and cut into ¾-inch cubes ●■
3 or 4	medium-sized unpeeled zucchini, halved lengthwise and sliced
¼	cup finely chopped fresh parsley leaves
2	teaspoons dried basil leaves, or 2 tablespoons chopped fresh basil
½	teaspoon dried thyme leaves, or 1½ teaspoons chopped fresh thyme ■
½	teaspoon dried oregano leaves, or 1½ teaspoons chopped fresh oregano ■
¼	teaspoon freshly ground black pepper, or to taste
¾	teaspoon salt ●■

Heat the oil in a Dutch oven or large heavy skillet. Add the onions and garlic and sauté until tender but not brown. Add the green pepper, and sauté for another 30 seconds. Stir in the tomatoes and their juice, eggplant, zucchini, herbs, pepper, and salt. Cover the pot and simmer, stirring occasionally, for about 30 minutes, or until all the vegetables are tender. Remove the lid and cook, stirring often, until most of the liquid has evaporated. Adjust the pepper to taste if necessary. Serve hot, at room temperature, or cold.

Makes about 8 servings.

NUTRI-STEP 1

- Decrease the oil to 2 tablespoons. Stir onions often to make sure that they don't stick.
- If fresh vine-ripened tomatoes are in season, substitute 6 large ones for the canned ones. If they are not very juicy, add a small amount of water or tomato juice to the pot.
- Leave the eggplant unpeeled.
- Decrease the salt to a scant ¾ teaspoon.

NUTRI-STEP 2

- Decrease the oil to 1½ tablespoons. Stir the onions often to make sure that they don't stick.
- If fresh vine-ripened tomatoes are in season, substitute 6 large ones for the canned ones. If they are not very juicy, add a small amount of tomato juice or water.
- Leave the eggplant unpeeled.
- Increase the thyme to ¾ teaspoon dried or 2 teaspoons fresh.
- Increase the oregano to ¾ teaspoon dried or 2 teaspoons fresh.
- Decrease the salt to a generous ½ teaspoon.

MUSTARD SAUCE FOR VEGETABLES

Use this light and tasty sauce to dress up broccoli, cauliflower, carrots, celery, or turnips.

1½	tablespoons butter or margarine •
1	tablespoon enriched all-purpose or unbleached white flour
1½	tablespoons Dijon or Dijon-style mustard
¼	teaspoon paprika
⅛	teaspoon salt •
¾	cup lowfat milk
1	tablespoon dry white table wine or dry sherry

Melt the butter in a small, heavy saucepan over medium-high heat. Add the flour and stir until the mixture is well blended and smooth. Cook, stirring constantly, for 1½ minutes. Remove the pan from the heat and stir the mustard, paprika, and salt into the flour mixture. Return the pan to the heat and add the milk in a slow, thin stream, stirring vigorously until the mixture is thoroughly blended and smooth. Cook, continuing to stir, until the sauce comes to a boil and thickens slightly. Add the wine and cook, stirring, for 1 minute longer. Serve immediately.

Makes about 1 cup sauce or enough to dress 5 to 5½ cups of cooked vegetables.

NUTRI-STEP 1

- Decrease the butter or margarine to 1 tablespoon.
- Decrease the salt to a pinch or omit.

Chapter 8

Grain and Legume Side Dishes

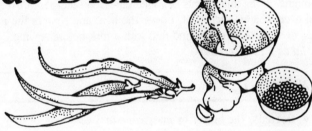

Dishes featuring whole grains and beans can be among the most nutritious, not to mention delicious and satisfying, in a cook's repertoire. And they are very easy on the budget, too.

This chapter includes nutritionally-improved versions of old favorites, such as New England-style baked beans, fried rice, and a hearty corn casserole. And there are also a number of recipes for less familiar but equally appealing dishes, which demonstrate the wonderful variety and versatility of grains and beans.

Just about all our rice dishes eventually suggest that whole grain brown rice be substituted for white rice. If you've eaten brown rice before, you know how delicious it can be. If you haven't, our special recipes are the best way to introduce this whole grain into your family's meals. We've designed and seasoned our recipes so that the difference between white and brown will hardly be noticed—although there's always the possibility that your family may like some dishes better with brown rice than with white!

By the way, our Vegetarian Main Dishes chapter also features several tasty recipes which highlight grains and beans. In smaller portions, some of them could be served as side dishes.

87

RICE AND CARROT PILAF

2	cups uncooked white rice ▪
4	cups water
1	large carrot, grated or shredded
1	small onion, finely shredded ▪
2	teaspoons butter or margarine ●▪
¾	teaspoon salt ●▪
⅛	teaspoon black pepper, preferably freshly ground
3 to 4	drops hot pepper sauce
⅛	teaspoon garlic powder
2	large bay leaves
	Pinch of ground cloves
⅛	teaspoon ground cinnamon ▪
⅛	teaspoon ground marjoram

Combine all the ingredients in a medium-sized saucepan. Cover and bring to a full boil over medium-high heat. Lower the heat and simmer the mixture for 20 minutes, or until tender. Stir and fluff with a fork before serving.

Makes 6 to 8 servings.

NUTRI-STEP 1

- Decrease the butter or margarine to 1 teaspoon or omit.
- Decrease the salt to a generous ½ teaspoon.

NUTRI-STEP 2

▪ Omit the white rice and SUBSTITUTE 2 cups of brown rice. Increase the cooking time to 45 to 50 minutes.
▪ Increase the onion to 1 medium-sized.
▪ Decrease the butter or margarine to 1 teaspoon or omit.
▪ Decrease the salt to a generous ½ teaspoon.
▪ Increase the cinnamon to ¼ teaspoon.

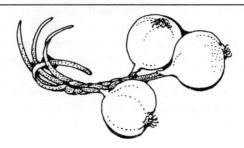

HERBED RICE

1½ cups uncooked white rice •
3 cups water
½ cup fresh parsley, finely chopped (coarse stems discarded)
½ cup finely chopped green onions (scallions), including tops
⅛ teaspoon dried thyme leaves
   Scant ¾ teaspoon salt •
⅛ teaspoon black pepper, preferably freshly ground

Combine all the ingredients in a medium-sized saucepan over high heat. Cover and bring to a boil. Lower the heat and simmer for 20 minutes, or until all the water is absorbed and the rice is tender. Stir the rice well before serving.

Makes 4 to 6 servings.

NUTRI-STEP 1

- Omit the white rice and SUBSTITUTE 1½ cups uncooked brown rice. Cook the brown rice for about 45 minutes, or until all the water is absorbed and the rice is tender.
- Decrease the salt to ½ teaspoon.

ORIENTAL FRIED RICE

1½ tablespoons peanut or corn oil •■
1 large celery stalk, including leaves, finely chopped
7 to 8 green onions (scallions), including tops, finely chopped
1 clove garlic, peeled and minced
3 to 4 medium-sized fresh mushrooms, sliced (optional)
1½ cups fresh bean sprouts (if unavailable, substitute 1 cup well-drained canned bean sprouts)
½ cup finely shredded cabbage •■
4½ cups cooked and cooled white rice ■
2½ tablespoons soy sauce •■
   Scant ¼ teaspoon freshly ground black pepper

Heat the oil in a large heavy skillet over high heat. Add the celery, green onions, and garlic and cook, stirring constantly, for 3 minutes. Add the mushrooms, bean sprouts, and cabbage and cook, stirring constantly, for 2 minutes. Stir in the rice, lower the heat to medium, and cook, stirring, for 3 to 4 minutes longer, or until the rice and vegetables are well blended. Add the soy sauce and pepper, and continue stirring until thoroughly and evenly incorporated into the rice mixture.

Makes 5 to 6 servings.

NUTRI-STEP 1

- Decrease the oil to 1 tablespoon. Stir the ingredients constantly and watch carefully to prevent them from sticking and burning.
- Increase the shredded cabbage to ¾ cup.
- Decrease the soy sauce to 2 tablespoons.

NUTRI-STEP 2

- Decrease the oil to 1 tablespoon. Stir the ingredients constantly and watch carefully to prevent them from sticking and burning.
- Increase the shredded cabbage to ¾ cup.
- Omit the white rice and SUBSTITUTE 4½ cups cooked and cooled brown rice.
- Decrease the soy sauce to 2 tablespoons.

SPANISH-STYLE BROWN RICE

This flavorful side dish is a good way to introduce your family to the appealing taste and texture of brown rice. The cooking technique is similar in many ways to the one used for pilafs; however, the seasoning is different.

2½	tablespoons olive or vegetable oil •
1	medium-sized onion, finely chopped
2	cloves garlic, peeled and minced
1	medium-sized green pepper, seeded and finely chopped
1¼	cups uncooked brown rice
1	16-ounce can tomatoes, including juice, coarsely chopped
1¾	cups hot water
1	teaspoon paprika
½	teaspoon salt •
¼	teaspoon chili powder, or more to taste •

Heat the oil in a large saucepan; then add the onion, garlic, and green pepper and cook until tender but not browned. Add the rice and cook, stirring constantly, for 2 minutes longer. Stir in chopped tomatoes and their juice, the hot water, paprika, salt, and chili powder. Bring to a boil, lower the heat, and cover tightly. Simmer, covered, for about 45 minutes, or until all the liquid is absorbed. Stir once before serving to evenly mix the rice and vegetables.

Makes 6 to 8 servings.

NUTRI-STEP 1

- Decrease the oil to 2 tablespoons. Stir the onions and other vegetables often to make sure they don't stick.
- Decrease the salt to ¼ teaspoon.
- Increase the chili powder to ½ teaspoon.

BROWN RICE AND LENTIL PILAF

2	teaspoons butter or margarine •
1	small onion, finely chopped
1	clove garlic, peeled and chopped
1	medium-sized celery stalk, finely chopped
1	cup uncooked brown rice
½	cup dry lentils, rinsed, sorted, and drained
3½	cups water
¼	teaspoon dry mustard
¼	teaspoon ground thyme
1	large bay leaf
¼	teaspoon celery seed
3 to 4	drops hot pepper sauce
	Pinch of ground cloves
½	teaspoon salt •
¼	teaspoon ground marjoram
⅛	teaspoon ground savory
¼	teaspoon prepared horseradish
¼	teaspoon black pepper, preferably freshly ground

Melt the butter in a medium-sized saucepan over medium heat. Add the onion, garlic, and celery and cook until the onion is soft. Stir frequently to prevent burning. Stir in the rice and lentils. Add the water and seasonings. Bring to a boil. Cover the pan, lower the heat, and simmer for 45 minutes, or until the water is absorbed and the rice and lentils are tender.

Makes 6 to 8 servings.

NEW ENGLAND-STYLE BAKED BEANS

3	cups dry Great Northern beans, sorted and rinsed
2½	tablespoons butter or margarine •
1	large onion, coarsely chopped
3	tablespoons chopped fresh parsley leaves
2	teaspoons dry mustard
¼	teaspoon ground ginger •
¼	teaspoon dried thyme leaves •
¼	teaspoon ground allspice
	Scant ⅛ teaspoon ground cloves
1	teaspoon salt •
	Generous ⅛ teaspoon black pepper, preferably freshly ground
1	tablespoon apple cider vinegar
¼	cup light molasses
1½	tablespoons packed dark brown sugar •

Cover the beans with about 3 inches of water in a 4-quart Dutch oven or similar ovenproof pot. Bring to a rolling boil over medium-high heat. Then turn off the heat and let stand for 1 hour, covered. If necessary, add more water to cover the beans, and once again, bring them to a simmer over medium-high heat. Lower the heat and simmer gently, covered, for 1 hour. Drain off and reserve 2½ cups of the bean cooking liquid. Turn the beans into a colander, discarding remaining liquid.

Rinse out and dry the Dutch oven or pot previously used. Add the butter to the pot, and melt over medium-high heat. Add the onion and parsley and cook, stirring, for 3 to 4 minutes, or until the onion is limp. Stir in the reserved bean liquid and all the remaining ingredients. Return the drained beans to the pot. Cover and bake in a 350-degree oven for 1 hour. Lower the oven temperature to 275 degrees, and bake for 2 hours longer. Remove the lid and continue baking for 30 to 35 minutes more, or until the beans are light brown and most of the excess moisture has been absorbed. Baked beans are good reheated.

Makes 6 to 8 servings.

- Decrease the butter or margarine to 1½ tablespoons.
- Increase the ginger to a scant ½ teaspoon.
- Increase the thyme to a scant ½ teaspoon.
- Decrease the salt to ¾ teaspoon.
- Decrease the dark brown sugar to 1 tablespoon.

HERBED WHITE BEANS WITH TOMATOES

1½	cups dry Great Northern beans, sorted and rinsed
2¼	cups water
2	medium-sized onions, cut into eighths
2	large cloves garlic, peeled and finely chopped
2	medium-sized celery stalks, including leaves, very coarsely sliced
1	medium-sized carrot, coarsely sliced
1	small turnip, peeled and coarsely chopped (optional)
¼	cup coarsely chopped fresh parsley leaves
¼	teaspoon dried thyme leaves
⅛	teaspoon dried marjoram leaves •
1	large bay leaf
⅛	teaspoon ground cloves
1⅛	teaspoons salt •
2	tablespoons butter or margarine •
2	medium-sized tomatoes, peeled, cored, and chopped
1	tablespoon fresh chives, or 1½ teaspoons dried chives
⅛	teaspoon black pepper, preferably freshly ground

Put the beans in a large saucepan and cover with 2 inches cold water. Place the pan over medium heat, bring to a full boil, and boil 2 minutes. Remove from the heat and let stand, covered, for 1 hour. Turn the beans into a colander, discarding the water.

Return the drained beans to the saucepan previously used, and add 2¼ cups water. Add the onions, garlic, celery, carrot, turnip, and parsley to the pan. Stir in the dried herbs, ground cloves, and salt. Bring to a boil over medium heat. Cover the pan, lower the heat, and simmer gently for 1 hour, stirring occasionally. Uncover the pan and simmer for 10 to 20 minutes longer, or until the beans are tender, stirring occasionally. Add the butter, chopped tomatoes, chives, and pepper. Continue simmering, uncovered, for 15 minutes longer, or until the tomatoes are soft and most of the excess liquid has evaporated. The dish may be served immediately or refrigerated and re-warmed at serving time. (Add a little water if necessary for reheating.)

Makes 5 to 6 servings.

NUTRI-STEP 1

- Increase the marjoram to ¼ teaspoon.
- Decrease the salt to 1 teaspoon.
- Decrease the butter or margarine to 1½ tablespoons.

SPICY BARBECUED BEANS

These delicious beans will zip up any meal. And there's no need to soak them before cooking as is often required.

1½	cups dry navy or pinto beans, sorted and rinsed
9	cups water
1	large onion, finely chopped
1	clove garlic, peeled and minced
2	bay leaves
1	15-ounce can tomato sauce
1	tablespoon packed light or dark brown sugar •
1	tablespoon dark molasses
¼	teaspoon onion powder
⅛	teaspoon garlic powder
	Pinch of ground cloves
¼	teaspoon chili powder
½	teaspoon dry mustard
⅛	teaspoon black pepper, preferably freshly ground
2 to 3	drops hot pepper sauce

In a large saucepan, combine the beans, water, onion, garlic, and bay leaves. Bring to a boil, cover, and lower the heat. Simmer, stirring occasionally, for about 1 hour and 30 minutes to 1 hour and 45 minutes, or until the beans are tender.

Drain the beans thoroughly in a colander and discard the bay leaves. Return the beans to the pan and add all the remaining ingredients. Cover and cook over very low heat for about 15 to 20 minutes, stirring often and checking to make sure the sauce is not sticking to the bottom of the pan.

Makes about 6 servings.

TEX-MEX RICE AND BEAN BAKE

This makes a very zesty and filling side dish. Because the rice and beans "complement" one another nutritionally, the casserole furnishes high-quality protein and could also be served as a main dish.

1¼	cups uncooked white rice •
1	cup water •
1½	tablespoons butter or margarine •
1	large onion, coarsely chopped
1	large celery stalk, including leaves, coarsely chopped
½	cup diced green pepper
¼	cup coarsely chopped fresh parsley leaves
1	16-ounce can tomatoes, including juice
1	8-ounce can tomato sauce
1	tablespoon dried chopped chives
½	teaspoon dried thyme leaves
1	small bay leaf, finely crumbled
1½	tablespoons mild chili powder
1	teaspoon paprika
¼	teaspoon salt •
1 to 2	tablespoons canned, chopped green chilies, well drained (or use more for a very "hot" dish)
1	15- or 16-ounce can kidney beans, well drained
2	tablespoons grated Longhorn or mild Cheddar cheese •

Bring the rice and water to a boil in a small Dutch oven (or other 2- to 3-quart stove-top *and* ovenproof pot) over medium-high heat. Lower the heat and simmer, covered, for 5 to 6 minutes, or until the water is absorbed. Turn the rice into a colander and let it drain for 5 minutes.

Rinse out and dry the pot. Add the butter to the pot, and put it over medium-high heat. Add the onion, celery, green pepper, and parsley. Cook, stirring, for 4 to 5 minutes, or until the vegetables are soft. Add the tomatoes, breaking them up with a spoon, then the tomato sauce, herbs, seasonings, and green chilies. Bring the mixture to a boil. Stir in the kidney beans and rice until well mixed. Remove the pot from the heat and sprinkle the cheese over the rice and beans.

Cover and bake in a preheated 350-degree oven for 30 minutes, or until the mixture is bubbly and the rice is just tender. If any excess moisture remains on the surface of the casserole, remove the lid and bake for about 5 minutes longer, or until evaporated.

Makes 5 to 6 side-dish servings.

NUTRI-STEP 1

- Omit the white rice and SUBSTITUTE brown rice.
- Increase the water to 1¾ cups. Cook the brown rice for 25 minutes, or until the water is absorbed. Then, let drain and proceed as directed in the basic recipe.
- Decrease the butter or margarine to 1 tablespoon. When cooking the vegetables, stir constantly and watch carefully to prevent them from sticking and burning.
- Omit the salt.
- Decrease the grated cheese to 1 tablespoon.

LIMA BEAN BAKE

2	cups dry lima beans, washed and sorted
2	teaspoons butter or margarine •
1	clove garlic, peeled and chopped
1	large onion, finely chopped
1	medium-sized celery stalk, finely chopped
1	15-ounce can tomato sauce
⅛	teaspoon black pepper, preferably freshly ground
¼	teaspoon dry mustard
2 to 3	drops hot pepper sauce
¾	teaspoon dried basil leaves
¼	teaspoon celery seed
⅛	teaspoon salt •

In a large heavy pot, combine 3 quarts of water and the lima beans and bring to a boil over high heat. Cover, lower the heat, and simmer for about 1 hour and 20 minutes, or until the beans are just tender. Remove from the heat and drain in a colander.

Melt the butter in a medium-sized skillet over medium heat. Add the garlic, onion, and celery and cook until the onion is limp. Put the lima beans in a 1½-quart casserole. Gently stir in the onion, garlic, and celery. Add all the remaining ingredients, and stir gently to mix. Bake, covered, in a preheated 325-degree oven for 30 minutes, or until hot and bubbly.

Makes 4 to 6 servings.

NUTRI-STEP 1

- Decrease the butter or margarine to 1 teaspoon and stir the vegetables well to prevent them from sticking.
- Omit the salt.

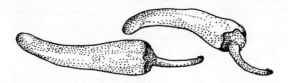

FESTIVE CORN CASSEROLE

Easy-to-prepare, healthful, economical, and tasty: For all these reasons, this is an appealing family side dish.

1	1-pound can cream-style yellow corn
1	1-pound can yellow corn kernels, well drained
1⅓	cups white or whole wheat bread crumbs (purchased or prepared in a blender from slightly stale bread)
1½	tablespoons instant minced onion
¼	cup chopped canned pimiento, well drained
2	tablespoons finely chopped green pepper
2	tablespoons finely chopped celery (optional)
⅛	teaspoon salt •
⅛	teaspoon black pepper, preferably freshly ground
1	tablespoon cold butter or margarine •

In a flat 9-inch square or similar casserole stir together cream-style corn, corn kernels, and 1 cup of the bread crumbs. (Reserve the remaining crumbs.) Add the onion, pimiento, green pepper, celery, salt, and black pepper to the casserole, stirring until thoroughly blended. Spread out the mixture to form an even layer. Sprinkle the reserved crumbs over the corn mixture. Dot the top of the casserole with butter. Bake in a preheated 375-degree oven for 30 to 35 minutes, or until the mixture is bubbly hot and the top is lightly browned.

Makes 6 to 7 servings.

NUTRI-STEP 1

- Omit the salt.
- Omit the butter; sprinkle the bread crumbs over the casserole and bake.

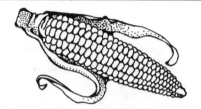

MEXICAN-STYLE CORN AND RICE

Because corn and rice combine to form a "complete" protein, this can serve as a light main dish as well as a side dish.

1	small onion, finely minced
2	teaspoons vegetable oil ●■
1½	cups uncooked white rice
2	cups water
¼	cup diced green pepper
½	teaspoon salt ●■
	Pinch of garlic powder
1	teaspoon chili powder ■
¼	teaspoon ground cumin (optional)
	Pinch of cayenne pepper
1½	cups fresh or frozen corn kernels
1	16-ounce can tomatoes, including juice

In a medium-sized saucepan over medium heat, cook the onion in the oil until it is soft. Add the rice, water, green pepper, salt, garlic powder, chili powder, cumin, and cayenne pepper. Stir in the corn and tomatoes, breaking up the tomatoes with a spoon. Bring to a boil over high heat. Cover, lower the heat, and simmer for 20 to 25 minutes, or until the liquid is absorbed and the rice is just tender.

Makes 5 to 6 side-dish servings.

NUTRI-STEP 1

- Omit the oil. Do not sauté the onion. Add the onion to the pan along with the rice, seasonings, and green pepper.
- Decrease the salt to ¼ teaspoon.

- Omit the oil. Do not sauté the onion. Add the onion to the pan along with the rice, seasonings, and green pepper.
- Omit the salt.
- Increase the chili powder to 1¼ teaspoons.

PLAIN-COOKED BULGUR, BUCKWHEAT GROATS, OR MILLET

BULGUR is kernels (or "berries") of whole wheat which have been parboiled, dried, and cracked into small pieces. (Cracked wheat is similar, but it has usually not been parboiled.) Both bulgur and cracked wheat contain all the nutrients of the whole wheat kernel, making them quite nutritious. Bulgur has an almost chewy texture, and a slightly nutty, very tasty flavor.

BUCKWHEAT is botanically not a grain; however, it is usually cooked and eaten like one. It is very high in protein, and is also rich in vitamins and minerals. Kernels of buckwheat—referred to as "groats" or "kasha"—can be purchased finely ground (sometimes called buckwheat "grits"), coarsely cracked, or whole. Buckwheat has a slightly nutty flavor which is a bit like bulgur, though a little stronger. However, the groats do not have the overpowering taste of buckwheat flour. Buckwheat is especially good when prepared as a pilaf.

MILLET is a nutritious whole grain which has been neglected by most Americans. This is unfortunate since, among the grains, millet has some of the best-quality protein and is one of the highest in iron. When the tiny, yellow spheres of whole millet are cooked, they become cream-colored and have a wonderful, mild flavor and a pleasing texture that sort of "tickles the tongue." In fact, the look and taste is very reminiscent of tiny bits of pasta or egg barley. Also, millet does not contain gluten, and can usually be eaten by those with wheat allergies.

Plain-cooked bulgur, buckwheat groats, and millet can all be cooked and used like rice. Just as with rice, you can vary the flavor by cooking them in bouillon or other liquid instead of plain water. (For instance, see our recipe for Millet and Cheese.) By increasing the liquid, they can also be cooked into nutritious and satisfying hot cereals.

Although some supermarkets are beginning to stock bulgur and millet, it may be necessary to get them at a health food store or by mail order. Buckwheat groats can be found in most supermarkets, sometimes in the specialty or foreign foods section.

RECIPE

2 cups water
¼ teaspoon salt •
1 cup uncooked bulgur, buckwheat groats, or whole millet

Bring water and salt to a boil. Add the bulgur, buckwheat, or millet and stir once. Then cover tightly. Reduce the heat to low, and simmer for about 15 to 20 minutes, or just until the grain has absorbed the liquid. Remove from the heat, and fluff with a fork to separate the grains. Serve hot, in a manner similar to "plain cooked" rice—that is, as a bed under meats or stews, as a side dish topped with a dab of butter or margarine, or as pilafs. (Also, millet is very good when substituted for rice in "rice pudding.")

Makes about 4 servings.

NUTRI-STEP 1

• Decrease the salt to ⅛ teaspoon or omit.

MILLET AND CHEESE

This tasty and very nutritious dish—a variation on macaroni and cheese—is a great way to serve millet, especially if the grain is unfamiliar to your family.

Note: For more information on millet, see the recipe for Plain-cooked Millet above.

3 cups water
1 cup uncooked whole millet
⅔ cup instant nonfat dry milk powder, divided
¼ to ½ teaspoon dry mustard, or to taste
Scant ⅛ teaspoon salt, or less to taste •
4 ounces (1 cup, packed) grated sharp Cheddar cheese •

Bring the water to a boil in a medium-sized saucepan. Stir in the millet and ⅓ cup of the milk powder. Cover, reduce the heat to low, and simmer for 20 minutes. (There should still be a little liquid left in the pan; if not, stir in a few additional tablespoons of water, and heat to simmering.) Slowly stir in the remaining ⅓ cup of milk powder, dry mustard, salt, and cheese. Continue stirring over low heat until the cheese is completely melted and the mixture is hot.

Makes about 6 servings as a side dish.

NUTRI-STEP 1

- Reduce the salt to a pinch or omit.
- Omit the regular Cheddar cheese and SUBSTITUTE 4 ounces (1 cup, packed) grated or very finely chopped lowfat or part-skim Cheddar-type cheese.

RANGE-TOP STUFFING

This range-top recipe is designed to be used with fresh or slightly stale bread cut into cubes. (Don't use packaged bread cubes, as the stuffing will be too dry.)

The recipe can also be baked inside a chicken; it makes enough for a 4-pound bird. Because the stuffing will absorb flavor and fat from the chicken during baking, you may want to reduce the butter or margarine by 1 tablespoon. Also, there's no need to cook the bread cubes in the frying pan first. Simply stir them into the rest of the ingredients and begin stuffing the bird.

3	tablespoons butter or margarine ●
1	medium-sized onion, finely chopped
2	medium-sized celery stalks, coarsely chopped
¼	teaspoon salt ●
⅛	teaspoon black pepper, preferably freshly ground
¼	teaspoon dry mustard
1	teaspoon dried marjoram leaves
¼	teaspoon ground sage
¼	teaspoon ground thyme
4	cups bread cubes, cut from fresh or slightly stale white or whole wheat bread ●

Melt the butter in a large heavy skillet over medium heat. Add the onion and celery and cook, stirring often, until the onion is soft. Stir in the salt, pepper, mustard, marjoram, sage, and thyme and mix thoroughly. Add the bread cubes and stir well until coated on all surfaces with the seasoned butter or margarine. Cook, uncovered, over medium heat for about 5 or 6 minutes longer.

Makes 4 servings.

Alternate Oven Method: If you are preparing an oven dinner, this stuffing can be baked in a 1½ -quart casserole. First cook the onion and celery in butter or margarine. Add the seasonings and mix well. Add the bread cubes and stir until well blended. Then turn the stuffing into the casserole, and bake at 350 degrees for 35 minutes.

NUTRI-STEP 1

- Decrease the butter or margarine to 2½ tablespoons.
- Decrease the salt to ⅛ teaspoon.
- Omit the white bread and USE whole wheat bread for cubes.

Chapter 9

Main Dishes—Beef

Many of the recipes in this chapter are family favorites—Spaghetti Sauce, Chili con Carne, Meatloaf, and Sloppy Joes. Others, such as Beef Stew with Red Wine or Hungarian Goulash, are special enough for company fare. But, whether homey or grand, they all call for lean cuts, such as round steak, chuck arm roast, flank steak, and lean ground beef. And most offer a flavorful combination of beef and vegetables. In fact, while all these dishes are hearty and satisfying, they almost always contain less meat than you would expect in similar recipes. This not only cuts down on fat, but it also helps stretch the family budget.

SPICY POT ROAST WITH VEGETABLES

1	3½- to 4-pound (bone-in) beef chuck arm roast, trimmed of all excess fat •
1	large onion, coarsely chopped
1	large celery stalk, including leaves, coarsely chopped
¼	cup chopped fresh parsley leaves
1	small turnip, coarsely chopped
1	8-ounce can tomato sauce
⅔	cup water
2	tablespoons packed light brown sugar
1	tablespoon apple cider vinegar
1	tablespoon dried chopped chives
½	teaspoon salt •
½	teaspoon chili powder
¼	teaspoon dry mustard
⅛	teaspoon ground allspice
⅛	teaspoon dried thyme leaves
⅛	teaspoon black pepper, preferably freshly ground
5 to 6	large potatoes, peeled and quartered
4	carrots, coarsely sliced
2	medium-sized turnips, peeled and quartered
6	small white onions, peeled, or 3 medium-sized yellow onions, peeled and halved
1	cup fresh or frozen whole string beans (optional)

Heat the oil in a large Dutch oven, and brown the roast well over medium-high heat. Add the onion, celery, parsley, and turnip and cook until the vegetables are limp. Reduce the heat to medium-low.

In a small bowl, combine the tomato sauce, water, brown sugar, vinegar, and all the herbs and spices. Stir until blended; then add the mixture to the pot. Cover the pot, and simmer the roast for 2¼ hours, stirring once or twice. Stir all the remaining vegetables into the pot and baste them with some of the pot liquid. Cover and cook, stirring occasionally, for 40 to 45 minutes, or until the vegetables are tender.

Makes 5 to 6 servings.

NUTRI-STEP 1

- Decrease the roast to 3 pounds.
- Decrease the salt to ¼ teaspoon. *And add* 1½ cups large fresh cauliflower flowerets with the potatoes and other vegetables.

SAUCY POT ROAST

 1   tablespoon vegetable oil •
 1   lean round roast (about 3 pounds), trimmed of all visible fat •
 1   medium-sized onion, thinly sliced
 1   clove garlic, finely minced or pressed
 ½   teaspoon dried marjoram leaves
 ½   teaspoon dried thyme leaves
 ½   teaspoon dried rosemary leaves
 1   medium-sized bay leaf
 ¼   teaspoon dry mustard
 1   6-ounce can tomato paste
1¼   cups water
 ⅓   cup dry sherry or dry white wine
1½   tablespoons packed dark brown sugar •
 ¼   teaspoon salt •
 ⅛   teaspoon black pepper, preferably freshly ground
     About 8 very small new potatoes, peeled •
 4   medium-sized carrots, cut into 2-inch chunks •

Heat the oil in a Dutch oven or other large heavy pot, and brown the roast on all sides. Add the onions and garlic, and cook for 1 minute, stirring.

In a small bowl, stir together all the remaining ingredients except the potatoes and carrots until well mixed. Pour this sauce over the roast, making sure the meat is well coated. Heat the sauce to boiling; then cover the pot tightly, and lower the heat to simmer.

Simmer the roast, basting often, for about 1 hour. Stir in the potatoes and carrots. Cover the pot and continue to simmer and baste the roast for about 1 hour longer, or until it is very tender. If the sauce seems to be drying out, stir in a little extra water. (Alternatively, the sauce-covered roast may be baked, covered, in a preheated 350-degree oven for about 3 hours, or until it is tender. Add the vegetables after the roast has baked 1½ hours.)

When the pot roast is done, remove from the heat and let stand for about 10 minutes before slicing. Remove the bay leaf. Serve with the vegetables and sauce from the pot.

Makes about 8 servings.

- Decrease the oil to 2 teaspoons. Rotate the roast often during browning.
- Decrease the size of the roast to about 2½ pounds. Decrease the cooking time about 10 to 20 minutes. Add the vegetables after the roast has simmered for about 45 minutes.
- Decrease the dark brown sugar to 1 tablespoon.
- Decrease the salt to a generous ⅛ teaspoon.
- Leave the potatoes unpeeled, but scrub them well.
- Increase the carrots to 6 medium-sized ones, cut into 2-inch chunks.

BELGIAN BEEF AND BEER STEW

¼   cup enriched all-purpose or unbleached white flour
¼   teaspoon salt •
⅛   teaspoon black pepper, preferably freshly ground
2   pounds lean stew beef, trimmed of all fat and cut into 1-inch cubes
3   tablespoons vegetable oil •
6   medium-sized onions, thinly sliced
2   cloves garlic, peeled and finely minced
1   bottle or can (11 to 12 ounces) regular or low-calorie ("light") beer •
1   medium-sized bay leaf
½   teaspoon dried thyme leaves
     About 2 pounds potatoes, peeled and cut into large chunks •
2   tablespoons chopped fresh parsley leaves

Mix together the flour, salt, and pepper; then dredge the beef cubes in the mixture, shaking off any excess. Set aside momentarily.

Heat the oil in a Dutch oven or large, deep ovenproof skillet (with a lid). Add the onions and garlic and sauté for about 2 minutes, or until the vegetables are limp. Add the beef cubes, and brown lightly on all sides. Add the beer, bay leaf, and thyme and mix well. Cover the pot, and simmer gently on top of the stove, or place in a preheated 325-degree oven. Cook for about 1½ to 2 hours, or until the meat is very tender. (It will take a little longer in the oven.)

When the stew is almost ready, put the potatoes in a saucepan with about 1 inch of water. Cover, bring to a boil, lower the heat, and steam for about 20 to 25 minutes, or until they are tender. Drain well. Transfer to a serving bowl.

Remove the bay leaf and ladle the stew over the cooked potatoes. Sprinkle the chopped parsley over the top just before serving.

Makes about 6 servings.

NUTRI-STEP 1

- Decrease the salt to a generous ⅛ teaspoon.
- Decrease the oil to 2 tablespoons. Stir the onions and beef often to make sure they don't stick. (Use a nonstick pan, if available.)
- Omit the regular beer and USE the low-calorie ("light") beer.
- Leave the potatoes unpeeled. If available, choose very small, thin-skinned new potatoes, and scrub them well before using. Leave whole while cooking and serving.

BEEF STEW WITH RED WINE

2	pounds lean stew beef, cut into ¾-inch cubes and trimmed of all visible fat
½	teaspoon black pepper, preferably freshly ground
2	tablespoons vegetable oil ●■
1	clove garlic, peeled and minced
1½	cups dry red table wine
1	16-ounce can tomatoes, including juice, puréed ●■
1	15-ounce can tomato sauce ●■
2	carrots, grated or shredded
2	large celery stalks, finely chopped or shredded
1	large onion, very finely chopped or grated
1	small turnip, peeled and grated or shredded
1	small broccoli stem, grated or shredded (Reserve the flowerets for another use.)
1	teaspoon dry mustard
¾	teaspoon salt ●■
4	large bay leaves
½	teaspoon ground thyme
1½	teaspoons sugar ●■
½	teaspoon dried basil leaves
⅛	teaspoon cayenne pepper
2	large carrots, cut into ½-inch-thick slices
10 to 15	small white onions, peeled

To Serve
4 to 5	cups hot cooked white or brown rice or bulgur wheat ■

Sprinkle the meat with pepper. Heat the oil in a large heavy pot or Dutch oven over medium-high heat. In batches, brown the meat on all sides in the oil. Drain off and discard any remaining oil. Add all the remaining ingredients to the pot except the sliced carrots, white onions, and rice. Lower the heat, cover, and simmer for 1 hour, stirring occasionally. Add the sliced carrots. Raise the heat to bring the stew to a boil again. Then lower the heat, remove the pot lid, and simmer for 20 minutes longer, allowing the sauce to cook down and thicken. Add the small white onions and stir into the sauce. Make sure the stew keeps simmering. Cook for 40 minutes longer, or until the onions are tender, stirring occasionally. (If the sauce becomes too thick, add a small amount of water, re-cover the pot, and continue cooking.) Serve the stew over hot cooked white or brown rice or bulgur.

Makes 7 to 8 servings.

NUTRI-STEP 1

- Decrease the oil to 1 tablespoon and stir meat almost constantly to prevent it from burning.
- Increase the tomatoes to 2 cans, including juice.
- Omit the tomato sauce.
- Decrease the salt to a generous ½ teaspoon.
- Decrease the sugar to 1 teaspoon.

NUTRI-STEP 2

- Decrease the oil to 1 tablespoon and stir the meat almost constantly to prevent it from burning.
- Increase the tomatoes to 2 cans, including juice.
- Omit the tomato sauce.
- Decrease the salt to a generous ½ teaspoon.
- Decrease the sugar to 1 teaspoon.

To Serve
- Omit the cooked white rice and USE cooked bulgur wheat or brown rice.

HUNGARIAN GOULASH

Because the distinctive character of Hungarian goulash comes mostly from the rich and savory taste of fine paprika, we prefer to use a good European variety. However, regular supermarket paprika can be substituted, if necessary, and will still yield a very pleasant dish.

1½	pounds very lean and well trimmed stew beef, cut into ¾-inch cubes ●■
1½	tablespoons vegetable oil
2	large onions, coarsely chopped
1	large turnip, peeled and coarsely chopped
1	clove garlic, peeled and minced
1	large potato, peeled and finely chopped ●■
1	cup canned tomatoes, including juice
1⅓	cups water
2	tablespoons imported "sweet" paprika, preferably Hungarian ●■
1	teaspoon packed light brown sugar
⅛	teaspoon caraway seeds
⅛	teaspoon black pepper, preferably freshly ground ●■
¾	teaspoon salt ●■

To Serve
4 to 5   cups hot cooked medium-wide or wide egg noodles ■

Pat the beef cubes dry with paper towels. Heat ½ tablespoon of the oil in a 3- to 4-quart Dutch oven (or similar heavy pot) over high heat until very hot but not smoking. Add about a third of the beef cubes and, stirring constantly, brown the meat on all sides. Remove the beef cubes from the pot with a slotted spoon and set aside. Repeat the browning process twice more, each time using ½ tablespoon oil and one third of the beef cubes.

When all three batches of beef cubes are browned and set aside, reduce the heat to medium and add the onions, turnip, and garlic to the pot. Cook, stirring constantly, for 4 to 5 minutes, or until the vegetables are soft. Add the potato and then the tomatoes, breaking them up with a spoon. Return the browned beef cubes and any juices to the pot. Stir in all the remaining ingredients except the noodles.

Bring the mixture to a boil; then lower the heat. Cover and simmer gently, stirring occasionally, for about 1 hour and 40 minutes, or until the beef is tender. If the sauce seems a bit thin, remove the lid, raise the heat to medium-high, and cook, stirring constantly, for about 5 minutes, or until the liquid is slightly reduced. Serve the goulash over hot cooked noodles. Hungarian goulash is very good made ahead and reheated.

Makes 5 to 6 servings.

NUTRI-STEP 1

- Decrease the beef cubes to 1⅓ pounds.
- Leave the potato unpeeled, but scrub it well. *And add* 1 finely chopped medium-sized carrot along with the potato.
- Increase the paprika to 2 tablespoons plus 1 teaspoon.
- Increase the black pepper to a scant ¼ teaspoon.
- Decrease the salt to a generous ½ teaspoon.

NUTRI-STEP 2

- Decrease the beef cubes to 1¼ pounds.
- Leave the potato unpeeled, but scrub it well. *And add* 1 finely chopped large carrot along with the potato.
- Increase the paprika to 2 tablespoons plus 1 teaspoon.
- Increase the black pepper to a scant ¼ teaspoon.
- Decrease the salt to ½ teaspoon.

To Serve
- Omit the regular egg noodles and SUBSTITUTE whole wheat noodles.

BEEF AND BARLEY BAKE

This is just one of the hearty and satisfying dishes that can be made with barley. The grain is available at most grocery stores and health food stores.

2 tablespoons vegetable oil •
1 pound lean stew beef, cut into ½-inch cubes and trimmed of all visible fat •
1 large onion, coarsely chopped
1 clove garlic, peeled and minced
2 celery stalks, thinly sliced
⅓ cup coarsely chopped fresh parsley leaves
1 small turnip, peeled and grated or shredded
2 medium-sized carrots (one grated or shredded, the other thinly sliced)
1 fresh broccoli stem, grated or shredded (Reserve the flowerets for another use.) •
1 16-ounce can tomatoes, including juice, puréed
1½ cups water
1 cup dry white table wine

¾	teaspoon salt ●
¼	teaspoon black pepper, preferably freshly ground
2	bay leaves
¼	teaspoon ground thyme
½	teaspoon dried basil leaves
½	teaspoon dried marjoram leaves
	Scant ½ teaspoon dry mustard
1	cup uncooked pearl barley

Heat the oil in a large heavy skillet over medium or medium-high heat. Add the beef, onion, garlic, and celery and cook until the beef is lightly browned. Stir frequently to brown the cubes on all sides. With a slotted spoon, remove the meat and vegetables to a 3-quart casserole with a tight-fitting lid. (Make sure any fat remaining in the pan is not transferred with the meat.) Add all the remaining ingredients to the casserole and stir to combine. Cover and bake in a preheated 350-degree oven for 2 hours, or until the liquid has been absorbed and the beef is tender. Fluff up the ingredients with a large spoon or fork before serving.

Makes 4 to 5 servings.

NUTRI-STEP 1

- Decrease the vegetable oil to 1½ tablespoons and stir the beef cubes and vegetables often to prevent them from sticking.
- Decrease the lean stew beef to ¾ pound.
- Increase the broccoli stalks to 2. Grate or shred one; peel and thinly slice the other.
- Decrease the salt to ½ teaspoon.

MARINATED FLANK STEAK

1	tablespoon vegetable oil
1½	tablespoons honey ●
1	small onion, coarsely chopped
¼	cup soy sauce ●
⅓	cup dry white table wine or dry sherry
1	teaspoon Worcestershire sauce
½	teaspoon fresh gingerroot, minced, or ¼ teaspoon ground ginger
1	clove garlic, peeled and minced
¼	teaspoon freshly ground black pepper
1	flank steak (about 1¼ pounds), trimmed of all visible fat

Combine all ingredients except steak in a small bowl. Stir the marinade until the honey dissolves.

Lay the steak in a shallow glass dish or enameled pan, and cover with half the marinade. Turn the steak over and cover with the remaining marinade. Refrigerate the steak, covered, for at least 12 hours or, preferably, 24 hours, turning and basting several times.

At serving time, drain the steak well, discarding the marinade. Put the steak on a broiler pan under a preheated broiler. Exact cooking time will vary depending on the thickness of the steak, but start with 6 to 8 minutes, or until nicely browned on the first side. Then turn the steak over, and broil for about 5 to 7 minutes on the second side. Keeping in mind that cooking will continue several minutes after the steak is removed from the broiler, check the meat for the desired degree of doneness by cutting into the thickest part. Broil longer, if necessary. When the steak is done, transfer it from the broiler to a platter and let stand for 5 minutes. On a cutting board, cut the steak across the grain into thin slices using a very sharp knife. Return the sliced meat to the platter and serve.

Makes 5 to 6 servings.

NUTRI-STEP 1

- Decrease the honey to 1 tablespoon.
- Decrease the soy sauce to 3 tablespoons.

ROUND STEAK AND POTATO DINNER

2   large onions, sliced
2   cloves garlic, peeled and chopped
1   tablespoon vegetable oil
¾   pound round steak, trimmed of all fat and cut into 3- by ¾-inch strips
1½   cups water
1¾   cups canned tomato purée
2   large bay leaves
1   tablespoon sugar
½   teaspoon salt •
⅛   teaspoon black pepper, preferably freshly ground
¼   teaspoon ground thyme
½   teaspoon apple cider vinegar
1   medium-sized carrot, ground or very finely chopped
1   medium-sized celery stalk, including leaves, ground or very finely chopped •
2   large potatoes, peeled and cut into ⅛-inch-thick slices •

In a large heavy skillet or Dutch oven over medium-high heat, sauté the onion and garlic in the oil until the onion is soft. Push the vegetables to one side. Add the meat and brown well. Add the water, tomato purée, seasonings, and vinegar and stir to mix well. Stir the carrots and celery into the sauce. Bring to a boil. Lower the heat, cover, and simmer for about 1½ hours, or until the sauce is slightly thickened and the vegetables and meat are tender. Add the potatoes to the pot, stirring them down under the meat and onions. Add more water if necessary to cover the potatoes completely. Cook for 20 to 25 minutes, stirring occasionally, until the potatoes are just tender.

Makes 4 to 5 servings.

NUTRI-STEP 1

- Decrease the salt to ¼ teaspoon.
- Omit the celery stalk and SUBSTITUTE ½ green pepper and 1 fresh broccoli stem, both ground or very finely chopped. (Reserve broccoli flowerets for another use.)
- Leave the potatoes unpeeled and scrub them well.

INDIVIDUAL STOVE-TOP MEATLOAVES

Meatloaves

1	pound lean ground beef
3	tablespoons tomato paste, from a 6-ounce can (Reserve the rest for the sauce below.)
1	large egg (or 2 large egg whites) •
1½	teaspoons prepared horseradish
⅛	teaspoon garlic powder
½	teaspoon salt •
¼	cup old-fashioned or quick-cooking rolled oats •
⅛	teaspoon black pepper, preferably freshly ground
1	medium-sized onion, finely chopped
1	small carrot, grated or shredded
1	small celery stalk, grated or shredded

Sauce

	Remaining tomato paste from a 6-ounce can (see above)
½	cup water
1½	teaspoons prepared horseradish
¼	teaspoon salt •
	Pinch of black pepper, preferably freshly ground

Combine all meatloaf ingredients in a medium-sized bowl. Mix with your hands or a fork until thoroughly blended. Form the mixture into 4 loaves, each about 4 by 2 inches.

Brown the loaves on the top and bottom in a large, heavy skillet over medium-low heat, turning them carefully with a spatula (pancake turner). If the loaves begin to burn during the browning, lower the heat slightly. When the loaves are nicely browned, cover and cook over very low heat for 15 minutes.

While the loaves are cooking, mix all the sauce ingredients and stir to blend well. Set aside.

With a large spoon, skim off and discard any fat in the skillet. Spoon the sauce over the loaves and cook, uncovered, for 10 to 15 minutes longer. Transfer the loaves to a serving platter with spatulas.

Makes 4 servings.

NUTRI-STEP 1

Meatloaves

- Omit the large egg and USE 2 large egg whites.
- Decrease the salt to a generous ¼ teaspoon.
- Increase the rolled oats to ⅓ cup.

Sauce

- Decrease the salt to ⅛ teaspoon.

MEATLOAF MILANO

1¼   pounds lean ground beef ●
1   large egg (or 2 large egg whites) ●
1   large onion, finely chopped
1   medium-sized celery stalk, including leaves, finely chopped ●
½   cup finely chopped fresh parsley leaves
⅓   cup finely chopped fresh mushrooms
2   cups white or whole wheat bread crumbs (purchased or homemade from slightly stale bread) ●
½   cup quick-cooking rolled oats ●
¾   teaspoon dried oregano leaves
½   teaspoon dried thyme leaves ●
¼   teaspoon black pepper, preferably freshly ground
¼   teaspoon celery salt
⅛   teaspoon garlic powder (optional)
½   teaspoon salt ●
1   8-ounce can tomato sauce

Combine all the ingredients except the tomato sauce in a large bowl. Add half the tomato sauce to the meat mixture, reserving the remainder for the meatloaf topping. Using your hands, mix all the ingredients thoroughly. Pack the mixture into an ungreased 9- by 5-inch loaf pan.

Bake, uncovered, in a preheated 350-degree oven for 1 hour. Remove the pan from the oven. Being careful not to dislodge the meatloaf from the pan, slowly tip the pan to one side. Holding the meatloaf in place with a spatula, drain off and discard all the fat. Spread the remaining tomato sauce evenly over the top of the meatloaf. Bake, uncovered, for 30 minutes longer, or until the meatloaf begins to shrink from the sides of the pan. Once again, drain off and discard all fat from the pan. Transfer the pan to a rack and let stand for 5 minutes. Loosen the meatloaf from the sides of the pan, cut into slices, and serve.

Makes 6 to 7 servings.

NUTRI-STEP 1

- Decrease the ground beef to 1 pound.
- Omit the large egg and USE 2 large egg whites.
- Increase the celery to 2 medium-sized stalks.
- Omit the white bread crumbs and USE whole wheat bread crumbs.
- Increase the rolled oats to ⅔ cup.
- Increase the dried thyme to ¾ teaspoon.
- Decrease the salt to ¼ teaspoon.

HAMBURGER STROGANOFF

1	pound lean ground beef ●■
2	medium-sized onions, coarsely chopped
1	large celery stalk, including leaves, coarsely chopped
1	cup coarsely sliced fresh mushrooms
1	beef bouillon cube
1½	cups warm water ●■
1½	tablespoons tomato paste
1	teaspoon Worcestershire sauce
¼	teaspoon black pepper, preferably freshly ground
¼	teaspoon salt ■
2½	cups uncooked medium-wide egg noodles ●■
½	cup plain lowfat yogurt

Brown the ground beef in a large, heavy skillet over medium-high heat. Drain off and discard all excess fat. Add the onions and celery to the pan and cook, stirring, for 4 to 5 minutes, or until the vegetables are limp. Add the mushrooms, stirring, and cook for 3 to 4 minutes longer. Dissolve the bouillon cube in the warm water, then stir into the skillet along with the tomato paste, Worcestershire sauce, pepper, and salt. When the mixture is thoroughly blended, add the noodles and moisten well with the pan liquid.

Lower the heat and, stirring frequently to prevent sticking, simmer the mixture, covered, for 7 to 9 minutes, or until the noodles are just cooked through. Stir the yogurt into the skillet and warm the stroganoff until heated through, but *not* boiling.

Makes 4 to 5 servings.

NUTRI-STEP 1

- Decrease the ground beef to ¾ pound.
- Increase the water to 1¾ cups.
- Increase the uncooked noodles to 2¾ cups.

NUTRI-STEP 2

- Decrease the ground beef to ¾ pound.
- Increase the water to 1¾ cups.
- Decrease the salt to ⅛ teaspoon.
- Omit the regular noodles and SUBSTITUTE whole wheat noodles; increase the noodles to 2¾ cups.

HAMBURGER SKILLET DINNER, ORIENTAL STYLE

1   pound lean ground beef •
1   large onion, peeled and coarsely chopped
2   tablespoons chopped fresh parsley leaves, or 1 tablespoon dried parsley flakes
1   small clove garlic, peeled and minced, or ¼ teaspoon garlic powder
1   large celery stalk, sliced crosswise into ¼-inch thick slices •
1   16-ounce can tomatoes, including juice
2¼   cups coarsely chopped cabbage •
1   teaspoon finely chopped fresh gingerroot, or 1 teaspoon ground ginger
1   teaspoon chili powder

⅛   teaspoon black pepper, preferably freshly ground
3   tablespoons soy sauce •
2   tablespoons water
1½   teaspoons cornstarch

To Serve
3½ to 4   cups hot cooked white or brown rice •

Brown the ground beef in a 12-inch (or similar) skillet over medium-high heat, stirring. Drain off and discard any excess fat. Add the onion, parsley, and garlic to the skillet and cook, stirring frequently, for 2 minutes. Stir in the celery and cook for 1 minute longer. Add the tomatoes and their juice, breaking up the tomatoes with a spoon. Then add the cabbage, ginger, chili powder, and pepper. Cook for 5 to 6 minutes.

Combine the soy sauce, water, and cornstarch in a small cup and stir until completely smooth and blended. Add to the skillet, stirring, and cook for 1 to 2 minutes longer, or until the mixture is thickened slightly and turns clear. Serve with rice.

Makes about 4 servings.

NUTRI-STEP 1

- Decrease the ground beef to ¾ pound.
- Increase the celery to 2 large stalks.
- Increase the chopped cabbage to 2¾ cups.
- Decrease the soy sauce to 2½ tablespoons.

To Serve
- Omit the cooked white rice and USE cooked brown rice.

FILIPINO-STYLE HAMBURGER SKILLET

2   medium-sized stalks fresh broccoli, including stems •
4   ounces thin rice noodles (or "rice sticks") available at Oriental or Filipino grocery stores, or 4 ounces thin spaghetti (vermicelli)
1   pound lean ground beef •
1   medium-sized onion, finely chopped
2   cloves garlic, peeled and finely minced
1   cup sliced fresh mushrooms
2   cups shredded cabbage
1   cup canned garbanzo beans (chick-peas), well drained
2½   tablespoons soy sauce •
2   tablespoons water

Cut the broccoli tops into small flowerets. Trim and discard ½ inch from the bottom of the stalks. Peel the woody covering from the thick part of the stalks and discard. Then cut the stalks into small slices. Set aside flowerets and the stem slices.

If using Oriental rice noodles or "rice sticks," break them into small pieces; then soak them in hot water until they are soft. Drain well. If using thin spaghetti, break it into 2-inch lengths and cook according to the package directions, omitting any salt. Drain well and set aside.

In a large deep skillet, brown the ground beef, breaking it up with a large spoon. Add the onions and garlic to the pan, and cook along with the meat. Then spoon off and discard any excess fat. Stir the reserved broccoli pieces along with the mushrooms, cabbage, garbanzos, soy sauce, and water into the skillet. Cover tightly, and steam the mixture for about 5 to 7 minutes, or until the broccoli is crisp-tender and brightly colored. Stir in the prepared noodles (either rice sticks or thin spaghetti), and heat, stirring, for 1 to 2 minutes longer to heat through.

Makes about 4 servings.

NUTRI-STEP 1

- Increase the broccoli to 3 medium-sized stalks.
- Decrease the ground beef to ¾ pound.
- Decrease the soy sauce to 2 tablespoons. *And add* ⅛ teaspoon ground ginger to the meat mixture.

BEEF AND BULGUR SKILLET

This quick skillet dinner makes a good introduction to bulgur wheat, which looks and tastes a bit like rice.

1	pound lean ground beef ●
1	medium-sized onion, finely chopped
1	clove garlic, peeled and minced
1	cup uncooked bulgur wheat
1	16-ounce can tomatoes, including juice
1	cup water
¼	teaspoon ground marjoram
¼	teaspoon ground savory
¼	teaspoon ground thyme
1 or 2	drops hot pepper sauce
2	large bay leaves

¾ teaspoon salt •
¼ teaspoon black pepper, preferably freshly ground
½ cup frozen green peas •

In a large, heavy skillet over medium heat, cook the ground beef, onion, and garlic until the onion is soft. Drain off any excess fat. Add the bulgur to the skillet and cook for 1 minute, stirring. Add the tomatoes, water, seasonings, and peas to the pan. Stir to blend well, breaking up the tomatoes with a spoon. Cover and simmer for about 18 to 20 minutes, or until the bulgur is tender.
Makes about 4 servings.

NUTRI-STEP 1

- Decrease the lean ground beef to ¾ pound. *And add* 1 finely sliced celery stalk along with the onion and garlic.
- Increase the frozen peas to 1 cup.
- Decrease the salt to ½ teaspoon.

STUFFED PEPPERS

4 large green peppers, seeded and cut in half lengthwise
¾ pound lean ground beef •
1 medium-sized onion, finely chopped •
1 clove garlic, peeled and minced
1 bay leaf

Sauce
1 15-ounce can tomato sauce
1 tablespoon apple cider vinegar
1 tablespoon sugar
¼ teaspoon black pepper, preferably freshly ground
½ teaspoon dry mustard
 Pinch of ground cloves
⅛ teaspoon salt •
1 cup water
1½ cups uncooked "instant" rice

Bring a large pot of water to a boil over high heat. Add the peppers, lower the heat, and boil, covered, for 2 to 4 minutes, depending on the crispness desired. Drain the peppers and set aside.
 Meanwhile, in a large saucepan over medium heat, combine the ground beef,

onion, garlic, and bay leaf. Cook, stirring, until the meat is brown. Drain off and discard any excess fat.

While the meat mixture is cooking, prepare the sauce. Stir the tomato sauce, vinegar, sugar, pepper, dry mustard, cloves, and salt together in a medium bowl. (The dry mustard must be stirred vigorously to incorporate it.) Add 1¼ cups of this sauce and the water to the meat mixture. (Reserve the remaining sauce to top the stuffed peppers.) Simmer the meat mixture covered, for 5 to 10 minutes. Remove the bay leaf, and stir the instant rice into the meat mixture. Remove from the heat and let stand, covered, for 5 minutes.

Arrange the drained green peppers in a shallow baking dish. Spoon some meat and rice mixture into each pepper. Top with the remaining seasoned tomato sauce, dividing it evenly. Bake, uncovered, in a preheated 350-degree oven for about 25 minutes, or until heated through.

Makes 4 servings.

NUTRI-STEP 1

- Decrease the lean ground beef to ½ pound.
- Increase the onions to 2. *And add* 1 stalk finely chopped celery along with the onion and garlic.

Sauce
- Omit the salt.

SWEET AND SOUR STUFFED CABBAGE

Here is a very appealing way to include cabbage—a cruciferous vegetable—in your diet. If you can find the curly leafed Savoy cabbage, try it in this dish. Not only is Savoy cabbage quite tasty, but the crinkly leaves are flexible and easy to fill.

1   medium-sized cabbage (about 1¼ pounds), trimmed and cored

Stuffing
1   pound very lean ground beef ●■
1   cup *cooked* white or brown rice ●■
1   small onion, grated
1   large egg (or 2 large egg whites) ●■
½   teaspoon salt ●■
⅛   teaspoon black pepper, preferably freshly ground ●■

Sauce
1   6-ounce can tomato paste
2   tomato paste cans water (1⅓ cups)

2 tablespoons apple cider vinegar
2 tablespoons light or dark brown sugar
1 medium-sized onion, finely chopped
¼ cup raisins (optional)

Place the whole cabbage in a large pot of boiling water, and cover. Turn off the heat, and let the cabbage soften in the hot water while you prepare the stuffing and sauce.

For the stuffing, use a fork or your hands to mix together the ground beef, cooked rice, onion, egg, salt, and pepper until very well combined. Set aside.

Combine all the sauce ingredients in a deep large skillet, electric frypan, or Dutch oven, and mix well. Heat to simmering, stirring occasionally.

Meanwhile, remove the cabbage from the hot water, and drain very well. Separate the leaves, and spread them on paper towels to dry.

To make the cabbage rolls, lay a softened cabbage leaf, ribbed-side down, on a plate; then place about 2 to 4 tablespoons of stuffing (or more, depending on the size of the leaf) in the center. Fold over the end of the leaf opposite the rib; then fold in the sides and roll up. Secure with a toothpick through the rib. Place the cabbage roll in the sauce, seam side down. Repeat until all the stuffing is used up. If there is any cabbage left, it may be chopped up and added to the sauce. Spoon some of the sauce over the tops of the rolls and then cover the pan tightly.

Simmer the cabbage rolls for about 1 hour, occasionally spooning sauce over them. Remove all the toothpicks before serving. (The stuffed cabbage won't unroll!)

Makes about 6 servings.

NUTRI-STEP 1

Stuffing
- Decrease the lean ground beef to ¾ pound.
- Increase the cooked rice to 1½ cups.
- Omit the large egg and USE 2 large egg whites.
- Decrease the salt to a generous ¼ teaspoon.
- Increase the pepper to a generous ⅛ teaspoon.

NUTRI-STEP 2

Stuffing
- Decrease the lean ground beef to ¾ pound.
- Omit the cooked white rice and USE cooked brown rice. Increase the rice to 1½ cups.
- Omit the large egg and USE 2 large egg whites.
- Decrease the salt to ¼ teaspoon.
- Increase the pepper to ¼ teaspoon.

ITALIAN-STYLE STUFFED EGGPLANT

2   medium-sized eggplants (approximately 1 pound each), or several very small Italian ones
½   pound lean ground beef
1   medium-sized onion, finely chopped
1   clove garlic, peeled and finely minced
1   16-ounce can tomatoes, including juice
1   medium-sized green pepper, seeded and finely chopped
½   teaspoon dried thyme leaves
½   teaspoon dried oregano leaves
½   teaspoon dried basil leaves
⅛   teaspoon black pepper, preferably freshly ground
½   teaspoon salt •
¼   cup fresh white or whole wheat bread crumbs •
¼   cup grated Parmesan cheese •

Slice the eggplants in half lengthwise; then use a melon baller, grapefruit spoon, or small knife to scoop out the pulp in the center, leaving a ½-inch-thick shell. Place the shells in a baking dish. Chop up the pulp, and set aside.

In a large skillet, brown the beef with the onion and garlic, breaking up the meat as it cooks. Spoon off any excess fat. Coarsely chop the tomatoes, and add them, along with their juice, to the skillet. Add the green pepper, herbs, black pepper, and salt, and the reserved chopped eggplant pulp. Cook for 5 minutes longer, stirring often. Remove from the heat, and stir in the bread crumbs.

Fill the prepared eggplant shells with the meat mixture. Sprinkle the tops with the cheese. Bake in a preheated 350-degree oven for 40 minutes, or until the cheese is melted and the eggplant shell is tender.

Makes about 4 servings.

NUTRI-STEP 1

- Decrease the salt to a generous ¼ teaspoon.
- Omit the white bread crumbs and USE whole wheat bread crumbs.
- Omit the Parmesan cheese and SUBSTITUTE ¼ cup grated or finely chopped lowfat or part-skim cheese, such as mozzarella.

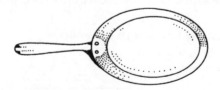

DON'T-TELL-'EM-IT'S-GOOD-FOR-'EM SPAGHETTI SAUCE

Salt and fat have been significantly decreased in this delicious recipe. The vitamin A- and C-rich vegetables add pleasing flavor and texture to the sauce.

1½	pounds lean ground beef ●■
2	medium-sized onions, coarsely chopped
3	large cloves garlic, peeled and chopped
2	large carrots, ground or very finely chopped ●■
2	celery stalks, including leaves, ground or very finely chopped ■
½	cup chopped green pepper
1	cup water (approximate) ●
4	15-ounce cans tomato sauce ●
2	6-ounce cans tomato paste ●
3	large bay leaves
2	teaspoons ground oregano ●■
2	teaspoons dried basil leaves
½	cup chopped fresh parsley leaves
¼	teaspoon black pepper, preferably freshly ground
¾	teaspoon salt ■

In a large heavy pot, cook the ground beef over medium heat until lightly browned. Drain off any excess fat and discard. Add the onion and garlic and cook, stirring, until the onion is soft. Add the carrots, celery, green pepper, and water to the browned meat, stirring. Add the tomato sauce, tomato paste, and all the herbs and seasonings. Stir well to blend. Lower the heat, cover, and simmer, stirring occasionally, for about 1½ hours, or until the sauce is slightly thickened and the vegetables are very soft. Serve on regular pasta or high-protein pasta. This sauce can be kept in the refrigerator several days or frozen for longer storage.

Makes about 8 servings.

NUTRI-STEP 1

- Decrease the meat to 1¼ pounds.
- Increase the carrots to 3. *And add* 2 ground or finely chopped fresh broccoli stems (reserve flowerets for another use) to the sauce when the other chopped vegetables are added.
- Increase the water to 4½ to 5 cups.
- Decrease the tomato sauce to 2 cans.
- Increase the tomato paste to 4 cans.
- Increase the ground oregano to 1 tablespoon.

Make a vegetarian sauce as follows:
- Omit the meat. Combine the vegetables directly with the tomato mixture and simmer, covered, for about 1½ hours, stirring occasionally.
- Increase the carrots to 4. *And add* 4 ground fresh broccoli stems (not flowerets) to the sauce when the other chopped vegetables are added.
- Increase the ground celery stalks to 4.
- Increase the ground oregano to 1 tablespoon.
- Decrease the salt to a generous ¼ teaspoon.

LASAGNE

Sauce

1	pound lean ground beef •
1	large onion, finely chopped
1	large clove garlic, peeled and minced
½	cup finely chopped celery
3	cups canned tomatoes, including juice
1	12-ounce can tomato paste
1	large bay leaf
¾	teaspoon dried oregano leaves •
½	teaspoon finely crumbled dried rosemary leaves
½	teaspoon dried basil leaves
¼	teaspoon dried marjoram leaves
⅛	teaspoon dried (hot) red pepper flakes
½	teaspoon salt •

Noodles and Filling

1	10-ounce package frozen chopped spinach, thawed
1	12-ounce carton lowfat cottage cheese (1½ cups) •
1½	cups part-skim ricotta cheese (if unavailable, substitute regular ricotta) •
16	lasagne noodles (approximately ¾ pound)
1	cup coarsely chopped fresh parsley leaves
8	ounces part-skim mozzarella cheese, shredded or grated
⅓	cup Parmesan cheese •

Brown the ground beef in a 4-quart (or similar) Dutch oven or pot over medium-high heat. Drain off any excess fat from the pan. Add the onion, garlic, and celery and cook, stirring, for 3 to 4 minutes, or until the vegetables are limp. Stir in the tomatoes, breaking them up with a spoon. Then add the tomato paste and all the herbs and seasonings. Bring the mixture to a boil and reduce the heat to low. Cover the pot loosely and simmer, stirring occasionally to prevent sticking, for 1½ hours, or until the sauce is well flavored and thick. While the sauce cooks, begin assembling the remaining ingredients. (If desired, the sauce may be made ahead and refrigerated or frozen until needed.)

To begin assembly of the lasagne, drain the thawed spinach in a colander for at least 30 minutes. Turn the cottage cheese into a sieve, and drain for at least 30 minutes or, preferably, 45 minutes. Then combine it with the ricotta.

Use your hands to squeeze as much excess moisture as possible from the spinach; then fluff it up with a fork and set it aside.

Cook the noodles in unsalted water according to the package directions, and drain well.

To assemble the lasagne, have ready a 9- by 13-inch (or similar) pan. Stir the parsley into the meat sauce. Spread a third of the meat sauce evenly over the bottom of the pan. Neatly top with 4 lasagne noodles, overlapping them to form a smooth layer. Spread half the cottage cheese–ricotta mixture over the noodles. Top the cheese mixture with half the spinach; then sprinkle with a fourth of the mozzarella and Parmesan. Top the cheeses with 4 more lasagne noodles. Evenly spread half the remaining meat sauce over the noodles. Top with a third of the remaining mozzarella and Parmesan. Top the cheeses with 4 more lasagne noodles and cover these with the remaining cottage cheese–ricotta mixture. Top the cheese mixture with the remaining spinach. Then top the spinach with half the remaining mozzarella and Parmesan. Top the cheeses with the last 4 noodles. Spread the remaining meat sauce over the noodles; then sprinkle with the remaining mozzarella and Parmesan.

Bake in a preheated 350-degree oven for 1 hour, or until the cheeses are melted and the lasagne is bubbly hot.

Makes 8 to 9 servings.

NUTRI-STEP 1

Sauce
- Decrease the ground beef to ¾ pound. **And add** ½ cup grated or shredded carrots to the sauce along with the celery.
- Increase the oregano to 1 teaspoon.
- Decrease the salt to ¼ teaspoon.

Noodles and Filling
- Increase the cottage cheese to 2 cups (one 1-pound carton).
- Decrease the ricotta cheese to 1 cup.
- Decrease the Parmesan cheese to ¼ cup.

CHILI CON CARNE

Here's one of our recipes in which the grated or shredded vegetables in the sauce "masquerade" as additional ground beef.

¾ pound lean ground beef •
1 large onion, coarsely chopped
1 clove garlic, peeled and minced
2 16-ounce cans tomatoes, including juice, puréed
1 small carrot, grated or shredded •
1 fresh broccoli stem, grated or shredded (reserve flowerets for another use)
2 16-ounce cans dark red kidney beans, drained
1 tablespoon plus 1 teaspoon chili powder, or to taste
½ teaspoon salt •
¼ teaspoon black pepper, preferably freshly ground

To Serve
   Hot cooked white or brown rice or Golden Yellow Corn Bread (page 226) •

In a large saucepan over medium heat, cook the ground beef, onion, and garlic until the meat is browned. Drain off the fat. Add all the remaining chili ingredients. Bring to a boil; then lower the heat, and simmer, covered, for about 45 minutes, stirring occasionally. Serve over hot cooked rice or with corn bread.
   Makes about 4 to 5 servings.

NUTRI-STEP 1

- Decrease the lean ground beef to ½ pound.
- Increase the carrot to 1 large. *And add* 1 celery stalk, finely chopped or shredded.
- Decrease the salt to ¼ teaspoon.

To Serve
- If serving over rice, omit the cooked white rice and USE brown rice.

LAYERED MEAT AND POTATO CASSEROLE

About 2 pounds potatoes, peeled and thickly sliced (about ⅜ inch thick) •
1   10-ounce package frozen chopped spinach, thawed and very well drained
1   pound very lean ground beef •
1   medium-sized onion, grated
2   green onions (scallions), including green tops, thinly sliced
1   medium-sized tomato, cored and finely chopped
2   tablespoons chopped fresh parsley leaves
½   teaspoon ground cinnamon
½   teaspoon salt •
¼   teaspoon black pepper, preferably freshly ground
1   large egg (or 2 large egg whites) •
    Paprika

Put the potatoes in a medium-sized saucepan with about 1 inch of water. Cover, bring to a boil, and steam the potatoes for about 15 to 20 minutes, or until just tender. Drain well, and cool slightly while preparing the meat layer.

Squeeze any remaining liquid from the spinach. In a medium-sized bowl, mix the spinach with the ground beef, onion, green onion, tomato, parsley, cinnamon, salt, pepper, and egg. Knead the mixture with your hands, or mix it with a fork, until it is very smooth and well combined. (Or mix it in a food processor.)

In a greased or nonstick spray-coated 10-inch square (or similar) shallow baking dish or casserole, layer half of the potato slices. Cover with all the meat mixture, pressing it into place. Top the meat with the remaining potato slices. Sprinkle the casserole with paprika.

Bake, covered, in a preheated 350-degree oven for 30 minutes. Then uncover, and bake for another 30 minutes, or until the top is golden brown.

Makes about 6 servings.

NUTRI-STEP 1

- Leave the potatoes unpeeled. Scrub the potatoes well before using. Use thin-skinned new potatoes, if available.
- Decrease the ground beef to ¾ pound. *And add* 1 large or 2 small grated unpeeled zucchini to the meat mixture. Before adding, squeeze out as much excess liquid from the grated zucchini as possible.
- Decrease the salt to ¼ teaspoon.
- Omit the large egg and USE 2 large egg whites.

SLOPPY JOES

¾   pound lean ground beef •
1   large onion, very finely chopped
1   medium-sized carrot, ground or very finely chopped
1   medium-sized celery stalk, including leaves, very finely chopped
1   cup ketchup •
¾   cup tomato sauce •
1   tablespoon sugar
1   tablespoon apple cider vinegar
⅛   teaspoon salt
     Pinch of black pepper, preferably freshly ground

To Serve
     Regular or whole wheat hamburger buns or English muffins •

In a medium-sized saucepan or skillet, over medium-high heat, cook the ground beef, stirring, until it is lightly browned. Drain off any excess fat. Stir the onion, carrot, and celery into the meat mixture, along with all the remaining ingredients. Cover, lower the heat, and simmer, stirring occasionally, for 35 to 40 minutes. Serve on hamburger buns or English muffins.
   Makes about 4 servings.

NUTRI-STEP 1

- Decrease the ground beef to ½ pound. *And add* 1 ground or finely chopped fresh broccoli stem (reserve the flowerets for another use) with the vegetables.
- Decrease the ketchup to ¼ cup.
- Increase the tomato sauce to 1½ cups. *And add* the following seasonings to the meat and tomato mixture: ⅛ teaspoon garlic powder, ¼ teaspoon dry mustard, a generous pinch of ground cloves.

To Serve
- Omit the regular hamburger buns or English muffins and USE whole wheat.

Chapter 10

Main Dishes— Lamb, Pork, and Veal

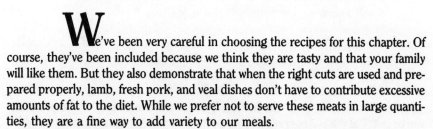

We've been very careful in choosing the recipes for this chapter. Of course, they've been included because we think they are tasty and that your family will like them. But they also demonstrate that when the right cuts are used and prepared properly, lamb, fresh pork, and veal dishes don't have to contribute excessive amounts of fat to the diet. While we prefer not to serve these meats in large quantities, they are a fine way to add variety to our meals.

One approach we've taken to make our lamb, pork, and veal dishes wholesome is to rely primarily on the least fatty cuts of meat. Generally, these include the more muscular or lean parts of the animal, such as the leg, shank, shoulder, and loin. In addition, we give directions for trimming off fat and "degreasing" dishes wherever necessary. And, we often use cooking methods like stewing, braising, and roasting to lend tenderness and succulence without requiring any added fat. Finally, most of our recipes are combination dishes which team relatively modest meat portions with savory (and healthful) varieties of vegetables and fruit.

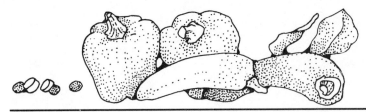

MEDITERRANEAN-STYLE LAMB AND VEGETABLE POT

Marinade
- 3 tablespoons lemon juice
- 2 tablespoons vegetable oil •
- 1¼ teaspoons dried marjoram leaves
- 1 teaspoon dried thyme leaves
- ½ teaspoon dried basil leaves
- 2 cloves garlic, peeled and minced
  Scant 1 teaspoon salt •
- ¼ teaspoon black pepper, preferably freshly ground

Meat and Vegetables
- 1½ pounds lamb (from the leg or shoulder), trimmed of all visible fat and cut into ¾-inch cubes •
- 1 large eggplant (about 1¼ pounds), peeled and cut into 1-inch chunks •
- 4 to 5 large onions, cut into eighths
- ¾ cup canned tomatoes (2 medium tomatoes, plus juice), broken up with a spoon
- 2 large green peppers, seeded and cut into 1½-inch chunks
- 1 large red bell pepper, seeded and cut into 1½-inch chunks (substitute another green pepper if red is unavailable)
- 1 small zucchini, cut into ¼-inch-thick slices •

Combine the lemon juice, oil, dried herbs, garlic, salt, and pepper in a large glass, stainless steel, or enameled bowl and stir until thoroughly blended. Add the lamb cubes and stir until they are well coated with the marinade. Cover and refrigerate the meat for at least 2½ to 3 hours, or as long as 8 hours, stirring several times.

Using a slotted spoon, transfer half the lamb from the marinade to a large Dutch oven or pot. Put the pot over high heat and brown the lamb lightly on all sides, stirring constantly. Remove the browned lamb from the pot, and set aside. Transfer the remaining lamb cubes to the pot. (Reserve any marinade.) Repeat the browning process with the second batch of cubes. Return the first batch to the pot, along with the eggplant cubes, any leftover marinade, and the onions. Cook the mixture, stirring, for 5 minutes. Stir the tomatoes, green and red peppers, and zucchini into the pot. Cover, lower the heat, and simmer, stirring occasionally, for about 30 minutes longer, or until the lamb is tender.

Makes 6 to 7 servings.

LAMB SHISH KEBAB

This shish kebab always wins raves—even from those who think they don't like lamb.

Marinade

⅓   cup vegetable oil •
¼   cup lemon juice •
½   teaspoon salt •
1   teaspoon ground marjoram
1   teaspoon ground thyme
1   clove garlic, peeled and chopped
1   medium-sized onion, coarsely chopped
½   cup snipped fresh parsley leaves

Meat and Vegetables

2   pounds lamb (from the leg or shoulder), trimmed of fat and cut into 1¼-inch cubes •
   About 14 small white onions, peeled and trimmed •
1½   large green peppers, trimmed, seeded, and cut into 1½-inch pieces •
2   medium-sized cucumbers, peeled and cut into 1-inch cubes

In a medium-sized bowl, combine all the marinade ingredients and mix well. Add the lamb and stir until well coated. Cover and refrigerate for at least 12 hours, or, preferably, 24 hours, stirring often.

Put the small white onions and green peppers in a medium-sized saucepan of boiling water. Parboil over medium heat for 3 to 4 minutes. Drain in a colander.

Alternate green peppers, onions, and cucumbers with lamb cubes on 4 or 5 large skewers. (Remove lamb cubes from the marinade as needed with a slotted spoon.)

Pack the skewers tightly, as this will help keep the vegetables from shifting as the skewers are turned during broiling.

Rest the ends of the skewers on the rim of a baking pan so that the fat from the meat can drip into the pan during broiling. Brush the vegetables lightly with the extra marinade. Broil about 4 inches from the heat for 25 to 30 minutes, depending on the degree of doneness desired; turn frequently so that the meat and vegetables can cook evenly. To serve, use a fork to push the meat and vegetables down and off skewers onto a large serving platter.

Makes 6 to 7 servings.

NUTRI-STEP 1

Marinade
- Decrease the vegetable oil to ¼ cup.
- Decrease the lemon juice to 3 tablespoons.
- Decrease the salt to ¼ teaspoon.

Meat and Vegetables
- Decrease the lamb to 1¾ pounds.
- Increase the small white onions to 18.
- Increase the green pepper to 2 large.

LAMB AND RICE PILAF

1   tablespoon butter or margarine •
1   pound lamb (from the leg or shoulder), trimmed of all fat and cut into 2- by ¼-inch strips •
1   large onion, coarsely chopped
2   cloves garlic, peeled and minced
1   celery stalk, coarsely chopped •
1½   cups uncooked white rice
2½   cups water
¾   cup canned tomatoes, chopped
½   teaspoon salt •
¼   teaspoon black pepper, preferably freshly ground
⅛   teaspoon cayenne pepper
½   teaspoon ground sage
½   teaspoon ground allspice
¼   teaspoon ground thyme

¾ cup coarsely chopped fresh parsley leaves
½ cup raisins •

Melt butter in a Dutch oven or large saucepan over medium heat. Add the lamb and brown on all sides. Turn the heat to medium-low and add the onion, garlic, and celery. Cook, stirring frequently, for 15 minutes. Stir in the rice, then the water and all the remaining ingredients. Raise the heat and bring the mixture to a boil. Then cover, lower the heat, and simmer for about 25 minutes, or until all the water is absorbed and the rice is tender.

Makes 4 to 6 servings.

NUTRI-STEP 1

- Decrease the butter or margarine to 2 teaspoons.
- Decrease the lamb to ¾ pound.
- Increase the celery stalks to 2.
- Decrease the salt to a scant ½ teaspoon.
- Increase the raisins to ¾ cup.

CREOLE-STYLE LAMB

---

1 tablespoon vegetable oil •■
1 pound lean lamb (from the leg or shoulder), trimmed of all fat and cut into 1¼-inch cubes
1 large onion, coarsely chopped
1 clove garlic, peeled and chopped
1 16-ounce can tomatoes, including juice, puréed
1 8-ounce can tomato sauce
1 medium-sized carrot, grated or shredded
1 small stem fresh broccoli, grated or shredded (Reserve the flowerets for another use.)
2½ cups green pepper, trimmed, seeded, and cut into 1-inch pieces •■
¼ cup coarsely chopped fresh parsley leaves
1 large bay leaf
¼ teaspoon black pepper, preferably freshly ground
½ teaspoon ground thyme
½ teaspoon ground marjoram
¼ teaspoon salt •■
3 to 4 drops hot pepper sauce

To Serve
3 cups hot cooked white or brown rice ■

Heat the oil in a large heavy skillet over medium heat. Add the lamb cubes, onion, and garlic and cook, stirring. When the meat is brown, add the tomatoes, tomato sauce, carrot, broccoli, green pepper, and parsley. Stir in all the seasonings and bring to a boil. Cover, lower the heat, and simmer for about 1½ hours, stirring occasionally. If the sauce becomes too thick, stir in a small amount of water. Serve over hot cooked rice.

Makes about 4 servings.

NUTRI-STEP 1

- Decrease the vegetable oil to 2 teaspoons and stir the vegetables and lamb almost constantly to prevent them from burning.
- Increase the green pepper to 3 cups.
- Decrease the salt to ⅛ teaspoon.

NUTRI-STEP 2

- Decrease the vegetable oil to 2 teaspoons and stir the vegetables and lamb almost constantly to prevent them from burning.
- Increase the green pepper to 3 cups.
- Decrease the salt to ⅛ teaspoon or omit.

To Serve
- Omit the hot cooked white rice and USE hot cooked brown rice.

MOUSSAKA

In this version of the popular Greek dish, the eggplant is steamed rather than fried, eliminating a large amount of fat and calories. Interestingly, we've found that many so-called "eggplant-haters" love Moussaka when it is prepared this way.

This recipe is perfect for company as it makes enough for a large group. Also, it can be prepared (and frozen) in advance and then baked shortly before serving.

Filling
2 medium-sized eggplants (about 1¼ pounds each), peeled and cut

into 1-inch cubes ●■
1½ pounds very lean ground lamb (or beef) ●■
1 large onion, finely chopped
1 clove garlic, peeled and minced

<table>
<tbody>
<tr><td>1</td><td>teaspoon dried basil leaves ■</td></tr>
<tr><td>½</td><td>teaspoon dried oregano leaves</td></tr>
<tr><td>2 to 4</td><td>teaspoons ground cinnamon, or to taste</td></tr>
<tr><td>⅛</td><td>teaspoon black pepper, preferably freshly ground ■</td></tr>
<tr><td>1</td><td>teaspoon salt ●■</td></tr>
<tr><td>1</td><td>6-ounce can tomato paste</td></tr>
<tr><td>⅔</td><td>cup dry red table wine or water</td></tr>
<tr><td>2</td><td>tablespoons white or whole wheat dry bread crumbs ●■</td></tr>
</tbody>
</table>

Topping

2	tablespoons butter or margarine ●■
¼	cup enriched all-purpose or unbleached white flour
2	cups hot skim milk, or ⅔ cup instant nonfat dry milk powder plus 1⅞ cups hot water
1	cup part-skim ricotta cheese (if unavailable, use regular ricotta)
1	large egg plus 2 large egg whites, lightly beaten ■
	Pinch of ground cinnamon
	Pinch of ground nutmeg
	Pinch of salt

For Layers

⅓	cup finely grated part-skim mozzarella cheese (if unavailable, use regular mozzarella)
3	tablespoons finely grated Parmesan cheese ●■

Put the eggplant cubes in a large saucepan with about 1 inch of water (or, even better, put them in the top of a steamer). Then steam until soft, about 10 to 15 minutes. Drain very well, and set aside.

Meanwhile, prepare the meat filling. In a large skillet, brown the meat while breaking it up with a spoon. As the meat browns, add the onion and garlic, and cook with the meat. When the meat is browned, spoon off and discard all excess fat from the skillet. Stir the basil, oregano, cinnamon, pepper, salt, tomato paste, and wine into the skillet. Bring to a boil, stirring constantly, then lower the heat and simmer for about 10 to 15 minutes, or until thick. Remove from the heat, and stir in the bread crumbs. Set aside.

For the topping, melt the butter in a medium-sized saucepan. Blend in the flour (with a wire whisk, if available) and cook, stirring constantly, for 1 minute. Gradually beat in the milk, and cook, stirring constantly, until the sauce thickens and boils. Remove from the heat and beat in the ricotta cheese. Then beat in the egg and egg whites, cinnamon, nutmeg, and salt.

To assemble the moussaka, layer half of the cooked eggplant cubes in the bottom of a greased or nonstick spray-coated 9- by 13-inch (or similar) casserole or baking pan. Mix the mozzarella and Parmesan cheese together. Sprinkle about one third of the grated cheese mixture over the eggplant; then evenly cover with all the meat filling. Sprinkle the meat with half of the remaining grated cheese, then top with the remaining eggplant cubes. Cover the layers with the ricotta topping and sprinkle the top of the casserole with the remaining grated cheese. (The casserole may be tightly covered with plastic wrap or foil, and frozen at this point. Thaw overnight in the refrigerator before baking.)

Bake the casserole, uncovered, in a preheated 375-degree oven for 40 to 50 minutes, or until the topping has set and is golden. Allow to stand for about 5 minutes before cutting into squares to serve. (This is also very good served reheated.)

Makes about 10 servings.

NUTRI-STEP 1

- Increase the eggplants to 2 large (about 1½ pounds each) or 3 small (about 1 pound each).
- Decrease the ground lamb (or beef) to 1¼ pounds.
- Decrease the salt to ¾ teaspoon.
- Increase the bread crumbs to 3 tablespoons.

Topping
- Decrease the butter or margarine to 1½ tablespoons.

For Layers
- Decrease the Parmesan cheese to 2 tablespoons.

NUTRI-STEP 2

- Increase the eggplants to 2 large (about 1½ pounds each) or 3 small (about 1 pound each). Remove the skin from the eggplants in stripes, so that some peel remains on each of the eggplants. Cut the eggplants into ½-inch cubes.
- Decrease the ground lamb (or beef) to 1 pound. **And add** 1 cup very finely chopped fresh broccoli to the meat mixture with the onions.
- Increase the basil to 1¼ teaspoons.
- Increase the black pepper to ¼ teaspoon.
- Decrease the salt to ½ teaspoon.
- Increase the bread crumbs to ¼ cup. Omit white bread crumbs and USE whole wheat bread crumbs.

Topping
- Decrease the butter or margarine to 1½ tablespoons.
- Omit the large egg plus 2 large whites and SUBSTITUTE 3 large egg whites.

For Layers
- Decrease the Parmesan cheese to 2 tablespoons.

LAMB STEW

2½ pounds lamb shanks (or shoulder neck slices)
1 tablespoon vegetable oil
1 large onion, coarsely chopped
2 cloves garlic, peeled and minced
4 cups water
1 beef bouillon cube
3 carrots, coarsely sliced
¼ cup uncooked pearl barley
¼ cup dry yellow split peas, sorted and rinsed
2 to 3 large bay leaves
¼ teaspoon ground thyme
¼ teaspoon salt •
⅛ teaspoon pepper, preferably freshly ground
3 large potatoes, peeled and cut into ½-inch cubes •

In a large pot or Dutch oven, brown the meat in the oil over medium-high heat, stirring occasionally. Remove the meat and set aside. Add the onion and garlic to the pot and sauté lightly, stirring occasionally. Return the meat to the pot and add all the remaining ingredients except the potatoes. Bring to a boil. Cover, lower the heat, and simmer, stirring occasionally, for about 1 hour and 15 minutes. Remove the meat from the pot and add the potatoes. Stirring and scraping the bottom of the pot frequently to prevent sticking, cook for about ½ hour longer, or until the potatoes are tender. While the potatoes are cooking, trim the meat from the bones, discarding any fat. Cut the meat into bite-sized pieces and return to the pot. Cook until just heated through.

Makes 4 to 5 servings.

NUTRI-STEP 1

- Decrease the salt to ⅛ teaspoon or omit.
- Wash the potatoes well and leave them unpeeled. Use thin-skinned new potatoes if available.

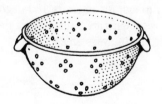

ORANGE-GLAZED PORK ROAST AND VEGETABLES

Glaze

- ⅓ cup frozen orange juice concentrate, thawed
- 2½ tablespoons prepared mustard, preferably Dijon or spicy brown style •
- 1½ tablespoons packed light brown sugar •
- 1 tablespoon instant minced onions
- 2 teaspoons mustard seeds
- ½ teaspoon salt •
- ⅛ teaspoon black pepper, preferably freshly ground
- 2 tablespoons water

Roast and Vegetables

- 1 4- to 4½-pound (bone-in) fresh pork shoulder arm (picnic) roast, trimmed of rind and all visible fat
- 4 to 5 carrots, cut into 1½-inch pieces
- 3 to 4 medium-sized onions, peeled and quartered
- 1 large rutabaga, peeled and cut into 1-inch chunks
- 2 to 3 medium-sized potatoes, peeled and quartered
- 10 to 12 medium-sized Brussels sprouts, trimmed of tough outer leaves
- ¼ cup water

Combine all the glaze ingredients in a small bowl. Stir until well mixed. Remove ¼ cup of the mixture from the bowl and reserve. (The reserved portion will be used to glaze the vegetables.)

Place the roast on a rack in a large roasting pan. Lightly baste all over with about a third of the glaze mixture remaining in the bowl. Roast the pork, uncovered, in a preheated 375-degree oven for 30 minutes. Baste with another third of the glaze mixture, and roast for 30 minutes more. Baste with the final third of the glaze and continue roasting, uncovered, for 1 hour longer.

Carefully remove the roast from the pan and set it aside. Remove the rack from the pan and set it aside. Discard any drippings in the roasting pan. Then wash out the pan and drain thoroughly. Add all the vegetables and the water to the pan. Pour the reserved ¼ cup of glaze over the vegetables and stir until they are all lightly coated with the mixture. Push the vegetables aside and return the pork roast to the pan. Cover the pan tightly with aluminum foil (or a lid) and return to the oven. Roast for 45 minutes and remove the foil. Roast for 15 minutes longer, or until the pork is cooked completely through (or registers 180 degrees when tested with a meat thermometer) and the vegetables are tender. Serve the whole roast or carved slices on a platter surrounded by the vegetables.

Makes 5 to 6 servings.

Glaze
- Decrease the prepared mustard to 2 tablespoons.
- Decrease the packed brown sugar to 1 tablespoon.
- Decrease the salt to a generous ¼ teaspoon.

PORK POT ROAST WITH VEGETABLES

1	4- to 4½-pound (bone-in) fresh pork shoulder arm (picnic) roast, trimmed of rind and all visible fat •
2	medium-sized onions, coarsely chopped
2	cloves garlic, peeled and minced
2	cups cabbage, coarsely chopped
1	large celery stalk, including leaves, finely chopped
1	apple, cored and coarsely chopped
2	tablespoons chopped fresh parsley leaves
1⅛	cups water
1	teaspoon salt •
1	small bay leaf
¾	teaspoon dried thyme leaves
½	teaspoon dry mustard
¼	teaspoon black pepper, preferably freshly ground •
	Pinch of ground cloves
4	large carrots, cut into 2-inch pieces
3	medium-sized potatoes, peeled and quartered
6 to 8	small white onions, peeled
1	large turnip, peeled and cut into eighths
10 to 12	medium-sized Brussels sprouts, trimmed of any tough outer leaves

In a very large heavy Dutch oven or pot over medium heat, lightly brown the pork roast in its own fat, turning frequently. As the roast begins to give off more fat, raise the heat to medium-high and brown well on all sides. Drain off and discard all the fat from the pot. Stir the onion and garlic into the Dutch oven. Cook, stirring, for 3 to 4 minutes, or until the onion is limp. Add the cabbage, celery, apple, parsley, and water to the pot. Then stir in the salt, bay leaf, thyme, mustard, pepper, and cloves. Bring the mixture to a boil. Cover, lower the heat, and simmer, stirring occasionally, for 1½ hours. With a large spoon, skim off and discard all the fat from the surface of the cooking liquid.

Add all the remaining ingredients to the Dutch oven in the order given, moistening each with some cooking liquid. Cover the pot and simmer for about 1 hour, or until the pork and vegetables are tender. Transfer the meat to a platter, and carve into slices. Place the vegetables and some of the cooking liquid in a large bowl, and serve separately.

Makes about 6 servings.

NUTRI-STEP 1

- Use a smaller pork roast (about 3¾ to 4 pounds).
- Decrease the salt to a generous ¾ teaspoon.
- Increase the black pepper to a generous ¼ teaspoon. *And add* about 6 1-inch-thick cabbage wedges to the pot during the last 30 to 35 minutes of cooking time. Lay the wedges snugly over the other vegetables, cover the pot, and continue cooking until the pork and vegetables are tender.

PORK CHOPS HAWAIIAN

Here's a tasty, festive, and easy-to-prepare pork, vegetable, and fruit combination. Soy sauce provides the salt in the recipe, and pineapple juice lends a natural sweetness. Contributing both appealing color and nutritional enrichment to the dish is sweet potato, a good source of carotene.

2	teaspoons vegetable oil
4 to 5	thick loin pork chops (about 4½ ounces each untrimmed), trimmed of all visible fat ●
1	1-pound, 3-ounce can juice-packed pineapple chunks, including juice
2½	tablespoons soy sauce ●
½	teaspoon apple cider vinegar
⅛	teaspoon black pepper, preferably freshly ground
3	tablespoons raisins
4	medium-sized onions, peeled and quartered
1	large sweet potato, peeled and cut into 1-inch chunks
2	large celery stalks, cut into ½-inch slices
2	tablespoons cold water
1	teaspoon cornstarch

Heat the oil in a 12-inch diameter or larger skillet over medium-high heat. Add the pork chops and, turning frequently to prevent burning, brown well on both sides.

Drain off and discard any fat in the pan. Add the juice from the canned pineapple to the skillet, along with the soy sauce, vinegar, pepper, and raisins. Lower the heat, cover the skillet, and simmer the chops for 20 minutes, turning occasionally. Add the onions, sweet potato, and celery. Cover again and simmer for 10 minutes longer. Add the pineapple chunks to the skillet. Simmer, covered, until the celery is just tender and the pork is cooked through, about 8 to 10 minutes longer (or a total cooking time of about 40 minutes).

With a slotted spoon, transfer the chops and vegetables to a serving platter. Stir together the water and cornstarch in a small bowl or cup until completely smooth and well blended. Add the cornstarch mixture to the liquid remaining in the skillet. Heat, stirring until the sauce is clear and slightly thickened. Spoon the sauce over the pork chops and vegetables, and serve.

Makes 4 to 5 servings.

NUTRI-STEP 1

- Use smaller pork chops; about 4 ounces (untrimmed) each.
- Decrease the soy sauce to 2 tablespoons. *And add* ⅔ cup small fresh cauliflower flowerets to the skillet along with the pineapple chunks.

PORK CHOP AND CABBAGE DINNER

2	teaspoons vegetable oil •
6	large pork chops, trimmed of all visible fat
1	15-ounce can tomato sauce
1	16-ounce can tomatoes, including juice, puréed
1	cup water
½	teaspoon dry mustard
⅛	teaspoon black pepper, preferably freshly ground
¼	teaspoon ground thyme
2	large bay leaves
½	teaspoon salt •
3 to 4	drops hot pepper sauce
1	tablespoon packed light brown sugar •
1	tablespoon apple cider vinegar
1	large onion, coarsely chopped
2	large carrots, cut into ¼-inch slices
4	cups potatoes, peeled and cut into ½-inch slices •
5	cups coarsely sliced cabbage

Heat the oil in a large heavy Dutch oven over medium-high heat. Add the pork chops and brown on both sides in batches. Return all the chops to the Dutch oven. Add the tomato sauce, tomatoes with their juice, water, and all the seasonings. Stir to combine well. Add the onions, carrots, and potatoes, and stir down into the sauce. Arrange the cabbage on top of the sauce. Turn the heat up and bring the mixture to a boil. Cover, lower the heat, and simmer for 1 hour, or slightly longer, until the potatoes and carrots are tender. Stir occasionally. Before serving, skim any excess fat from the surface of the sauce and discard. Then stir the cabbage down into the sauce.

Makes 6 servings.

NUTRI-STEP 1

- Omit the vegetable oil and coat the pot with nonstick spray coating before browning the chops.
- Decrease the salt to ¼ teaspoon.
- Decrease the light brown sugar to a scant 1 tablespoon.
- Leave the potatoes unpeeled and scrub them well.

PORK CHOPS IN ORANGE SAUCE

This dish tastes best if the flavorful sauce is allowed to cook down to the consistency of thick gravy.

2   teaspoons vegetable oil •
4   large pork chops, trimmed of all visible fat
     Black pepper, preferably freshly ground, to taste
2   cups orange juice
1   medium-sized onion, coarsely chopped
10   whole cloves
½   teaspoon dried marjoram leaves
¼   teaspoon salt •

Heat the oil in a large heavy skillet over medium heat. Sprinkle the chops with pepper and brown them in the oil. Add all the remaining ingredients and bring to a boil. Cover, lower the heat, and simmer for 1 hour, stirring occasionally. During the last half hour, set the cover of the skillet ajar so the sauce begins to cook down. Skim any excess fat from the sauce and discard. When the chops are very tender, turn up the heat and continue cooking down the sauce until it resembles thick gravy. Discard the cloves.

Makes 4 servings.

- Omit the oil and coat the pan with nonstick vegetable spray.
- Decrease the salt to ⅛ teaspoon.

CASSOULET AMÉRICAIN

Cassoulet, a hearty French casserole made of sausage, various other meats, and beans, was the inspiration for the recipe which follows. It features fresh pork sausage baked along with well-seasoned Great Northern beans. Our dish is much easier to prepare than real cassoulet, however. And it's also far, far lower in fat.

Although salt isn't listed as an ingredient in Cassoulet Américain, it's not a salt-free dish. The salt is in the bouillon, which, as a result, we decrease in Nutri-Step 1.

Note: Our cassoulet calls for homemade Pork Sausage Patties (see page 294).

2	cups dry Great Northern beans, sorted and rinsed
6	cups water
1	medium-sized onion, peeled and stuck with 1 clove
1	large bay leaf
8 to 10	fresh or frozen (thawed) homemade Pork Sausage Patties
2	large onions, peeled and finely chopped
1	celery stalk, including leaves, finely chopped
1	large turnip, peeled and finely chopped
2	large cloves garlic, peeled and minced
1	cup beef broth or bouillon ●■
1	cup canned imported Italian tomatoes, including juice, puréed
½	teaspoon dried thyme leaves
¼	teaspoon freshly ground black pepper
	Scant ⅛ teaspoon ground allspice

Topping
1	cup dry white bread crumbs ■
¼	cup chopped fresh parsley leaves
1	tablespoon butter or margarine, melted ●■

Combine the beans, water, onion stuck with a clove, and bay leaf in a 4-quart or larger Dutch oven over high heat. Bring to a full boil, and boil for 1 minute. Then turn off the heat and let the pot stand, covered, for 1 hour. Heat the beans to boiling once again, lower the heat, and simmer the beans, covered, for 1 hour and 15 to 20 minutes, or until they are tender. Reserve ½ cup of the bean cooking liquid and drain the beans in a colander. Discard the cooked onion and bay leaf.

Put the sausage patties in a large heavy skillet over medium-high heat. Cook until nicely browned on both sides, about 12 to 14 minutes. Remove the patties from the skillet, and lay them on paper towels to drain. Drain off and discard all but 1 teaspoon of fat from the skillet. Return the pan to the heat and add the chopped onion, celery, turnip, and garlic. Cook, stirring constantly and scraping any sausage bits from the bottom of the pan, for 4 to 5 minutes, or until the vegetables are limp. Remove the skillet from the heat and add the drained cooked beans to the skillet. Stir to mix with the vegetables.

To assemble the casserole, turn half the drained beans and vegetables back into the Dutch oven used to cook the beans. Lay the sausage patties over the beans and then cover the patties with the remaining beans.

Combine the bouillon, puréed tomatoes and juice, thyme, pepper, and allspice in a medium-sized bowl, stirring to blend. Pour the bouillon mixture into the Dutch oven, adding only enough to come almost to the top layer of beans. (Discard any extra bouillon mixture.)

In a small bowl stir together the bread crumbs, parsley, and butter until well mixed. Sprinkle the crumb mixture over the top of the casserole. Place the casserole on a rack in the upper half of a preheated 375-degree oven. Bake, uncovered, for 30 minutes. Stir the crumb layer lightly to ensure even browning and bake the casserole, uncovered, for 30 to 35 minutes longer. If the top seems dry, occasionally add a bit of the reserved bean cooking liquid. Cassoulet is very good served reheated.

Makes 4 to 5 main-dish servings.

NUTRI-STEP 1

- Decrease the bouillon to ¾ cup. Add ¼ cup of the reserved bean cooking liquid to the bouillon. Then combine the bouillon with the puréed tomatoes and seasonings, and proceed as directed.

Topping
- Decrease the melted butter or margarine to ½ tablespoon.

NUTRI-STEP 2

- Decrease the bouillon to ¾ cup. Add ¼ cup of the reserved bean cooking liquid to the bouillon. Then combine the bouillon with the puréed tomatoes and seasonings, and proceed as directed.

Topping
- Decrease the white bread crumbs to ½ cup. *And add* ½ cup whole wheat bread crumbs to the white bread crumbs.
- Decrease the melted butter or margarine to ½ tablespoon.

SWEET AND SOUR PORK

The colorful assortment of fruit and vegetables in this dish not only boosts nutrition but lends eye and taste appeal.

Sauce
½   cup juice from 1 15½-ounce can juice-packed pineapple chunks (reserve pineapple chunks)
1   tablespoon plus 2 teaspoons cornstarch
3½   tablespoons apple cider vinegar •
2   tablespoons soy sauce •
2   tablespoons packed light brown sugar •
    Generous ⅛ teaspoon freshly ground black pepper

Pork and Vegetables
¾   pound boneless very lean pork loin, trimmed of all fat and cut into ½-inch cubes •
2½   tablespoons peanut or corn oil •
2   medium-sized carrots, thinly sliced
2   large onions, cut into eighths
1   medium-sized green pepper, seeded and cut into 1-inch chunks
1   medium-sized red bell pepper, seeded and cut into 1-inch chunks (if unavailable, substitute another green pepper)
1   large celery stalk, sliced into ½-inch pieces •
1   large, tart unpeeled apple, cored and cut into 1-inch chunks
⅔   cup very coarsely chopped celery cabbage or green cabbage
1   teaspoon very finely minced fresh gingerroot, or ¾ teaspoon ground ginger
1   large tomato, peeled, cored, and cut into eighths
    Drained pineapple chunks (from a 15½-ounce can)

For the sauce, combine ½ cup juice drained from canned pineapple in a cup with the cornstarch. Stir until the mixture is smooth. Add all remaining sauce ingredients and stir until the sugar dissolves. Set the sauce aside.

Pat the pork cubes completely dry with paper towels. Heat the oil in a heavy, 12-inch diameter (or larger) skillet over high heat. When the oil is very hot but not smoking, add the pork cubes, stirring constantly. Continue to stir and cook the pork for about 4 to 5 minutes, or until browned on all sides.

Add the carrots, onions, green and red peppers, celery, apple, celery cabbage, and gingerroot to the skillet, stirring. Stir constantly and cook over high heat for 5 to 6 minutes. Stir the reserved sauce mixture briefly, then pour it into the skillet. Cook, stirring constantly, for 2 minutes, or until the liquid is slightly thickened and clear. Lower the heat to medium and continue cooking, stirring constantly, for 4 minutes longer. Add the tomato and pineapple chunks and cook for about 2 minutes longer, or until the vegetables are cooked through but still hold some shape. Serve with Oriental Fried Rice (page 89), if desired.

Makes 4 servings.

NUTRI-STEP 1

Sauce
- Decrease the vinegar to 3 tablespoons.
- Decrease the soy sauce to 1½ tablespoons.
- Decrease the light brown sugar to 1½ tablespoons.

Pork and Vegetables
- Decrease the pork to ⅔ pound.
- Decrease the oil to 1½ tablespoons. Watch the pork and vegetables carefully and stir constantly to prevent them from sticking and burning.
- Increase the celery stalks to 2 large ones.

PORK AND MIXED CHINESE VEGETABLES

Pork and Marinade
- ¾ pound boneless pork loin or shoulder, trimmed of all fat and cut into ½-inch cubes •
- 1 tablespoon soy sauce
- 1 clove garlic, peeled and minced
- ¾ teaspoon minced fresh gingerroot, or ½ teaspoon ground ginger

Sauce
- 1½ teaspoons cornstarch
- ⅓ cup water
- 2 tablespoons dry white wine or chicken broth
- 2 tablespoons soy sauce •
- 1 tablespoon ketchup
- 1½ teaspoons light brown sugar
- 1½ teaspoons apple cider vinegar
  Pinch of cayenne pepper, or more to taste

Vegetables
- 1 large onion, coarsely chopped
- 1½ cups fresh broccoli flowerets, sliced in half lengthwise
- 1 6- to 8-ounce package frozen Chinese pea pods, rinsed and well drained

5 to 6	fresh medium-sized mushrooms, sliced in half
1	cup celery cabbage or green cabbage, cut into bite-sized chunks
1	celery stalk, coarsely sliced
1	cup fresh bean sprouts or canned sliced water chestnuts
1½	tablespoons peanut or vegetable oil

To Serve
3½ to 4   cups hot cooked white or brown rice

To prepare the pork and marinade, combine the pork cubes with soy sauce, garlic, and ginger in a medium-sized bowl, stirring to mix. Cover and refrigerate for 10 minutes.

To prepare the sauce, stir together the cornstarch and water in a small bowl or cup until smooth. Stir in the wine, remaining soy sauce, ketchup, brown sugar, vinegar, and cayenne. Set the mixture aside.

To ready the vegetables, combine the onion, broccoli, and pea pods in one bowl, and the mushrooms, celery cabbage, and celery in another. Rinse the bean sprouts or water chestnuts and put into a colander to drain.

Heat the oil in a very large skillet over medium-high heat until hot but not smoking. Add the pork and marinade to the pan and cook, stirring, for about 6 to 7 minutes, or until the pork cubes are cooked through. Push the pork to one side, and add the onion, broccoli, and pea pods to the pan. Cook, stirring, for 1 minute, then push to one side. Stir in the mushrooms, celery cabbage, and celery and cook for 1 minute longer. Stir the reserved sauce mixture and add it to the skillet, along with the drained sprouts or water chestnuts.

Stirring constantly, cook about 2 minutes longer, or until the sauce is clear and slightly thickened and the vegetables are tender-crisp. Serve immediately along with white or brown rice.

Makes 4 to 5 servings.

NUTRI-STEP 1

Pork and Marinade
- Decrease the pork to ⅔ pound.

Sauce
- Decrease the soy sauce to 1½ tablespoons.

Vegetables
Add 1 cup small fresh cauliflower flowerets to the skillet when the onion, broccoli, and pea pods are added.

SAVORY VEAL GOULASH

1	pound boneless lean veal shank or shoulder, cut into ¾-inch cubes •
1	tablespoon butter or margarine •
½	tablespoon vegetable oil •
1	large onion, finely chopped
2	cups coarsely sliced fresh mushrooms
1	medium-sized celery stalk, including leaves, finely chopped
4	medium-sized carrots, cut into ¼-inch-thick slices
4 to 5	medium-sized potatoes, peeled and cut into 1-inch cubes
⅓	cup dry white table wine or chicken broth
⅓	cup water (approximate)
½	teaspoon salt •
⅛	teaspoon dried basil leaves
⅛	teaspoon black pepper, preferably freshly ground
2	tablespoons commercial sour cream •
2	tablespoons plain lowfat yogurt

In a 4-quart or similar Dutch oven over medium heat, brown the veal lightly in the butter and oil, stirring constantly. Add the onion, mushrooms, and celery and cook, stirring, for 5 to 6 minutes longer, or until the vegetables are limp and the juices are released. Stir in the carrots, potatoes, wine, water, salt, basil, and pepper. Cover and lower the heat. Simmer very gently, stirring frequently to prevent sticking, for 20 to 25 minutes, or until the vegetables and meat are just tender. Add a bit more water if necessary to prevent the mixture from boiling dry. Remove the pot from the heat and add the sour cream and yogurt. Stir until well blended and serve.

Makes 4 to 5 servings.

NUTRI-STEP 1

- Decrease the veal to ¾ pound.
- Decrease the butter or margarine to 2 teaspoons.
- Decrease the vegetable oil to 1 teaspoon. *And add* ⅔ cup finely diced fresh cauliflower flowerets along with the celery.
- Decrease the salt to a generous ¼ teaspoon.
- Decrease the sour cream to 1 tablespoon.

VEAL SHANKS DUTCH OVEN DINNER

1   tablespoon butter or margarine
1½ teaspoons vegetable oil
2¼ pounds cross-cut veal shanks (about 5 to 6 2-inch-thick pieces),
    trimmed of all fat
1   large onion, coarsely chopped
1   medium-sized turnip, peeled and coarsely chopped
1   medium-sized celery stalk, including leaves, coarsely chopped
3   tablespoons chopped fresh parsley leaves (optional)
1   clove garlic, peeled and minced
1   16-ounce can imported Italian tomatoes, including juice
1   cup chicken broth or bouillon
1   large bay leaf
⅛   teaspoon black pepper, preferably freshly ground
¼   teaspoon salt •
½   medium-sized lemon, well-washed, seeded, and halved
4   large carrots, cut into 1½-inch pieces
4   medium-sized potatoes, peeled and cut into 1-inch chunks
6   small white onions, peeled

Combine the butter and oil in a 4-quart or larger Dutch oven or similar heavy pot over high heat. Add veal shank pieces and, turning frequently, brown well on all sides. Remove the shank pieces from the pot and set them aside. Lower the heat to medium and add the chopped onion, turnip, celery, parsley, and garlic to the pot, stirring. Cook the vegetables, stirring, for 6 to 7 minutes, or until they are soft. Add the tomatoes, breaking them up with a spoon. Then stir the broth, bay leaf, pepper, salt, and lemon pieces into the vegetables. Return the veal to the pot.

Bring the mixture to a boil, lower the heat, and simmer, covered, for 35 to 40 minutes. Add the carrots and simmer, covered, 15 minutes longer. Stir the potatoes and white onions into the pot, cover, and continue simmering for about 40 minutes more, or until the veal and vegetables are tender. Remove and discard the bay leaf and lemon pieces. The dish may be served immediately or refrigerated and served reheated.

Makes 4 to 5 servings.

NUTRI-STEP 1

- Decrease the salt to ⅛ teaspoon. *And add* ¾ cup small fresh cauliflower flowerets to the pot during the last 20 minutes of cooking.

VEAL CHOPS PAPRIKAS

  2 teaspoons butter or margarine
  1 teaspoon vegetable oil
4 to 5 meaty loin or shoulder veal chops, trimmed of all visible fat
  2 medium-sized onions, thinly sliced into rings
  2 large red bell peppers, seeded, sliced in half lengthwise, and cut into half rings (if unavailable, substitute green peppers)
  1 cup canned tomatoes (3 medium-sized tomatoes, plus juice)
 1½ teaspoons paprika, preferably imported spicy-style ●
  ¼ teaspoon salt ●
  ⅛ teaspoon freshly ground black pepper

Heat the butter and oil in a large heavy skillet over medium-high heat. Add the chops and, turning frequently to prevent sticking, brown them well on both sides. Add the onions and bell peppers to the skillet and, stirring constantly, cook for 5 to 6 minutes longer, or until the vegetables are limp. Add the tomatoes and their juice to the skillet, breaking them up with a spoon. Then add all the remaining ingredients. Turn the heat to low and cover the skillet. Cook, stirring occasionally, for about 20 to 25 minutes longer, or until the chops are just cooked through and the vegetables are very tender. If necessary, add a tablespoon or two of water to the skillet to prevent the vegetables from drying out and burning. Spoon some of the vegetable mixture over each chop and serve.

Makes 4 to 5 servings.

NUTRI-STEP 1

Add ½ cup finely chopped carrot to the skillet along with the onions and bell peppers.
- Increase the paprika to 2 teaspoons.
- Decrease the salt to a generous ⅛ teaspoon.

Chapter 11

Main Dishes— Poultry

T he following recipes show the versatility of poultry—cooked whole and in pieces, boned and unboned, with vegetables and with fruit. Chicken and turkey dishes are so popular and inexpensive to prepare, as well as healthful, that we have made this one of our larger recipe chapters. Poultry is high in protein and niacin, but generally much lower in fat than red meats such as beef and pork. (We have not included any duck or goose recipes because these particular birds *are* rather fatty, and they are also quite expensive.)

Most chicken fat is in and right under the skin. This is why many of our chicken recipes have Nutri-Steps directing you to remove the skin before cooking. Just pull off and discard the skin—it should come loose fairly easily—and then use a small knife to scrape off any visible fat left behind on the meat.

If you've ever tried this easy preparation technique, you know that it also has another distinct advantage. It allows seasonings to permeate the nutritious part of the chicken during cooking rather than being absorbed by the skin as in most traditional recipes. Of course, our recipes have been specifically designed to keep the chicken moist and tender even though it's being cooked "in the buff."

QUICK OVEN-FRIED CHICKEN

An easy and economical lowfat recipe, this chicken offers good taste and a crispy crust.

8 to 10	**meaty chicken pieces (about 2 to 2¼ pounds)** •
1½	**tablespoons butter or margarine** •
⅔	**cup enriched all-purpose or unbleached white flour**
½	**teaspoon dried parsley flakes**
½	**teaspoon chili powder**
½	**teaspoon paprika**
⅛	**teaspoon onion powder**
¼	**teaspoon dried dillweed**
¼	**teaspoon celery salt**
	Generous ⅛ teaspoon salt •

Preheat the oven to 350 degrees. Pat the chicken pieces dry with paper towels. Put the butter in a 9- by 13-inch or similar baking dish, and place it in the oven until the butter is melted. Remove from the oven.

Combine the flour and all the seasoning ingredients in a heavy paper bag and shake to mix. Add the chicken to the bag a few pieces at a time, and shake until thoroughly coated with the seasoning mix. Tap off any excess seasoning mix from the chicken. Dip the top surface of each piece into the melted butter in the baking dish, then turn skin side (buttered side) up and arrange in the dish.

Bake chicken in a preheated 350-degree oven for 30 minutes. Turn the chicken over with a fork, and continue baking for 20 to 25 minutes, or until the pieces are golden brown and cooked through.

Makes 4 to 5 servings.

NUTRI-STEP 1

- Remove the skin from the chicken pieces.
- Omit the butter or margarine from the recipe. Place the coated chicken pieces in a very lightly greased baking dish, and bake for 20 minutes on the top side. Turn pieces over and bake for 20 minutes longer on the bottom side. Turn again and bake for 20 to 25 minutes longer.
- Omit the salt.

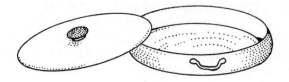

CHICKEN IN RED WINE

9 to 10   meaty chicken pieces •
   1½   tablespoons butter or margarine
    1   large onion, coarsely chopped
    1   clove garlic, peeled and minced
    ¼   cup coarsely chopped fresh parsley leaves
    2   cups coarsely sliced fresh mushrooms
    1   large bay leaf
    ½   teaspoon dried thyme leaves
    ½   teaspoon salt
    ¼   teaspoon freshly ground black pepper
   1¼   cups dry red table wine
    1   celery stalk, cut into ¼-inch-thick slices

To Serve
3½ to 4   cups hot cooked white or brown rice •

Arrange the chicken pieces on a broiler pan under a preheated broiler. Broil for about 5 minutes, or until the pieces are well browned. Then turn them over and broil for 5 minutes, or until well browned on the second side. Remove the pan from the broiler and set aside. Lay the chicken pieces on paper towels and let drain.

In a 4-quart or similar Dutch oven or pot, melt the butter over medium-high heat. Add the onion, garlic, parsley, and mushrooms. Cook, stirring constantly, for 5 to 6 minutes, or until the vegetables are limp. Stir in the herbs, seasonings, and wine. Add the chicken pieces, moistening with the cooking liquid. Bring the mixture to a simmer, cover tightly, and turn the heat to medium-low. Simmer for 25 minutes. Stir in the sliced celery and cook for 7 to 9 minutes longer, or until the celery pieces are cooked through but still slightly crunchy. Arrange the chicken on a bed of rice. Discard the bay leaf. Spoon the wine and vegetables over the chicken and rice.

Makes 4 to 6 servings.

NUTRI-STEP 1

- Remove the skin from the chicken pieces. Omit the broiling of the chicken pieces. Instead, melt the butter and cook the vegetables in the Dutch oven. Then add the skinless chicken pieces along with the herbs, seasonings, and wine. Increase the cooking time to 35 minutes. Then add the celery and cook for 12 to 15 minutes longer.

To Serve
- Omit the cooked white rice and USE cooked brown rice.

CHICKEN MARENGO

Here's our nutritionally-improved version of an international favorite which features a tasty variety of vegetables and herbs. We've cut way down on the amount of ripe olives usually included in the classic recipe because they are so high in fat. If you wish, the olives can be omitted.

About 3 pounds meaty chicken pieces •
Paprika
2   tablespoons olive oil or vegetable oil •
8   ounces peeled fresh or frozen pearl (tiny white) onions, or 1 large onion, cut into eighths
2   cloves garlic, peeled and minced
1   cup sliced fresh mushrooms
2   medium-sized carrots, cut into ½-inch slices •
1   16-ounce can tomatoes, including juice, coarsely chopped
¼   cup dry sherry or white table wine
¼   cup pitted ripe (black) olives (optional) •
½   teaspoon dried thyme leaves •
¾   teaspoon dried basil leaves •
1   bay leaf, crumbled
½   teaspoon salt •
⅛   teaspoon black pepper, preferably freshly ground •
1   tablespoon enriched all-purpose or unbleached white flour
1   tablespoon cold water

To Serve (optional)
Hot cooked white or brown rice or hot cooked regular or whole wheat noodles •

Sprinkle the chicken pieces lightly with paprika. Set aside.

Heat the oil in a Dutch oven or large saucepan and brown chicken lightly on all sides. Add the onions and garlic, and cook, stirring often, until they are tender. Then stir in the mushrooms, carrots, tomatoes and their juice, sherry, olives, thyme, basil, bay leaf, salt, and pepper.

Reduce the heat and cover the pan tightly. Simmer, stirring occasionally, for about 1 hour, or until the chicken is very tender. Use a slotted spoon to remove the chicken pieces and vegetables to a serving platter. Cover with aluminum foil to keep warm.

In a small cup, mix together the flour and water until smooth. Stir this paste into the liquid remaining in the pan. Cook until the sauce boils and thickens slightly. Pour some of the sauce over the chicken, and serve the rest on the side (with cooked rice or noodles, if desired).

Makes 4 to 5 servings.

- Remove and discard all the skin and visible fat from the chicken pieces.
- Decrease the oil to 1 tablespoon. Use a nonstick skillet and watch the chicken carefully so it does not stick.
- Increase the carrots to 3 medium.
- Omit the olives.
- Increase the thyme to ¾ teaspoon.
- Increase the basil to 1 teaspoon.
- Decrease the salt to ¼ teaspoon.
- Increase the black pepper to a generous ⅛ teaspoon.

To Serve
- If serving with rice or noodles, omit the white rice or regular noodles and USE brown rice or whole wheat or spinach noodles.

APRICOT CHICKEN

The apricots in this flavorful dish are a good source of vitamin A. The alcohol in the rum evaporates during cooking, leaving behind an intriguing, Caribbean-like flavor.

	About 2½ to 3 pounds meaty chicken pieces •
	Enriched all-purpose or unbleached white flour
2	tablespoons butter or margarine •
2	teaspoons vegetable oil •
1	large onion, peeled and finely chopped
½	cup dark rum
1	cup water
	Generous ¼ teaspoon ground ginger, or more to taste •
1½	tablespoons packed light or dark brown sugar •
½	teaspoon salt •
⅛	teaspoon black pepper, preferably freshly ground
1	cup dried apricot halves (about 6 ounces)

To Serve

Hot cooked white or brown rice or Plain-Cooked Millet (page 100) •
About 2 tablespoons chopped fresh parsley, for garnish (optional)

Lightly coat the chicken pieces with flour, shaking off any excess.

In a large, deep, heavy skillet or electric frypan, heat the butter with the oil until hot. Add the onion and sauté until tender but not browned. Add the chicken to the skillet, and lightly brown on all sides. Pour the rum over the chicken, and let sizzle for about 2 minutes.

Meanwhile, mix together the water, ginger, brown sugar, salt, and pepper. Pour this mixture over the chicken. Add the apricot halves to the skillet between the chicken pieces. Make sure the apricots are covered with the cooking liquid.

Cover the skillet and simmer over low heat for about 40 to 45 minutes, or until the chicken is tender. Occasionally baste the chicken and apricots, and rotate the chicken pieces. (If the sauce gets too thick, stir in a few additional tablespoons of water.) Use a large spoon or tongs to transfer the chicken pieces from the skillet to a bed of hot, cooked rice or millet. Put the apricots on top of the chicken pieces, and pour the sauce over all. Sprinkle with chopped parsley, if desired, and serve.

Makes about 5 servings.

NUTRI-STEP 1

- Remove all the skin and visible fat from the chicken pieces.
- Decrease the butter or margarine to 1½ tablespoons. Watch the chicken carefully so it does not stick.
- Decrease the oil to 1 teaspoon.
- Increase the ground ginger to ½ teaspoon or to taste.
- Decrease the brown sugar to 1 packed tablespoon.
- Decrease the salt to ¼ teaspoon.

To Serve

- If serving with rice, omit the cooked white rice and USE cooked brown rice.

CHICKEN IN BARBECUE SAUCE

3   pounds meaty chicken pieces •
2   medium-sized onions, cut in eighths
1   recipe Barbecue Sauce (page 292)

Arrange the chicken pieces in a shallow 9- by 13-inch or similar baking dish. Tuck the onion wedges in among the chicken pieces. Pour half of the barbecue sauce recipe (¾ cup) over the chicken. Cover the baking dish tightly with aluminum foil or the baking dish top, and bake in a preheated 375-degree oven for 30 minutes. Remove the cover, turn the chicken pieces, and spread on the remaining barbecue sauce. Bake, uncovered, for 30 minutes longer. If a crisper exterior is desired, brown the chicken under the broiler for 5 minutes before serving.

Makes 4 to 6 servings.

NUTRI-STEP 1

- Remove the skin from the chicken pieces before arranging them in the baking dish.

    Note: The Barbecue Sauce recipe contains additional Nutri-Steps.

SPICY MOROCCAN-STYLE CHICKEN IN SAUCE

The aromatic spices in this easy dish penetrate the chicken as it cooks, giving it such a wonderful flavor that you won't even notice all the skin has been removed. The chicken is "stewed" in a small amount of liquid, keeping the meat very moist and tender. After the chicken is done, its well-seasoned broth becomes a tasty lowfat sauce.

	About 3 pounds meaty chicken pieces, skin and all visible fat removed
1½	cups water
¾	cup chopped fresh parsley leaves
1	large onion, grated or very finely chopped
½	teaspoon ground turmeric
½ to ¾	teaspoon black pepper, or to taste, preferably freshly ground
¾ to 1	teaspoon ground ginger
¾ to 1	teaspoon ground cinnamon
1	tablespoon butter or margarine •
½	teaspoon salt •

To Serve

| | Hot cooked white or brown rice or hot Plain-Cooked Millet (page 100) • |
| 2 | tablespoons slivered almonds • |

Put the chicken pieces in a large saucepan (about 4-quarts), Dutch oven, or soup pot.

In a small bowl, combine the water, parsley, onion, turmeric, pepper, ginger, cinnamon, butter, and salt. Pour the seasoned liquid over the chicken pieces. (The liquid may not cover all the chicken pieces.) Cover and bring to a boil. Then lower the heat and simmer for about 1 hour, or until the chicken is very tender. Occasionally rotate the chicken so that each piece is immersed in the broth for part of the cooking period.

Use a slotted spoon or tongs to remove the chicken pieces from the pot onto a bed of hot, cooked rice or millet. Cover with aluminum foil to keep it warm. Bring the chicken broth remaining in the pot to a rapid boil, and quickly reduce it by half or until concentrated enough for a sauce. Pour this sauce over the chicken pieces. Sprinkle the almonds on top for garnish and serve.

Makes about 5 servings.

NUTRI-STEP 1

- Decrease the butter or margarine to 1½ teaspoons.
- Decrease the salt to ¼ teaspoon.

To Serve
- If serving with rice, omit the white rice and USE brown rice.
- Decrease the almonds to 1 tablespoon or omit.

CHICKEN AND RICE RANGOON

Who says brown rice is too "healthy" to taste good? In this recipe the rice is as delicious as the chicken it complements.

3	tablespoons soy sauce ●
2	teaspoons curry powder ●
½	teaspoon chili powder ●
⅛	teaspoon ground cinnamon
	Pinch of saffron threads (optional)
¼	teaspoon salt
8 to 10	meaty chicken pieces ●
1½	tablespoons peanut or corn oil
2	medium-sized onions, peeled and chopped
1	large celery stalk, including leaves, chopped
1	large turnip, peeled and coarsely chopped
2⅓	cups warm water
1	large bay leaf
1	cup uncooked brown rice, rinsed and well drained
¼	cup raisins

Combine the soy sauce, curry powder, chili powder, cinnamon, saffron, and salt in a large bowl. Add the chicken pieces and toss until well coated with the seasoning mixture. Cover and refrigerate the chicken for 10 minutes.

Heat the oil in a 4-quart or larger Dutch oven or heavy pot over medium-high heat. Using tongs, transfer the chicken from the bowl to the Dutch oven. Set the bowl, along with any remaining seasoning mixture, aside.

Brown the chicken pieces lightly on all sides. Add the onions, celery, and turnip to the chicken. Cook, stirring, for about 4 minutes, or until the onion is soft. Add the water to the bowl used for the chicken marinade. Then pour the liquid over the chicken.

Stir the bay leaf, rice, and raisins into the pot. Cover with a tight-fitting lid and lower the heat. Simmer, stirring occasionally to prevent rice from sticking, for 45 to 50 minutes, or until the chicken and rice are tender. Remove the bay leaf and serve.

Makes 4 to 5 servings.

NUTRI-STEP 1

- Decrease the soy sauce to 2 tablespoons.
- Increase the curry powder to 2¼ teaspoons.
- Increase the chili powder to ¾ teaspoon.
- Remove and discard the skin from the chicken pieces before placing the chicken in the seasoning mixture. *And add* 1 small, coarsely chopped carrot to the pot along with the turnip.

QUICK ORANGE–GINGER CHICKEN

2	cups uncooked chicken white meat, cut into bite-sized pieces (meat from 3 breast halves)
	Black pepper, preferably freshly ground, to taste
1	cup coarsely sliced fresh mushrooms
1	tablespoon vegetable oil •
2	celery stalks, coarsely sliced
1	medium-sized onion, chopped
1¾	cups orange juice
¼	cup water
1	tablespoon soy sauce •
⅛	teaspoon garlic powder
1	teaspoon ground ginger
1	8-ounce can sliced water chestnuts, drained
2	cups "instant" rice

Sprinkle the chicken lightly with pepper. In a large skillet, sauté chicken and mushrooms in the oil over medium-high heat. When the chicken has turned white, add the celery, onion, orange juice, water, soy sauce, garlic, ginger, and water chestnuts to the pan. Cover and cook over medium-low heat for about 8 minutes, or until the chicken is tender. Stir in the rice and remove from the heat. Let stand for 5 minutes, or until the liquid is absorbed and the rice is tender.

Makes 4 to 5 servings.

NUTRI-STEP 1

- Decrease the vegetable oil to 2 teaspoons and stir the ingredients constantly. Or use a nonstick pan.
- Decrease the soy sauce to 2 teaspoons.

CHINESE-STYLE CHICKEN AND CAULIFLOWER

1	cup chicken broth or bouillon
2½	tablespoons soy sauce •
1	tablespoon dry sherry
1 to 2	teaspoons grated fresh gingerroot, or ½ teaspoon ground ginger
1½	tablespoons vegetable oil •
4	large chicken breast halves, skinned, boned, and cut into ¾-inch squares
2	green onions (scallions), thinly sliced
1	medium-sized head fresh cauliflower, trimmed and cut into small flowerets
1	medium-sized green pepper, seeded and cut into ¾-inch squares
½	cup fresh mushrooms, sliced
2	tablespoons cornstarch
2	tablespoons cool water

To Serve

Hot cooked white or brown rice •

In a small bowl, stir together the chicken broth, soy sauce, sherry, and gingerroot. Set aside.

Heat the oil in a wok or a large, deep skillet. Add the chicken pieces and the green onions, and stir-fry (that is, stir constantly while gently tossing) over medium-high heat until the chicken is almost cooked through and is opaque (about 2 to 3 minutes). Stir in the cauliflower, green pepper, and mushrooms, and pour the reserved liquid over all. Cover the wok or skillet tightly, and steam the mixture about 5 to 8 minutes or until the cauliflower is crisp-tender.

In a small cup, dissolve the cornstarch in the water; then add to the liquid in the pan and heat, stirring constantly, until the sauce thickens (about 30 seconds to 1 minute). Serve over the cooked rice.

Makes 4 to 6 servings.

NUTRI-STEP 1

- Decrease the soy sauce to 2 tablespoons.
- Decrease the oil to 1 tablespoon. Use a nonstick pan, if available.

To Serve
- Omit the white rice and serve over hot cooked brown rice.

CHICKEN BREASTS IN CURRIED CASHEW SAUCE

In this recipe, the acid in the buttermilk acts as a meat tenderizer and flavor enhancer. The buttermilk is also the basis for a creamy lowfat sauce.

1	cup commercial buttermilk
1	clove garlic, peeled and very finely minced
½	teaspoon salt •
4 or 5	large chicken breast halves •
	Enriched all-purpose or unbleached white flour
2	tablespoons vegetable oil •
¼	cup water
1	medium-sized onion, finely chopped
⅛	teaspoon ground ginger •
1	teaspoon curry powder •
3	tablespoons chopped unsalted cashews •

To Serve

      Hot cooked white or brown rice or Plain-Cooked Bulgur (page 100) •

1   tablespoon chopped unsalted cashews for garnish

Mix the buttermilk, garlic, and salt together in a large bowl. Add the chicken, cover, and refrigerate for at least 1 hour. Remove the chicken breasts from the marinade and drain them well. (Reserve the marinade.) Dredge the chicken in the flour, shaking off any excess.

Heat the oil in a large skillet and brown the chicken breasts on both sides. Add the water to the skillet, cover tightly, and steam the chicken over low heat for 50 minutes, or until very tender. Remove the chicken from the skillet with tongs, and place it on a bed of cooked rice or bulgur on a serving platter. Cover with aluminum foil to keep it warm.

Add the onion to the pan juices, and cook until it is tender but not browned.

Mix the ginger, curry powder, and 3 tablespoons of the cashews with the reserved buttermilk marinade. Then add the mixture to the skillet. Heat, stirring constantly, for about 2 to 3 minutes, or until the sauce cooks down and thickens to the desired consistency. Pour the sauce over the chicken. Garnish the chicken with the cashews and serve.

Makes 4 to 5 servings.

NUTRI-STEP 1

- Decrease the salt to ¼ teaspoon.
- Remove and discard all the skin and any visible fat from the chicken pieces.
- Decrease the oil to 1½ tablespoons. Use a nonstick skillet and watch the chicken carefully so it does not stick.
- Increase the ginger to a generous ⅛ teaspoon or more to taste.
- Increase the curry powder to 1¼ teaspoons or more to taste.
- Decrease the cashews to 2 tablespoons.

To Serve
- If serving with rice, omit the white rice and USE brown rice.

CHICKEN TARRAGON

1½	tablespoons butter or margarine ●
4 to 5	large chicken breast halves ●
1	medium-sized onion, finely chopped
1	large clove garlic, peeled and minced
2	tablespoons chopped fresh parsley leaves
1½	tablespoons chopped fresh chives, or 2 teaspoons dried chives
2	teaspoons dried tarragon leaves ●
½	cup dry white table wine
1½	teaspoons lemon juice ●
½	teaspoon salt ●
⅛	teaspoon black pepper, preferably freshly ground

Melt butter in a large, heavy deep-sided skillet over medium-high heat. Add the chicken pieces and brown them lightly on all sides. Add the onion, garlic, and parsley and cook, stirring, for 3 to 4 minutes longer, or until the onion is limp.

Stir in all the remaining ingredients and bring to a boil. Lower the heat and simmer, covered, for 20 minutes. Remove the cover and simmer for 20 to 25 minutes longer, or until the chicken is just tender and most of the liquid has evaporated from the skillet. Spoon some of the pan juices over each chicken breast and serve. *Makes 4 to 5 servings.*

NUTRI-STEP 1

- Decrease the butter to 1 tablespoon.
- Remove and discard the skin and visible fat from the chicken breasts.
- Increase the tarragon to 2¼ teaspoons.
- Increase the lemon juice to 2 teaspoons.
- Decrease the salt to ¼ teaspoon.

CHICKEN AND VEGETABLES IN LEMON–MUSTARD SAUCE

It's remarkable that such a simple combination of ingredients can produce such a delicious and attractive dish. The recipe is also exceptionally healthful, featuring lean chicken pieces and vitamin A-rich carrots in a lowfat, low-salt sauce. (The only salt in the dish comes from the prepared mustard.)

The dish tastes best when made with Dijon or Dijon-style mustard, but regular prepared mustard may be substituted if absolutely necessary.

1½	tablespoons butter or margarine •
1	large onion, chopped
5 to 6	large chicken breast halves, skin and visible fat removed
1	pound carrots (about 5 medium), peeled and cut into 2½- by ½-inch sticks
5 to 6	small white onions, peeled
2	tablespoons lemon juice •
2	tablespoons Dijon or Dijon-style mustard •
2	tablespoons packed light brown sugar •
⅓	cup water (approximate)

Melt the butter in a large deep skillet over medium-high heat. Add the chopped onion and cook, stirring, for 3 minutes. Add the chicken pieces, meaty-side down, and cook for 6 to 8 minutes, or until lightly browned. Then turn the chicken pieces meaty side up. Lay the carrot sticks and whole small white onions around the chicken breasts.

Stir together the lemon juice, mustard, and brown sugar in a small bowl. Gradually add ⅓ cup water and stir until blended. Carefully pour the mixture over the chicken and vegetables, being sure to moisten all pieces well with sauce. Allow the mixture to come to a boil. Lower the heat, cover, and simmer for about 35 minutes, or until the carrots are tender and the chicken breasts are cooked through. Occasionally baste the chicken and vegetables with sauce during cooking. Add 1 to 2 tablespoons more water as necessary to prevent the ingredients from boiling dry. Arrange the chicken breasts on a large serving platter and surround with the carrots and onions. Top the platter with any sauce remaining in the skillet and serve.

Makes 5 to 6 servings.

NUTRI-STEP 1

- Decrease the butter or margarine to 2 teaspoons. Stir the chopped onion constantly and watch the onion and chicken breasts carefully to prevent them from burning.
- Decrease the lemon juice to 1½ tablespoons.
- Decrease the Dijon mustard to 1½ tablespoons.
- Decrease the packed light brown sugar to 1½ tablespoons.

CRUSTY ITALIAN-SEASONED OVEN-FRIED CHICKEN

2   pounds mixed chicken breasts, drumsticks, and thighs, all skin and visible fat removed
¾   cup enriched all-purpose or unbleached white flour •
1   large egg (or 2 large egg whites) •
⅔   cup lowfat or skim milk •
¼   teaspoon salt •
     About 2 cups homemade Italian-style Crumb Coating Mix (page 290)

Pat the chicken pieces dry with paper towels.

Put the flour in a sturdy paper bag. Add chicken pieces and shake until uniformly coated with flour.

Combine the egg, milk, and salt in a pie pan or soup plate, and beat with a fork until well blended and smooth. Spread about 1 cup of the Crumb Coating Mix on a sheet of wax paper. (Reserve the remainder.) Dip the flour-coated chicken pieces in the egg-milk mixture one at a time until they are completely covered with liquid. Allow any excess liquid to drip back into the pan. Carefully roll the pieces in the coating mixture until coated all over with crumbs. Gently shake off any excess crumbs. (Add more crumb coating mix to the wax paper as needed.) Place the coated chicken pieces on a lightly greased or nonstick spray-coated baking sheet.

Bake the chicken, uncovered, in a preheated 400-degree oven for 25 minutes. Gently lift the pieces from the pan surface and turn over with a spatula. Continue baking for 20 to 25 minutes longer, or until the pieces are crusty-brown and cooked through.

Makes 4 to 5 servings.

NUTRI-STEP 1

- Decrease the white flour to ½ cup. *And add* ¼ cup whole wheat flour to the paper bag along with the white flour.
- Omit the large egg and USE 2 large egg whites.
- Omit the lowfat milk and USE skim milk.
- Decrease the salt to ⅛ teaspoon.

CHICKEN CATALONIA

Here is a simple skillet dinner inspired by the wonderful Spanish dish paella.

2	tablespoons olive oil or vegetable oil •
8 to 10	chicken thighs and/or drumsticks •
1	teaspoon chili powder
1	large onion, coarsely chopped
1	large clove garlic, peeled and minced
¼	cup coarsely chopped mixed green and red bell peppers (or use all green if red bell peppers are unavailable)
½	cup finely chopped celery
½	cup finely chopped carrot
¼	cup finely chopped fresh parsley leaves
1	16-ounce can tomatoes, including juice
⅛	teaspoon freshly ground black pepper •
	Pinch of dried thyme leaves •
	Scant ⅛ teaspoon saffron threads, or ⅛ teaspoon ground turmeric
½	teaspoon salt •
⅔	cup water
1	cup uncooked white rice, rinsed and drained
1	cup frozen green peas

Heat the oil in a very large (12-inch or larger) skillet over medium-high heat. Sprinkle the chicken pieces with chili powder and brown them on all sides in the oil.

Add the onion, garlic, green and/or red pepper, celery, carrot, and parsley to the skillet and cook, stirring for 3 to 4 minutes, or until the vegetables are limp. Add the tomatoes and their juice to the skillet, breaking them up with a spoon. Stir all the seasonings, water, and rice into the skillet. Bring the mixture to a boil, stirring constantly. Turn the heat to low, cover the pan, and simmer gently for 30 minutes, stirring occasionally to prevent the rice from sticking.

Stir the green peas into the rice and cook, covered, for 5 minutes longer. Remove the cover, fluff up the rice with a fork, and continue cooking for about 3 minutes longer, or until the chicken pieces and peas are just tender.

Makes 4 to 5 servings.

NUTRI-STEP 1

- Decrease the oil to 1½ tablespoons.
- Remove and discard the skin from the chicken pieces. Then sprinkle the pieces with chili powder. When browning the chicken, turn it frequently to prevent the pieces from sticking to the pan. Proceed as directed.
- Increase the black pepper to a scant ¼ teaspoon.
- Increase the dried thyme leaves to ⅛ teaspoon.
- Decrease the salt to a generous ¼ teaspoon.

ROAST CHICKEN AND HERB STUFFING

1	roasting chicken (about 4¼ to 4½ pounds)
1½	cups water
6	cups cubed, slightly stale white bread or commercial bread cubes ●■
2½	tablespoons butter or margarine ●■
2	medium-sized celery stalks, including leaves, finely chopped
1	large onion, finely chopped
3	tablespoons coarsely chopped fresh parsley leaves
½	cup coarsely chopped fresh mushrooms
½	cup thinly sliced water chestnuts, drained (optional)
1	tablespoon dried chopped chives
¾	teaspoon dried sage leaves, crumbled ■
½	teaspoon celery seed
¼	teaspoon dried marjoram leaves
¼	teaspoon dried thyme leaves
⅛	teaspoon black pepper, preferably freshly ground
¾	teaspoon salt ■

Remove the neck and giblets from the chicken cavity. (Set chicken aside.) Rinse the giblets and neck, and put in a small saucepan with the water. Bring to a boil over medium-high heat. Lower the heat and simmer, uncovered, for 15 minutes, or until the resulting stock is reduced to ½ cup. Discard the giblets and neck and set the stock aside. (While the stock simmers, ready the other ingredients.)

If homemade bread cubes are used, put them in a roasting pan, and toast in a preheated 350-degree oven for 15 minutes, stirring occasionally. If commercial bread cubes are used, omit the toasting process.

Melt the butter in a large skillet over medium-high heat. Add the celery, onion, and parsley. Cook, stirring, for 4 to 5 minutes, or until the vegetables are limp. Add the mushrooms and cook, stirring, for 3 minutes longer. Remove the skillet from the heat, and add the water chestnuts and all the seasonings. Turn the toasted bread cubes into the skillet, and stir the ingredients until thoroughly mixed. Pour the reserved stock over the bread cubes and stir until the stuffing mixture is evenly moistened.

Rinse the chicken inside and out and pat it dry. Fill the chicken neck and body cavities with the stuffing (stuff firmly but not tightly).

Place the chicken breast side up on a rack in a roasting pan. Roast the chicken at 350 degrees until a meat thermometer inserted between thigh and breast registers 185 degrees, about 2 hours and 15 minutes. (As an alternate test of doneness, prick the meat between the thigh and breast; if juices run clear rather than pink, the chicken is done.) Transfer the chicken to a platter and serve.

Makes about 5 to 6 servings.

NUTRI-STEP 1

- Decrease the white bread cubes to 3 cups. *And add* 3 cups whole wheat bread cubes to the skillet along with the white bread cubes.
- Decrease the butter or margarine to 1½ tablespoons.

NUTRI-STEP 2

- Omit the white bread cubes and SUBSTITUTE 6 cups whole wheat bread cubes.
- Decrease the butter or margarine to 1½ tablespoons.
- Increase the sage leaves to 1 teaspoon.
- Decrease the salt to ½ teaspoon.

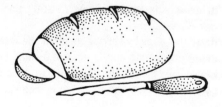

GLAZED CORNISH HENS WITH MANDARIN-RICE STUFFING

Here is the perfect dish when you want to serve something special. The vitamin C-rich orange juice glaze adds a golden sheen to the hens. And mandarin oranges contribute a wonderful flavor to the stuffing.

Stuffing
2   tablespoons butter or margarine •
1   medium-sized onion, finely chopped
1   medium-sized celery stalk, finely chopped
¼   teaspoon dried thyme leaves
¼   teaspoon dried oregano leaves
¼   teaspoon dried marjoram leaves •
¼   teaspoon dried basil leaves •
½   teaspoon salt •
     Generous ¼ teaspoon black pepper, preferably freshly ground
2   cups *cooked* white rice •
1   cup fresh white or whole wheat bread crumbs •
1   11-ounce can mandarin orange sections, drained with ¼ cup of juice reserved

Cornish Hens and Glaze
5 to 6   Cornish hens, weighing approximately 1 pound each
         Grated peel of 1 small lemon (yellow part only)
¼   cup frozen orange juice concentrate, thawed
1   tablespoon orange-flavored liqueur

Melt the butter in a large skillet over medium-high heat. Add the onion and celery and cook, stirring, for 4 to 5 minutes, or until the vegetables are limp. Stir all the seasonings, rice, and bread crumbs into the skillet. Cook, continuing to stir, for 4 to 5 minutes longer, or until the ingredients are heated and thoroughly mixed. Remove the skillet from the heat and stir in the mandarin oranges, along with the reserved ¼ cup of their juice. Set the stuffing mixture aside.

Remove and discard the giblets and necks packed with the hens. Trim off and discard any visible fat (but not the skin) from the hens. Rinse the hens inside and out and pat dry with paper towels. Divide stuffing mixture among the hens, and fill the body cavities firmly, but not tightly. Rub the skin of the hens with half the grated lemon peel. (Reserve remaining peel for the glaze.)

Place the hens breast side up in a large roasting pan. Roast in a preheated 375-degree oven for 45 minutes.

Meanwhile, prepare the glaze by stirring together the reserved grated lemon peel with the orange juice concentrate and liqueur in a small bowl or cup.

Drain off and discard all fat from the roasting pan. Baste each hen well with the glaze. Return the pan to the oven and roast the hens for about 15 minutes longer, or until the skins are golden brown and the birds are cooked through. Transfer the hens to a platter. Lightly baste with any remaining glaze and serve whole.

Makes 5 to 6 generous servings.

NUTRI-STEP 1

- Decrease the butter or margarine to 1½ tablespoons.
- Increase the marjoram to ½ teaspoon.
- Increase the basil to ½ teaspoon.
- Decrease the salt to a scant ½ teaspoon.
- Omit the cooked white rice and SUBSTITUTE cooked brown rice.
- Omit the white bread crumbs and USE whole wheat bread crumbs.

TURKEY AND VEGETABLE POT

This makes a tasty, economical, and wholesome one-dish supper. The flavor is even better when the dish is prepared ahead and reheated.

2½	tablespoons butter or margarine •
4 to 5	medium-sized green onions (scallions), green tops chopped and reserved, and white parts cut into 1-inch lengths
2	medium-sized onions, quartered
⅓	cup chopped fresh parsley leaves
1	small celery stalk, including leaves, coarsely chopped
5	cups water
2¾ to 3	pounds turkey wings
¼	cup dry Great Northern beans, sorted and rinsed
1	teaspoon salt •
¼	teaspoon black pepper, preferably freshly ground
4	medium-sized carrots, coarsely sliced
3 to 4	medium-sized potatoes, peeled and cut into 1-inch cubes •
¼	cup medium egg noodles
1	medium-sized rutabaga, peeled and cut into 1-inch cubes
2½	cups fresh cauliflower flowerets, coarsely sliced
1½	cups cabbage, cut into 1½-inch chunks

Melt the butter in a large Dutch oven or pot over medium-high heat. Add the chopped green onion tops (reserve white parts), onions, parsley, and celery and cook, stirring, for 4 to 5 minutes, or until the vegetables are limp. Add the water, turkey wings, beans, salt, and pepper. Cover and bring to a boil. Lower the heat and simmer for 1¾ to 2 hours, or until the turkey wings are tender. Remove the turkey from the pot and set aside to cool. Skim off any fat from the surface of the broth with a large spoon.

In layers, add the carrots, potatoes, white parts of green onions, noodles, rutabaga, cauliflower, and, finally, the cabbage to the pot. Return to the heat and simmer, covered, for 30 to 35 minutes longer, or until the carrots and potatoes are just tender.

While the vegetables cook, remove the turkey from the bones and cut into bite-sized pieces. Discard the turkey skin and bones. Return the meat to the pot, stir the mixture well, and reheat to boiling.

Makes 4 to 5 servings.

NUTRI-STEP 1

- Decrease the butter or margarine to 1½ tablespoons.
- Decrease the salt to ¾ teaspoon.
- Leave the potatoes unpeeled and scrub them well before using.

ROLLED, STUFFED TURKEY CUTLETS

This nutritious yet very elegant dish is a great way to introduce your family to buckwheat (kasha). It also demonstrates the appealing versatility of turkey—one of the leanest and most healthful meats. Presliced and packaged boneless turkey breast cutlets are available at many supermarkets (in the fresh meat section). You can also cut them yourself, or have the butcher do it for you.

This recipe specifically calls for finely ground buckwheat groats (sometimes called buckwheat "grits"), because they have a more delicate texture than coarse or whole groats, and they form a more compact stuffing. If you have difficulty obtaining finely ground groats, you can use a food processor or blender to grind whole or coarse buckwheat groats into smaller pieces. Buckwheat is a very good source of high-quality protein as well as many vitamins and minerals. For more information on buckwheat, see the recipe for Plain-Cooked Buckwheat (page 100).

Note: The stuffing part of this recipe can be served as a pilaf-type side dish on its own. In that case, omit the egg or egg whites, and use any style buckwheat groats desired.

1   tablespoon butter or margarine
1   tablespoon vegetable oil •
1   medium-sized onion, finely chopped
1   cup finely chopped celery
1   cup sliced fresh mushrooms

2 cups chicken or turkey broth, divided
½ teaspoon dried thyme leaves •
½ teaspoon dried rubbed sage •
¼ teaspoon salt •
⅛ teaspoon black pepper, preferably freshly ground
¾ cup finely ground buckwheat groats
1 pound thinly sliced boneless turkey breast cutlets
1 large egg (or 2 large egg whites), beaten •
2 tablespoons dry white table wine, dry vermouth, or dry sherry
   Fresh parsley sprigs or chopped parsley leaves for garnish

Heat the butter and oil in a large skillet. Add the onion and sauté until it is tender but not brown. Set aside 2 tablespoons of the sautéed onion. To the remainder in the skillet, add the celery and mushrooms and sauté for about 2 minutes longer. Add 1½ cups of the broth, along with the thyme, sage, salt, and pepper. Bring to a boil, stir in the buckwheat, and lower the heat. Cook, stirring constantly, until all the moisture is absorbed and the buckwheat forms a compact mass (about 5 minutes). Remove from the heat to cool.

Put the turkey cutlets between two sheets of heavy plastic wrap or wax paper. Use a rubber mallet or rolling pin to pound and flatten the turkey meat to a ⅛-inch thickness, being careful not to tear the meat. (Pounding it does not require much effort.)

When the turkey cutlets are ready, stir the egg into the cooled buckwheat mixture. Divide the buckwheat stuffing among the turkey cutlets (use about ¼ cup for each), and spread it evenly over the meat. Roll up each cutlet (from the longer side) like a jelly roll. Place the rolled cutlets seam side down next to each other in a 7- by 11-inch or similar baking dish.

Mix the remaining ½ cup of broth with the white wine and pour over the turkey rolls. Sprinkle the reserved sautéed onions on top. Bake in a preheated 350-degree oven for about 25 minutes, or until the turkey is cooked through. Baste often with the pan juices during baking.

To serve, transfer the baked turkey rolls to a serving platter. Pour any extra pan juices on top. Garnish with sprigs of fresh parsley or chopped fresh parsley.

Makes 4 to 6 servings.

NUTRI-STEP 1

- Decrease the oil to 1 teaspoon. Stir the onions often to make sure they don't stick.
- Increase the thyme to ¾ teaspoon.
- Increase the sage to ¾ teaspoon.
- Decrease the salt to ⅛ teaspoon or omit.
- Omit the large egg and USE 2 large egg whites.

TURKEY MARSALA

Although this is traditionally made with thinly-sliced boneless veal scallops, our recipe substitutes very thin, raw turkey cutlets cut from the breast. Presliced and packaged boneless turkey cutlets are available at many supermarkets (in the fresh meat section), or you can have a butcher cut them or do it yourself. When prepared in the same manner as veal in the following recipe, these turkey cutlets look and taste very much like their more expensive counterparts.

1½	pounds thinly sliced boneless turkey breast cutlets
¼	teaspoon black pepper, preferably freshly ground
¼	teaspoon salt •
	About ¼ cup enriched all-purpose or unbleached white flour
2	tablespoons butter or margarine •
1	tablespoon vegetable oil
	About ⅔ cup dry Marsala wine, or dry Madeira
3 to 4	tablespoons chicken broth

Put the turkey cutlets between 2 sheets of heavy plastic wrap and pound gently with a rubber mallet or rolling pin until the meat is about ⅛ inch thick. Be careful not to tear the meat.

Mix together the pepper, salt, and flour in a medium-sized bowl. Coat the cutlets with this mixture, shaking off any excess.

Heat the butter and oil until hot in a large skillet. Quickly brown the cutlets on both sides, in two or more batches if necessary. (This will take only about 2 minutes on each side; do not overcook or it may toughen.) When all the cutlets are ready, return them to the skillet and pour the Marsala over them. Bring to a boil and cook for about 1 minute. Then remove the cutlets to a hot serving platter.

Add the broth to the pan and stir, scraping up all the browned bits on the bottom. Boil the sauce for about 30 seconds, or until it is thickened and slightly reduced. Pour over the cutlets and serve immediately.

Makes 4 to 6 servings.

NUTRI-STEP 1

- Decrease the salt to ⅛ teaspoon.
- Decrease the butter or margarine to 1 tablespoon. Use a nonstick skillet if available and watch the cutlets carefully as they brown.

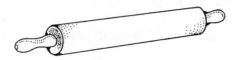

TURKEY HASH

Try this great way to use up leftover turkey after a holiday. Imitation bacon bits give this hash its traditional flavor, but they can be left out if preferred.

3   tablespoons butter or margarine, divided •
1   medium-sized onion, finely chopped
½   medium-sized green bell pepper, seeded and finely chopped
½   medium-sized ripe, red bell pepper, seeded and finely chopped (if unavailable, substitute additional chopped green pepper)
2   tablespoons imitation bacon-flavored bits (optional)
2   cups diced, cooked turkey meat
2   cups peeled and coarsely shredded raw potato •
1   large egg (or 2 large egg whites) •
½   teaspoon salt •
⅛   teaspoon black pepper, preferably freshly ground •

Melt 1 tablespoon of the butter in a large nonstick skillet. Add the onion, green pepper, and red pepper and sauté until tender. Transfer the mixture to a bowl and stir in the remaining ingredients.

Melt 1 tablespoon of the remaining butter in the skillet and distribute it evenly over the inner surface. Turn out all the turkey mixture into the skillet, and press it into one large "pancake."

Turn the heat to low and cover the skillet. Cook for about 15 to 20 minutes without disturbing. Invert the hash "pancake" onto a large platter. Melt the remaining 1 tablespoon of butter in the skillet as before. Slide the "pancake" back into the skillet, browned side up. Cover and cook for 15 to 20 minutes longer, or until all the potato shreds are completely cooked through. Serve the hash warm, cut into wedges.

Makes about 4 servings.

NUTRI-STEP 1

- Decrease the butter or margarine to 2 tablespoons plus 2 teaspoons. Use only 2 teaspoons to sauté the onion and pepper. Stir often so the vegetables don't stick.
- Leave the potatoes unpeeled. Use thin-skinned new potatoes, if available, and scrub well before using.
- Omit the large egg and USE 2 large egg whites.
- Decrease the salt to a generous ¼ teaspoon.
- Increase the black pepper to ¼ teaspoon.

TURKEY–ZUCCHINI SKILLET DINNER

Since this calls for cooked turkey, it's a marvelous way to use up leftovers.

1½	tablespoons butter or margarine ●
1	teaspoon vegetable oil
1	medium-sized onion, finely chopped
1	medium-sized green pepper, seeded and cut into ½-inch squares
3	cups diced, cooked turkey meat
2	medium-sized zucchini, cut into ½-inch cubes
1	medium yellow squash, cut into ½-inch cubes ●
½	cup raisins
2	tablespoons slivered almonds (optional) ●
¼	teaspoon curry powder
⅛	teaspoon black pepper, preferably freshly ground
⅛	teaspoon ground cumin
⅛	teaspoon ground allspice
⅛	teaspoon salt ●
2	cups hot cooked white or brown rice or Plain-Cooked Bulgur (page 100) ●

Heat the butter and oil in large skillet over medium-high heat. Add the onion and sauté until it is tender but not brown. Then add all the remaining ingredients except the cooked rice or bulgur. Stir constantly until the green pepper and squash are cooked through. If desired, add more curry powder to taste. Stir the cooked rice or bulgur into the turkey mixture, or serve the turkey mixture on a bed of rice or bulgur.

Makes about 4 servings.

NUTRI-STEP 1

- Decrease the butter or margarine to 1 tablespoon. Be sure to stir ingredients constantly and use a nonstick skillet, if available.
- Increase the yellow squash to 2 medium ones.
- Omit the almonds.
- Decrease the salt to a pinch or omit.
- If using rice, omit the white rice and USE brown rice.

Chapter *12*

Main Dishes— Fish and Shellfish

T his chapter includes an appealing assortment of fish and shellfish recipes that our families enjoy. In these dishes, fresh vegetables add color and taste, light sauces let the subtle flavor of the fish shine through, and innovative presentations pique interest. And that's a real plus, since fish scores quite well on its own merit. It's very high in protein, low in fat, and low in calories, making it ideal for family meals.

Many of our recipes call for skinless fillets because these are easily obtained, and also because we feel fillets are the best way to introduce diners to the delights of a fish feast. Later, you might want to try our whole stuffed baked fish—a real showstopper.

You can use fresh fish in these recipes, or frozen fish that has been thawed before cooking. For best taste, thaw fish in the refrigerator overnight. If the specific type of fish called for in a recipe isn't available, try substituting another, similar kind.

This chapter also includes several recipes for canned tuna and salmon because they are the favorites of so many people. Besides, we know how convenient and easy canned fish can be.

You will also find some wonderful shellfish recipes which feature shrimp and crabmeat. Shellfish is high in protein and low in fat, but it is also relatively high in cholesterol. However, this need not be a problem unless you must avoid cholesterol for special reasons.

FISH CROQUETTES

These taste remarkably like Maryland crab cakes, but they are much lower in cholesterol and cost a lot less to prepare.

1   **pound fresh or frozen (thawed) skinless fillets of lean white fish, such as cod, haddock, turbot, or flounder**
2   **large eggs (or 1 large egg plus 2 large egg whites) ●■**
3   **tablespoons mayonnaise ●■**
1   **tablespoon plain lowfat yogurt ●■**
1   **teaspoon dry mustard ■**
¾   **teaspoon salt ●■**
½   **teaspoon celery seed ■**
½   **teaspoon Worcestershire sauce**
¼   **teaspoon black pepper, preferably freshly ground**
     Pinch of ground cloves
     Pinch of ground mace
     Pinch of cayenne pepper, or more to taste ■
1   **cup fresh white or whole wheat bread crumbs ●■**
2   **tablespoons vegetable oil ■**

To Serve (optional)
     About 8 pieces of toasted white or whole wheat bread or English muffin halves ●■

Place the fish in one layer in a large skillet. Cover the fish with water and bring to a boil. Lower the heat, cover the skillet, and simmer gently until the fish is tender and just beginning to flake, about 10 to 15 minutes, depending on the thickness of the fillets. Remove the fish from the skillet with a slotted spoon or spatula, draining well. Refrigerate the fish until cool, then flake into ¾-inch pieces.

In a medium-sized bowl, beat together the egg, mayonnaise, yogurt, dry mustard, salt, celery seed, Worcestershire sauce, black pepper, cloves, mace, cayenne pepper, and bread crumbs. Let stand for about 5 minutes, so the bread crumbs can absorb some of the moisture. (The mixture should be rather stiff.) Gently stir the flaked fish into the bread crumb mixture, being careful not to break up the lumps of fish too much.

In a nonstick skillet, heat the oil until hot, but not smoking. Form the fish mixture into patties using about ¼ cup for each. Fry the croquettes over medium-high heat until browned on both sides. Drain well on paper towels. If desired, serve each croquette on a piece of toasted bread or an English muffin half. (*Note:* Leftover croquettes are good cold!)

Makes about 8 fish croquettes or 4 servings.

NUTRI-STEP 1

- Omit the 2 large eggs and USE 1 large egg plus 2 large egg whites.
- Decrease the mayonnaise to 2 tablespoons.
- Increase the yogurt to 2 tablespoons.
- Decrease the salt to ½ teaspoon.
- Omit the white bread crumbs and USE whole wheat bread crumbs.

To Serve
- Omit the white bread or English muffins, and USE whole wheat bread or whole wheat English muffins.

NUTRI-STEP 2

- Omit the 2 large eggs and SUBSTITUTE 3 large egg whites.
- Decrease the mayonnaise to 2 tablespoons.
- Increase the yogurt to 2 tablespoons.
- Increase the dry mustard to 1⅛ teaspoons.
- Decrease the salt to ¼ teaspoon.
- Increase the celery seed to a generous ½ teaspoon.
- Increase the cayenne pepper to a scant ⅛ teaspoon.
- Omit the white bread crumbs and USE whole wheat bread crumbs.
- Decrease the oil to 1½ tablespoons. Watch the croquettes carefully to be sure they don't stick or burn. During frying, frequently loosen the bottoms of the croquettes from the pan with a pancake turner or metal spatula.

To Serve
- Omit the white bread or English muffins and USE whole wheat bread or whole wheat English muffins.

FISH WITH CREOLE SAUCE

Never mind the long list of ingredients—this savory dish is really rather easy to prepare.

Sauce
1½	tablespoons butter or margarine •
1	medium-sized onion, finely chopped
1	celery stalk, including leaves, finely chopped
¼	cup chopped green pepper
3	tablespoons finely chopped fresh parsley leaves
1	clove garlic, peeled and minced
1	16-ounce can tomatoes, including juice
½	teaspoon chili powder
⅛	teaspoon sugar
⅛	teaspoon dried thyme leaves
⅛	teaspoon salt
1	medium bay leaf
	Pinch of cayenne pepper, or more to taste

Fish
2	tablespoons apple cider vinegar
2	tablespoons lemon juice
1	small onion, peeled and quartered
1	celery top, coarsely chopped
¼	teaspoon dry mustard
¼	teaspoon celery seed
1	small bay leaf, crumbled
⅛	teaspoon dried tarragon leaves
⅛	teaspoon black pepper, preferably freshly ground
⅛	teaspoon salt •
½	cup water
1½	pounds fresh or frozen (thawed) skinless cod fillets, well drained (or substitute a similar white-fleshed fish)

To Serve
4	cups hot cooked white or brown rice (optional)

To prepare creole sauce, melt the butter in a medium saucepan over medium-high heat. Add the onion, celery, green pepper, parsley, and garlic and cook, stirring, for 3 minutes, or until the vegetables are limp. Stir in the tomatoes and their juice, breaking them up with a spoon. Then add all the remaining sauce ingredients. Lower the heat to medium-low and simmer, stirring occasionally, for 12 to 15 minutes. While the sauce simmers, prepare fish.

To braise the fish, combine the vinegar, lemon juice, onion, celery, all the seasonings, and ¼ cup of the water in a large deep-sided skillet. Bring to a boil over medium-high heat and simmer, stirring occasionally, until all the excess moisture evaporates from the pan. Add the remaining ¼ cup of water to the pan, and bring to a simmer once again. Place cod fillets in the skillet, spooning some of the pan liquid over each. Simmer the fillets for 3½ to 4 minutes, basting once or twice with the liquid. Gently turn the fillets over and cook for about 3 minutes longer, or until the fish is opaque and begins to flake when touched with a fork. Immediately remove the skillet from the heat. With a slotted spoon transfer the fish to a serving platter, or to a bed of hot cooked rice. Spoon the hot creole sauce over the fillets and serve.

Makes 4 to 5 servings.

NUTRI-STEP 1

Sauce
- Decrease the butter or margarine to 1 tablespoon. Stir the vegetables constantly and watch carefully to prevent them from burning. *And add* ¼ cup finely chopped carrot along with the green pepper.

Fish
- Decrease the salt to a pinch or omit.

CRAB "STUFFED" FLOUNDER

Many recipes for this dish are loaded with mayonnaise and butter. This savory and healthful version, however, is very low in fat.

12	ounces fresh or frozen (thawed) crabmeat
3	tablespoons mayonnaise •
2	tablespoons plain lowfat yogurt •
1	teaspoon dry mustard
1	teaspoon instant minced onions
⅛	teaspoon cayenne pepper
1	cup fresh white or whole wheat bread crumbs •
1 to 1½	pounds fresh or frozen (thawed) flounder fillets
	Paprika

Combine crabmeat, mayonnaise, yogurt, mustard, onions, cayenne pepper, and ⅔ cup of the bread crumbs and mix lightly. Spread the crab mixture in a greased or nonstick spray-coated, 6- by 10-inch or similar baking dish so the bottom of the dish is covered.

Arrange the fillets on top. Sprinkle the flounder with the remaining ⅓ cup of bread crumbs and the paprika.

Bake, uncovered, in a preheated 475-degree oven for about 20 minutes, or until the flounder is done and flakes with a fork.

Makes 4 to 5 servings.

NUTRI-STEP 1

- Decrease the mayonnaise to 2 tablespoons.
- Increase the yogurt to 3 tablespoons.
- Omit the white bread crumbs and USE whole wheat bread crumbs.

FISH ROLLS STUFFED WITH SPINACH AND RICE

Here is a healthful fish dinner that will not only delight your family, but is special enough for company as well.

2½ tablespoons lemon juice ●■
 3 tablespoons butter or margarine, melted ●■
 ½ teaspoon salt ●■
 ⅛ teaspoon freshly ground black pepper
 1 cup *cooked* white or brown rice ●■
 1 10-ounce package frozen chopped spinach, thawed and very well drained
 ⅔ cup shredded Cheddar or Colby cheese ●■
 2 pounds skinless flounder or sole fillets (evenly sized, if possible)
    Paprika for garnish

In a small bowl, mix together the lemon juice, butter, salt, and pepper.

In a medium-sized bowl, mix together the rice, spinach, cheese, and about a third of the lemon-butter mixture.

Spread the rice-spinach-cheese mixture on the smooth, skinned surface of each fish fillet, dividing the mixture evenly among all the fillets. Roll up the fillets, and place them seam side down, close to each other in a 7- by 12-inch or similar baking dish. Pour the remaining butter mixture over the fish rolls, and sprinkle them lightly with paprika.

Bake, uncovered, in a preheated 375-degree oven for about 25 minutes, or until the fish just flakes when touched with a fork. Spoon the sauce from the pan over the rolls, and serve immediately.

Makes about 6 servings.

NUTRI-STEP 1

- Increase the lemon juice to 3 tablespoons.
- Decrease the butter or margarine to 2½ tablespoons.
- Decrease the salt to a generous ¼ teaspoon.
- Increase the cooked rice to 1¼ cups.
- Decrease the cheese to ½ cup.

NUTRI-STEP 2

- Increase the lemon juice to 3 tablespoons.
- Decrease the butter or margarine to 2 tablespoons.
- Decrease the salt to a scant ¼ teaspoon.
- Increase the cooked rice to 1¼ cups. Omit the cooked white rice and USE cooked brown rice.
- Omit the regular Cheddar or Colby cheese and SUBSTITUTE ½ cup low-fat or part-skim Cheddar, Colby, or similar cheese.

FISH AND VEGETABLE LAYERED CASSEROLE

When this casserole is divided into portions, colorful layers of green, white, and red are revealed. The casserole is easy to assemble, and very low in calories and fat.

2   tablespoons butter or margarine •
1   medium-sized onion, thinly sliced
1   clove garlic, peeled and finely minced
1   16-ounce can tomatoes, drained and coarsely chopped •
1   medium-sized green pepper, seeded and thinly sliced
¾   teaspoon dried basil leaves •
½   teaspoon dried thyme leaves
¼   teaspoon salt •
⅛   teaspoon freshly ground black pepper
1   pound fresh spinach, rinsed well, trimmed, and cooked 3 minutes in only the liquid clinging to the leaves, OR 1 10-ounce package frozen chopped spinach, thawed and very well drained
    Pinch *each* of salt and black pepper to season spinach
1   pound fresh or frozen (thawed) skinless fish fillets, such as flounder, sole, cod, turbot, or other lean white fish

Melt the butter in a medium-sized skillet. Add the onion and garlic and sauté until tender but not browned. Stir in the tomatoes, green pepper, basil, thyme, salt, and pepper and cook, stirring constantly, until most of the liquid has evaporated. Remove from the heat and set aside.

Lightly grease (or coat with nonstick vegetable spray) a 7- by 12-inch or similar baking dish. Mix the spinach and pinches of salt and pepper together in the bottom of the dish. Spread the fish fillets on top, then top the fillets with the reserved tomato mixture. Cover with foil or a lid, and bake in a preheated 400-degree oven for about 20 minutes, or until the spinach is piping hot and the fish is tender.

Makes about 4 servings.

NUTRI-STEP 1

- Decrease the butter or margarine to 1 tablespoon. Stir the onions and other vegetables often to make sure they don't stick.
- If available, SUBSTITUTE 3 to 4 cored and chopped fresh vine-ripened tomatoes for the canned ones.
- Increase the basil to 1 teaspoon.
- If using canned tomatoes, decrease the salt to ⅛ teaspoon.

OVEN-FRIED FISH

Serve our crispy, Italian-seasoned "oven-fried" fish instead of ordinary pan-fried fillets. Oven-frying is much easier than regular frying, and much more healthful too.

1½   pounds fresh or frozen (thawed) boneless, skinless haddock, or similar firm, white fish fillets
⅔   cup enriched all-purpose or unbleached white flour •
1   large egg •
⅔   cup lowfat or skim milk •
   About 1½ cups Italian-style Crumb Coating Mix (page 287)
1½   tablespoons butter or margarine, melted •
   Fresh lemon wedges for serving with fillets

Pat the fish fillets completely dry with paper towels.

Place the flour in a paper bag; then add the fillets and shake until they are completely coated with flour.

With a fork, beat the egg and milk together in a pie pan or soup plate until well blended and smooth. Spread half the crumb coating mix on a sheet of wax paper. (Reserve the remainder.) Dip the flour-coated fillets in the egg-milk mixture one at a time, until they are completely covered with liquid. Then hold up the fillets and allow any excess liquid to drip back into the pan. Carefully roll the fillets in the coating mix until coated all over with crumbs. Gently shake off any excess crumbs. (Add more crumb coating mix as needed.) Lay the fillets, slightly separated, on a lightly greased or nonstick spray-coated baking sheet. Drizzle some of the melted butter over each fillet.

Bake the fillets in a preheated 550-degree oven until the coating begins to look lightly browned and crispy (about 7 minutes for small fillets and 8 to 9 minutes for larger ones). Turn the fillets over with a metal spatula, and bake for 6 to 8 minutes longer, or until nicely browned and crisp. Serve the fillets along with the lemon wedges. The fish may also be served with Tartar Sauce (page 292), if desired.

Makes 4 to 5 servings.

NUTRI-STEP 1

- Decrease the white flour to ⅓ cup. *And add* ⅓ cup whole wheat flour to the paper bag along with the white flour.
- Omit the large egg and SUBSTITUTE 2 large egg whites.
- Omit the lowfat milk and USE ⅔ cup skim milk.
- Decrease the butter or margarine to 1 tablespoon.

SOLE (OR FLOUNDER) VERONIQUE

¼	cup dry white table wine
½	cup water
1	bay leaf
2	tablespoons finely minced onion
⅛	teaspoon dried tarragon leaves
⅛	teaspoon black pepper, preferably freshly ground
1 to 1½	pounds skinless fillets of sole, flounder, or other delicate lean white fish
2	tablespoons butter or margarine, softened •
2	tablespoons enriched all-purpose or unbleached white flour
¼	cup instant nonfat dry milk powder
¼	teaspoon salt •
1 to 1½	cups seedless green grapes, stemmed, rinsed, and dried
¼	cup finely shredded Swiss cheese •

In a 10-inch skillet, mix together the wine, water, bay leaf, onion, tarragon, and pepper. Add the fish fillets, in one layer if possible. (The liquid in the skillet need not cover the fish.) Heat to simmering, cover tightly, and poach the fish gently for 5 minutes. (*Note:* If you must stack the fillets, they may need to cook a few minutes longer. However, be careful not to overcook the fish, or it may dry out.)

Carefully remove the cooked fish fillets and bay leaf with a slotted spoon or spatula, reserving the poaching liquid. Place the fillets in an ovenproof serving platter with slightly raised sides or a shallow baking dish, making sure the fish is well drained. Discard the bay leaf.

In a small bowl, mix together the softened butter with the flour until completely combined. Stir this "paste" into the cooking liquid left in the skillet, along with the milk powder and salt. Heat, stirring constantly, until the sauce thickens and boils. Spoon the sauce over the fish. Scatter the grapes over the sauce and sprinkle the cheese on top. Briefly place under a preheated broiler just until the cheese is melted and the sauce is bubbling.

Makes 4 to 6 servings.

NUTRI-STEP 1

- Decrease the butter or margarine to 1½ tablespoons.
- Decrease the salt to ⅛ teaspoon.
- Omit the regular Swiss cheese and SUBSTITUTE 3 tablespoons finely shredded or very finely chopped lowfat or part-skim Swiss-style cheese.

FISH GLAZED WITH TOMATO SAUCE

Serve this attractive and appealing cold dish as the first course of a large dinner, or as a luncheon main course. It is particularly well suited for a warm weather meal. (Note: In this recipe, the fish skin is left intact to hold each individual piece of fish together throughout preparation, and also to add natural gelatin to the glaze. If desired, the skin may be carefully removed before the fish is covered with the glaze and refrigerated.)

1	8-ounce can tomato sauce
½	cup water (or more, if necessary)
3	tablespoons lemon juice
½	cup chopped fresh parsley leaves
½	teaspoon dried basil leaves
⅛	teaspoon black pepper, preferably freshly ground

¼ teaspoon salt •
1½ tablespoons vegetable oil •
2 pounds 1-inch or thicker fish fillets (with skin intact), cut into 6 to 8 serving-size pieces

To Serve
Salad greens

In a large skillet, combine the tomato sauce, water, lemon juice, parsley, basil, pepper, salt, and oil. Bring to a boil, lower the heat, and simmer for 5 minutes. Add the fish pieces, preferably in one layer, and cook, covered, about 20 minutes, basting often. Use a slotted spoon or spatula to transfer the cooked fish to a dish or platter with raised sides. If the sauce is thin, boil it down until it thickens. Pour the sauce over the fish.

Cover and refrigerate the sauce-covered fish until chilled. Natural gelatin from the fish will jell the sauce so that it forms an attractive red glaze. Serve the glazed fish cold. Use a wide spatula to carefully place each serving on a bed of greens.

Makes 6 to 8 servings.

NUTRI-STEP 1

- Decrease the salt to ⅛ teaspoon.
- Decrease the oil to 1 tablespoon.

FISH BAKED WITH RED ONIONS AND ORANGES

This unusual combination is really quite tasty with all sorts of fish, even stronger-tasting varieties like bluefish. Although the recipe calls for fillets, you can use a whole, dressed fish instead. For a whole fish, follow the directions below, except cover the fish during baking, and bake it for about 25 to 30 minutes, or until the fish is just tender.

2 pounds skinless fish fillets of your choice
2 tablespoons grated orange peel (colored part only)
2 medium-sized oranges, peeled and thickly sliced
1 medium-sized red onion, thinly sliced and separated into rings
2 tablespoons butter or margarine, melted •
2 teaspoons honey
½ cup orange juice
⅛ teaspoon ground ginger
¼ teaspoon black pepper, preferably freshly ground

Place the fish in a greased or nonstick spray-coated baking dish, preferably in one layer. Sprinkle with the orange peel. Arrange the orange and onion rings attractively on top of the fish. Mix together the melted butter, honey, orange juice, ginger, and pepper, and pour the sauce over the fish. Cover the baking dish with foil or a lid.

Bake, covered, in a preheated 400-degree oven for about 15 to 20 minutes, or until the fish just flakes when touched with a fork. Baste the fish with sauce once or twice during the baking period, and just before serving.

Makes about 6 servings.

NUTRI-STEP 1

- Decrease the butter or margarine in the sauce to 1 tablespoon.

SALMON FLORENTINE

The word "Florentine" in a recipe title usually indicates that it contains spinach. In this dish, spinach forms a bed for canned salmon, turning a convenience food into an appealing dinner.

1	15½-ounce can salmon, including liquid
2	tablespoons dry sherry or dry white table wine
½	cup lowfat or skim milk (approximately) •
2	tablespoons butter or margarine •
1	small onion, finely chopped
1	clove garlic, peeled and finely minced
3	tablespoons enriched all-purpose or unbleached white flour
1	tablespoon chopped fresh parsley leaves
⅛	teaspoon dried dillweed, or to taste
⅛	teaspoon freshly ground black pepper
	Pinch of salt •
12	ounces to 1 pound fresh spinach, trimmed, well rinsed, and cooked for 3 minutes in the water clinging to the leaves, OR 1 10-ounce package frozen chopped spinach, thawed and very well drained
¼	cup grated Swiss cheese •

Drain the liquid from the salmon can into a small cup, and mix the sherry into it. Stir in the milk. You should have 1 cup liquid altogether; add more milk if necessary. Set aside.

Melt the butter in a small saucepan. Add the onion and garlic and cook until tender but not browned. Blend in the flour and cook, stirring constantly, for about 1 minute. Gradually stir the reserved liquid into the cooked flour mixture. Continue heating, stirring constantly, until the mixture thickens and boils. Remove from the heat. Coarsely flake the salmon and stir it into the sauce along with the parsley, dill-weed, pepper, and salt.

Spread the spinach in the bottom of an 8-inch round or oval baking dish or similar casserole. Spread the salmon mixture evenly on top. Sprinkle with the grated cheese. Bake, uncovered, in a preheated 350-degree oven for about 20 minutes, or until the cheese melts and the spinach and sauce are hot and bubbly.

Makes about 4 servings.

NUTRI-STEP 1

- Omit the lowfat milk and USE skim milk.
- Decrease the butter or margarine to 1½ tablespoons.
- Omit the salt.
- Omit the regular Swiss cheese and SUBSTITUTE ¼ cup grated or finely chopped lowfat or part-skim Swiss-style cheese.

SALMON PILAF

This is especially easy to prepare—the perfect dish when you're worn out after a long day's work. Turmeric colors the pilaf a nice bright yellow, and bouillon gives it good flavor; so it's pretty hard to tell that the rice is actually brown!

2	tablespoons butter or margarine ●
1	medium-sized onion, finely chopped
1	clove garlic, peeled and finely minced
1	cup uncooked brown rice
¼	teaspoon salt ●
⅛	teaspoon black pepper, preferably freshly ground
¼	teaspoon turmeric
1	15½-ounce can salmon, including liquid
1¾	cups chicken bouillon or broth
3	tablespoons chopped fresh parsley leaves

Melt the butter in a 2-quart saucepan or stove-top casserole. Add the onion and garlic and sauté until tender but not browned. Add the rice and sauté a minute longer. Then stir in the salt, pepper, turmeric, liquid from the can of salmon, and chicken bouillon. Flake the salmon coarsely and add it to the rice mixture along with the parsley, stirring so that the ingredients are mixed well. Bring the mixture to a boil, cover tightly, and lower the heat so the mixture simmers.

Cook for about 40 to 45 minutes, or until the rice is almost tender and most of the liquid is absorbed. Remove the cover and cook for about 5 minutes longer, or until the rice is tender and almost all the liquid is absorbed. Stir once before serving.

Makes about 4 servings.

NUTRI-STEP 1

- Decrease the butter or margarine to 1 tablespoon. Stir the onions often to make sure they don't stick.
- Decrease the salt to a generous ⅛ teaspoon.

BAKED STUFFED FISH

Just about any white-fleshed fish that's suitable for baking can be prepared using the following recipe. However, striped bass is especially good fixed this way.

Stuffing

2	tablespoons butter or margarine ●■
3 to 4	green onions (scallions) including tops, finely chopped
⅔	cup finely chopped fresh mushrooms
1	tablespoon chopped fresh parsley leaves (optional)
2	cups dry white bread crumbs ●■
⅛	teaspoon freshly ground black pepper
⅛	teaspoon freshly grated lemon peel (yellow part only)
⅛	teaspoon salt ■
1	tablespoon water
1½	teaspoons fresh lemon juice

Fish

1	dressed (head and innards removed) and boned *whole* white-fleshed fish (striped bass, sea trout, haddock, etc.), weighing about 3 pounds
1	tablespoon fresh lemon juice
⅛	teaspoon salt
¼	cup dry white table wine or dry sherry
	Lemon wedges for garnish

For the stuffing, melt the butter in a medium-sized skillet over medium-high heat. Stir the green onions, mushrooms, and parsley into the skillet and cook, stirring, for 4 to 5 minutes, or until the vegetables are limp. Add the bread crumbs, pepper, lemon peel, salt, water, and 1½ teaspoons lemon juice to the skillet. Cook, stirring, for 4 to 5 minutes longer. Remove the pan from the heat and set the stuffing aside.

Rub the fish all over, inside and out, with 1 tablespoon lemon juice. Sprinkle the fish all over very lightly with salt. Fill fish cavity with stuffing mixture. Place the stuffed fish on the dull side of a large sheet of heavy duty aluminum foil, being careful not to puncture the foil. Pour the wine over the fish. Tightly wrap the fish in foil. Transfer the foil-encased fish to a baking pan. Bake in a preheated 425-degree oven for 20 minutes. Roll back the foil to expose the fish. Baste the fish with some of the wine and baking juices inside the foil. Bake for about 20 to 25 minutes longer, or until the fish is tender and the flesh just begins to flake when touched with a fork. To serve, cut the fish crosswise into slices. Serve portions with lemon wedges.

Makes about 5 to 6 servings.

NUTRI-STEP 1

Stuffing
- Decrease the butter or margarine to 1½ tablespoons.
- Decrease the white bread crumbs to 1 cup. *And add* 1 cup whole wheat bread crumbs (made from slightly stale bread) to the skillet along with the white bread crumbs.

NUTRI-STEP 2

Stuffing
- Decrease the butter or margarine to 1½ tablespoons.
- Omit the white bread crumbs and SUBSTITUTE 2 cups whole wheat bread crumbs (made from slightly stale bread).
- Decrease the salt to a pinch.

TUNA "SPECIALS"

The tops of these quick and satisfying open-faced sandwiches can be "decorated" with sliced cucumber, bean sprouts, grated carrot, lettuce, or whatever strikes your fancy.

4   regular or whole wheat English muffins •
2   6½-ounce cans water-packed tuna, drained
¼   cup mayonnaise •
2   tablespoons plain regular or lowfat yogurt •
1   celery stalk, finely chopped
2   tablespoons finely chopped green or red bell pepper •
      Grated onion or onion powder, to taste
      Black pepper, preferably freshly ground, to taste
8   thin slices part-skim or lowfat (or regular) Swiss, Jarlsburg, mozzarella, or other cheese •
8   slices tomato (optional)

Split the English muffins and lightly toast the halves. In a medium-sized bowl, mix together the tuna, mayonnaise, yogurt, celery, green pepper, onion, and black pepper. Divide the tuna mixture evenly among the muffin halves, and spread evenly. Top each tuna sandwich with a slice each of cheese and tomato.

Heat in a 350-degree toaster oven or conventional oven for about 10 minutes (or heat for a couple of minutes in a microwave oven on "high"), until the cheese melts and the tuna mixture is warmed through. Serve hot. Sandwiches are easiest to eat with a knife and fork.

Makes 8 "specials," about 4 servings.

NUTRI-STEP 1

- Omit the regular English muffins and USE whole wheat English muffins.
- Decrease the mayonnaise to 3 tablespoons.
- Increase the yogurt to 3 tablespoons.
- Increase the chopped green or red bell pepper to 3 tablespoons. *And add* ¼ cup grated carrot to the tuna mixture.
- Omit the regular cheese and USE lowfat or part-skim cheese.

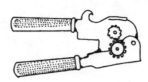

SPICY TUNA CREOLE SKILLET

Colorful and low in calories and cost, this tasty dish is a cinch to fix. Go easy on the cayenne if you don't particularly like spicy-hot foods.

2　tablespoons vegetable oil •
1　large onion, finely chopped
1　clove garlic, peeled and finely minced
1　green pepper, seeded and diced
2　celery stalks, thinly sliced
1　16-ounce can tomatoes, including juice
1　bay leaf
½　teaspoon dried thyme leaves
1　teaspoon paprika
⅛　teaspoon cayenne pepper, or to taste
¼　teaspoon salt •
2　6½-ounce cans water-packed tuna, drained and coarsely flaked

To Serve
Hot cooked white or brown rice, or 4 plain, hot, baked potatoes •

Heat the oil in a large skillet. Add the onion, garlic, green pepper, and celery and sauté until tender but not brown. Add the tomatoes and their juice, breaking up the tomatoes with a spoon. Then add the bay leaf, thyme, paprika, cayenne, and salt, and mix to combine. Simmer, stirring occasionally, for 15 to 20 minutes, or until the flavors have blended and the mixture has thickened. Gently stir in the tuna, and simmer for about 5 minutes longer. Remove the bay leaf. Serve over a bed of hot, cooked rice or over cut-open and lightly-fluffed baked potatoes.
Makes about 4 servings.

NUTRI-STEP 1

- Decrease the oil to 1 tablespoon. Stir the onions, garlic, green pepper, and celery often so that they don't stick.
- Decrease the salt to a generous ⅛ teaspoon.

To Serve
- If serving over rice, omit the hot cooked white rice and USE hot cooked brown rice.

CRUNCHY TUNA–BROCCOLI CASSEROLE

2 medium-sized stalks fresh broccoli, including stems ●■
2½ tablespoons butter or margarine ●■
1 medium-sized onion, finely chopped
1 clove garlic, peeled and finely minced
¾ cup sliced fresh mushrooms
3 tablespoons enriched all-purpose or unbleached white flour
2 cups hot lowfat milk ●■
½ teaspoon dried thyme leaves
¼ teaspoon salt ■
⅛ teaspoon black pepper, preferably freshly ground
1 8-ounce can water chestnuts, drained and thinly sliced
2 6½-ounce cans water-packed tuna, drained
2 cups (3-ounce can) chow mein noodles, divided ●■

Cut the broccoli tops into small flowerets. Trim and discard the bottom ½ inch from the stalks. Peel the woody covering from the thick part of the stem and discard. Cut the stem into small pieces. Set aside the flowerets and stem pieces.

Melt the butter in a large saucepan. Add the onion and garlic and cook, stirring, until tender but not browned. Stir in the mushrooms, and cook for a few minutes longer until they begin to release some juices. Mix in the flour and cook, stirring constantly, for about 1 minute. Gradually stir in the hot milk, thyme, salt, and pepper. Continue to cook, stirring constantly, until the sauce thickens and boils. Stir in the water chestnuts and reserved broccoli, and cook for about 2 minutes longer.

Coarsely flake the drained tuna and add it to the sauce along with 1½ cups of the chow mein noodles. Turn the mixture into a greased or nonstick spray-coated 2- to 2½-quart casserole. Bake, covered, in a 350-degree oven for 30 minutes, or until hot and bubbly, and the broccoli is crisp-tender. Before serving, sprinkle the remaining ½ cup chow mein noodles on top.

Makes about 5 servings.

NUTRI-STEP 1

- Increase the broccoli to 2 large stalks or 3 small stalks, including stems.
- Decrease the butter or margarine to 2 tablespoons.
- Omit the lowfat milk and SUBSTITUTE 2 cups hot skim milk or ⅔ cup instant nonfat dry milk plus 1⅞ cups hot water. (If using milk powder and water, it is not necessary to mix them together first; just stir the water into the saucepan, and then stir in the milk powder.)
- Decrease the chow mein noodles to 1 cup. Add ⅔ cup to the tuna mixture, and sprinkle ⅓ cup on top of the casserole.

- Increase the broccoli to 3 medium-sized stalks, including stems.
- Decrease the butter or margarine to 1½ tablespoons. Stir the onions often to make sure they don't stick or burn.
- Omit the lowfat milk and SUBSTITUTE 2 cups hot skim milk or ⅔ cup instant nonfat dry milk plus 1⅞ cups hot water. (If using milk powder and water, it is not necessary to mix them together first; just stir the water into the saucepan, and then stir in the milk powder.)
- Decrease the salt to a scant ¼ teaspoon.
- Omit the chow mein noodles and SUBSTITUTE ⅓ cup fresh white or whole wheat bread crumbs. Use all crumbs as a topping, and sprinkle over casserole BEFORE baking.

SHRIMP JAMBALAYA

The special combination of herbs and spices in this popular and healthful Creole stew gives it a tantalizing aroma and taste.

2 tablespoons peanut or vegetable oil •
1 cup green onions (scallions), including tops, coarsely chopped
1 celery stalk, including leaves, finely chopped
1 clove garlic, peeled and finely minced
⅓ cup coarsely chopped fresh parsley leaves
1 16-ounce can tomatoes, preferably imported Italian tomatoes, including juice
1 cup chicken broth or bouillon
1 cup water
2 large bay leaves
1 teaspoon mild chili powder •
½ teaspoon dried thyme leaves
½ teaspoon ground allspice
⅛ teaspoon freshly ground black pepper
   Pinch of cayenne pepper, or to taste
   Pinch of saffron threads (optional)
½ teaspoon salt •
1¼ cup uncooked white rice, rinsed and drained
   About 1 pound fresh or frozen, peeled and deveined (small or medium-sized) shrimp

Combine the oil, onions, celery, garlic, and parsley in a 4-quart or larger heavy pot over medium-high heat. Cook, stirring constantly, for 5 to 6 minutes, or until the vegetables are soft. Add the tomatoes and their juice, breaking the tomatoes up with a spoon. Then add the chicken broth, water, and all the seasonings. Bring the mixture to a boil, and stir in the rice. Turn the heat to medium-low and cover the pot. Simmer for 30 minutes, stirring frequently to prevent the rice from sticking. Add a bit of water, if necessary, to prevent the mixture from boiling dry. Stir the shrimp into the rice mixture and continue simmering, covered, for about 10 minutes, or until the rice is just tender and the shrimp are pink and curled. Serve immediately.

Makes about 5 servings.

NUTRI-STEP 1

- Decrease the oil to 1 tablespoon. Stir the vegetables constantly and watch carefully to prevent them from burning and sticking. *And add* 1 large carrot, finely chopped, along with the celery.
- Increase the chili powder to 1¼ teaspoons.
- Decrease the salt to a generous ¼ teaspoon.

SHRIMP CURRY

Curry

2	tablespoons butter or margarine ●■
1	large onion, coarsely chopped
3	medium-sized celery stalks, including leaves, coarsely chopped
1	large clove garlic, peeled and minced
1	medium-sized carrot, coarsely chopped ●■
1	large tart unpeeled apple, cored and coarsely chopped
1	small turnip, peeled and coarsely chopped
¼	cup coarsely chopped green pepper
¼	cup enriched all-purpose or unbleached white flour
1	large ripe tomato, peeled, cored, and chopped
1½ to 2	tablespoons mild curry powder
¼	teaspoon ground nutmeg
¼	teaspoon black pepper, preferably freshly ground ■

⅛ to ¼	teaspoon cayenne pepper
	Scant ⅛ teaspoon ground allspice
⅛	teaspoon dried basil leaves
1	large bay leaf
	Pinch of dried thyme leaves
½	teaspoon salt ■
1¾	cups beef broth or bouillon
1	cup dry white table wine
1¼	pounds fresh or frozen shelled and deveined medium-sized shrimp ●■
1¼	cups lowfat milk

To Serve
| 5 to 6 | cups hot cooked white or brown rice ■ |

Garnishes (select 3 or 4 of the following)
½	cup raisins
½	cup well-drained juice-packed pineapple tidbits
½	cup grated or shredded carrots
½	cup thinly sliced green onions (scallions), including tops
½	cup diced unpeeled tart apple tossed in 1 teaspoon lemon juice

Melt the butter in a heavy 3-quart or larger pot over medium-high heat. Add the onion, celery, and garlic. Cook, stirring, for 4 to 5 minutes, or until the vegetables are limp. Add the carrot, apple, turnip, and green pepper. Cook, stirring, for 3 minutes. Gradually stir the flour into the vegetables, blending until completely smooth. Cook the mixture for 2 minutes longer stirring constantly. Add the tomato, all the spices, herbs, and salt. Slowly stir in the beef broth and then the wine. Bring the mixture to a boil, stirring. Turn the heat to low, cover, and simmer for 30 to 35 minutes, stirring occasionally to prevent sticking.

While curry simmers, prepare 3 or 4 of the garnishes. Place each garnish in a small serving dish.

Add the shrimp and milk to the curry and simmer, uncovered, for 6 to 8 minutes longer, or until the shrimp are pink and just cooked through. Transfer the curry to a serving bowl. Pass hot cooked rice and garnishes along with the curry. A homemade or commercial chutney may also accompany the curry, if desired.

Makes 5 to 6 servings.

NUTRI-STEP 1

Curry
- Decrease the butter or margarine to 1½ tablespoons.
- Increase the carrots to 2 medium, coarsely chopped. *And add* ½ cup coarsely chopped fresh cauliflower flowerets along with the carrot.
- Decrease the shrimp to 1 pound.

Curry
- Decrease the butter or margarine to 1½ tablespoons.
- Increase the carrots to 2 medium, coarsely chopped. *And add* ½ cup coarsely chopped fresh cauliflower flowerets along with the carrot.
- Increase the black pepper to a generous ¼ teaspoon.
- Decrease the salt to a generous ¼ teaspoon.
- Decrease the shrimp to 1 pound.

To Serve
- Omit the white rice and USE brown rice.

QUICK SHRIMP SKILLET

2½	tablespoons butter or margarine •
5 to 6	green onions (scallions), including tops, coarsely chopped
1	medium-sized celery stalk, including leaves, coarsely chopped
1	small carrot, finely chopped
6 to 7	medium-sized fresh mushrooms, coarsely sliced
	Scant ¾ teaspoon dried thyme leaves •
⅛	teaspoon freshly ground black pepper
¼	teaspoon salt •
12	ounces medium-sized cleaned and deveined fresh or frozen shrimp
⅔	cup water
1	cup "instant" white rice

Melt the butter in a large skillet over medium-high heat. Add the green onions, celery, carrot, and mushrooms to the pan, and cook, stirring, for 7 to 8 minutes, or until the onion and mushrooms are tender but not browned. Stir the thyme, pepper, salt, and shrimp into the vegetables. Cook, stirring, for 6 to 7 minutes, or until the shrimp are curled and pink. Stir the water and rice into the skillet, and bring the mixture to a boil. Cover the skillet and remove from the heat. Let stand for about 5 minutes longer, or until the rice is tender. Fluff up the rice with a fork and serve.
  Makes about 4 servings.

NUTRI-STEP 1

- Decrease the butter or margarine to 1½ tablespoons.
- Increase the thyme to a generous ¾ teaspoon.
- Decrease the salt to ⅛ teaspoon.

Chapter 13

Main Dishes—
Vegetarian

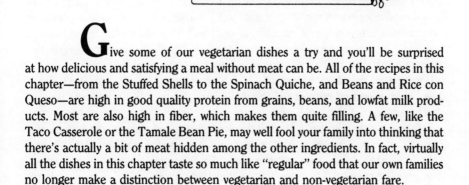

Give some of our vegetarian dishes a try and you'll be surprised at how delicious and satisfying a meal without meat can be. All of the recipes in this chapter—from the Stuffed Shells to the Spinach Quiche, and Beans and Rice con Queso—are high in good quality protein from grains, beans, and lowfat milk products. Most are also high in fiber, which makes them quite filling. A few, like the Taco Casserole or the Tamale Bean Pie, may well fool your family into thinking that there's actually a bit of meat hidden among the other ingredients. In fact, virtually all the dishes in this chapter taste so much like "regular" food that our own families no longer make a distinction between vegetarian and non-vegetarian fare.

EGGPLANT, PASTA, AND CHEESE CASSEROLE

Eggplant and Pasta
1   large eggplant (about 1¾ pounds), peeled and cut crosswise into ¾-inch-
    thick slices
3   ounces uncooked spaghetti, broken into 2-inch lengths (about 1 cup of
    pieces)

Sauce
1   green onion (scallion) including top, coarsely chopped
1   small clove garlic, peeled and minced
1   small celery stalk, including leaves, very coarsely sliced
1   16-ounce can tomatoes, including juice
1   6-ounce can tomato paste
½   cup water
2   teaspoons dried basil leaves
¼   teaspoon salt •
⅛   teaspoon black pepper, preferably freshly ground

Cheeses
¼   cup grated Parmesan cheese •
8   ounces grated or shredded part-skim mozzarella (if unavailable
    substitute regular mozzarella)

Lay the eggplant slices on an aluminum foil-lined broiler pan. Broil under a preheated broiler for 6 to 8 minutes, or until well browned on top. Turn the slices over
and continue broiling 6 to 8 minutes, or until well browned on the second side.

While the eggplant broils, cook the spaghetti in unsalted water according to the
package directions until almost tender. Then, turn into a colander and let drain.

Combine all the sauce ingredients in a blender or food processor fitted with a
steel blade. Blend or process for about 30 seconds, or until the mixture is completely puréed. Set the sauce aside.

To assemble the casserole, lay half the broiled eggplant slices in the bottom of a
2-quart casserole. Top with a third of the sauce. Then sprinkle a third of the Parmesan and mozzarella cheeses over the sauce. Lay the cooked spaghetti in an even
layer over the cheeses. Then, top the spaghetti with another third of the sauce and
cheeses. Place the remaining eggplant slices in the casserole. Top with the remaining sauce and cheeses.

Bake the casserole, uncovered, in a preheated 375-degree oven for 45 minutes,
or until the cheese melts and the mixture is bubbly hot. The casserole is also good
made ahead and reheated.

Makes 5 to 6 servings.

BEANS AND PASTA SKILLET

A tasty and satisfying main dish, this provides plenty of high-quality protein. If you decide to use dry beans, they can be cooked in advance. See the cooking note below.

2½	cups uncooked corkscrew (or other shaped) regular pasta ■
2	tablespoons vegetable oil ●■
2	medium-sized onions, finely chopped
2	cloves garlic, peeled and minced
3	celery stalks, including leaves, thinly sliced ●■
¾	teaspoon dried basil leaves ■
¾	teaspoon dried rubbed sage
⅛	teaspoon dry mustard
¾	teaspoon salt ●■
⅛	teaspoon freshly ground black pepper
1⅓	cups dry white beans (navy or Great Northern), cooked and drained (see note below), or 2 16-ounce cans white beans, drained
⅓	cup lowfat or skim milk ●■
6	ounces (1½ cups, packed) grated cheese, such as Cheddar, Colby, or Longhorn ●■

Cook the pasta according to the package directions, but omit the salt. Drain well and set aside.

Heat the oil in a large deep skillet or electric frypan. Add the onion, garlic, and celery and sauté until tender but not brown. Stir in the basil, sage, dry mustard, salt, and pepper. Then mix in the beans, milk, and cooked pasta. Add the grated cheese to the skillet and continue stirring over medium heat until the cheese melts and is bubbly.

Makes about 6 main-dish servings.

Note: To cook dry white beans, sort and rinse them well. Put them in a saucepan with about 4 cups of water. Cover and bring to a boil. Boil for 3 minutes. Turn off the heat and let the beans stand, covered, for 1 hour. Bring to a boil again and boil for about 1½ to 2 hours, or until tender. Drain well before using. The beans may be cooked in advance and refrigerated or even frozen.

NUTRI-STEP 1

- Decrease the oil to 1½ tablespoons. Use a nonstick skillet, if available, and stir the onions and celery often to make sure they don't stick.
- Increase the celery to 4 stalks.
- Decrease the salt to ½ teaspoon.
- Omit the lowfat milk and USE skim milk.
- Decrease the grated cheese to 5 ounces (1¼ cups, packed). Use part-skim or lowfat Cheddar-type cheese, if available. If it's too soft to grate, finely chop the cheese instead.

NUTRI-STEP 2

- Omit the regular pasta and SUBSTITUTE whole wheat or soy-enriched pasta.
- Decrease the oil to 1½ tablespoons. Use a nonstick skillet, if available, and stir the onions and celery often to make sure they don't stick.
- Increase the celery to 4 stalks.
- Increase the basil to 1 teaspoon.
- Decrease the salt to ¼ teaspoon.
- Omit the lowfat milk and USE skim milk.
- Decrease the grated cheese to 4 ounces (1 cup, packed). Use part-skim or lowfat Cheddar-type cheese, if available. If it's too soft to grate, finely chop the cheese instead.

FETTUCCINE WITH RICOTTA SAUCE

Although this pasta dish tastes similar to Fettuccine Alfredo, it is much lower in fat and higher in protein.

8   ounces regular fettuccine pasta •
1½   cups part-skim ricotta cheese (if unavailable, substitute regular ricotta)

⅓ cup lowfat plain yogurt •
2 tablespoons commercial sour cream •
1 large egg •
¼ cup finely grated Parmesan cheese
⅛ teaspoon salt •
⅛ teaspoon white or black pepper, preferably freshly ground
½ teaspoon dried basil leaves
2 tablespoons finely chopped fresh parsley leaves

Cook the fettuccine according to the package directions, omitting the salt.

Meanwhile, put the ricotta, yogurt, sour cream, egg, and Parmesan cheese into a food processor or blender. Process until smooth. (Or, press the mixture through a fine sieve.) Put the ricotta mixture into the top of a double boiler, and slowly heat over simmering water, stirring constantly, until the sauce is warmed through. (Do not overheat, or the sauce may develop an unpleasant texture.) Remove from the heat, and stir in the salt, pepper, and basil.

Drain the pasta well, and transfer it to a serving bowl. Pour the warm sauce over the hot pasta and toss gently so all the pasta is coated with sauce. Sprinkle the top with parsley and serve immediately.

Makes about 2 main-dish servings, or about 4 side-dish servings.

NUTRI-STEP 1

- Omit the regular fettuccine and SUBSTITUTE whole wheat, spinach, or soy-enriched fettuccine.
- Increase the yogurt to ½ cup.
- Omit the sour cream.
- Omit the large egg and SUBSTITUTE 2 large egg whites.
- Decrease the salt to a pinch or omit.

MACARONI AND CHEESE

3 cups uncooked elbow macaroni or other pasta ■
½ cup lowfat milk
1 cup lowfat cottage cheese
⅛ teaspoon garlic powder
8 ounces (2 cups) grated Cheddar cheese (or part-skim Longhorn cheese) •■
¼ teaspoon salt •■
Pinch of black pepper, preferably freshly ground

In a medium saucepan, cook the macaroni according to the package directions, omitting the salt. Drain well in a colander. Turn the macaroni into an 8- by 10-inch or similar baking dish. Stir in all the remaining ingredients. Bake in a preheated 350-degree oven for about 30 minutes, or until all the liquid has been absorbed and the macaroni is heated through.

Makes 4 to 5 servings.

Note: If you're in a hurry, make this macaroni and cheese dish as a stove-top dinner. Simply decrease the milk to ¼ cup. After draining the cooked macaroni, return it to the cooking pot. Stir in all the remaining ingredients. Cover and cook over low heat, stirring frequently, for about 3 to 4 minutes or until the cheeses are melted.

NUTRI-STEP 1

- Decrease the grated Cheddar or part-skim Longhorn cheese to 6 ounces (1½ cups).
- Decrease the salt to ⅛ teaspoon.

NUTRI-STEP 2

- Omit the regular macaroni and SUBSTITUTE 3 cups whole wheat macaroni, and cook according to package directions, omitting the salt.
- Decrease the grated Cheddar or part-skim Longhorn cheese to 6 ounces (1½ cups).
- Decrease the salt to ⅛ teaspoon or omit.

STUFFED SHELLS

20 to 24   jumbo pasta shells (each about 2 inches long)

Filling
    1½   cups part-skim ricotta cheese (if unavailable, substitute regular ricotta) •
    2   cups lowfat cottage cheese •
    2   cups shredded part-skim mozzarella cheese (if unavailable, substitute regular mozzarella)
    ¼   cup grated Parmesan cheese
    ¼   teaspoon salt •

1	teaspoon dried oregano leaves
	Pinch of ground nutmeg
¾	cup finely chopped fresh parsley leaves
⅛	teaspoon black pepper, preferably freshly ground

Sauce

2	teaspoons vegetable oil •
1	medium-sized onion, finely chopped
1 to 2	cloves garlic, peeled and minced
2	15-ounce cans tomato sauce
½	teaspoon dried oregano leaves
½	teaspoon dried basil leaves
⅛	teaspoon black pepper, preferably freshly ground

Cook the pasta shells in unsalted boiling water for about 20 to 25 minutes or until almost tender.

Meanwhile, mix together all the filling ingredients and refrigerate until needed.

To make the sauce, heat the oil in a small saucepan over medium-low heat. Add the onion and garlic and cook until very tender, stirring frequently. Stir in all the remaining sauce ingredients, cover, and lower the heat. Simmer, stirring occasionally, for about 15 minutes.

Pour half of the sauce into a shallow 9- by 13-inch or slightly smaller baking dish. Drain the cooked shells. When cool enough to handle, stuff the shells with the filling mixture. Arrange the stuffed shells over the sauce in the baking dish. Top with the remaining sauce. Bake, uncovered, in a preheated 350-degree oven for about 35 minutes, or until the sauce is bubbly and the shells are heated through.

Makes 5 to 6 servings.

NUTRI-STEP 1

Filling
- Decrease the ricotta cheese to 1 cup.
- Increase the cottage cheese to 2½ cups.
- Omit the salt.

Sauce
- Decrease the vegetable oil to 1 teaspoon. Stir the onion and garlic very carefully to prevent them from burning.

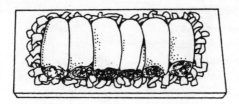

QUICK ITALIAN-STYLE PASTA CASSEROLE

2½ cups uncooked pasta, such as spirals, small shells, or elbows •

Sauce
- 1 15-ounce can tomato sauce
- ½ teaspoon dried oregano leaves
- ¼ teaspoon dried basil leaves
- 1 teaspoon instant minced onions
- ¼ teaspoon garlic powder
- ⅛ teaspoon black pepper, preferably freshly ground
- ⅛ teaspoon salt •

Cheeses
- 1 cup lowfat cottage cheese
- ¾ cup (3 ounces) grated or finely cubed mozzarella cheese
- 3 tablespoons grated Parmesan cheese •

In a large saucepan, cook the pasta according to the package directions, omitting the salt from the water. Drain well.

While the pasta is cooking, mix together all the sauce ingredients in a small bowl.

Turn the drained pasta into a 2-quart casserole. Stir the cottage cheese, mozzarella, and 2 tablespoons of the Parmesan cheese into the pasta, mixing well. Pour the sauce mixture over the pasta and cheese mixture. Sprinkle the top of the casserole with the remaining Parmesan cheese. Bake in a preheated 350-degree oven for about 25 minutes, or until heated through.

Makes about 4 servings.

NUTRI-STEP 1

- SUBSTITUTE whole wheat pasta for one half (or all) of the regular pasta.

Sauce
- Omit the salt.

Cheeses
- Decrease the grated Parmesan cheese to 2 tablespoons. Use half for the filling and half for the topping.

SPINACH GNOCCHI

Unlike many other dumplings, these "naked ravioli," as they are sometimes called in Italy, are as light and delicate as can be. The topping on the gnocchi (pronounced "nyok'-kee") can be varied to suit your taste (see one alternate suggestion below).

Gnocchi
2   **10-ounce packages frozen chopped spinach, thawed and very well drained**

2   **large eggs (or 1 large egg plus 2 large egg whites) ●■**

1½   **cups part-skim ricotta cheese (if unavailable, substitute regular ricotta)**

⅓   **cup finely grated Parmesan cheese ●■**

¼   **cup finely grated or shredded lowfat or part-skim cheese, such as mozzarella ●■**

2½   **tablespoons enriched all-purpose or unbleached white flour ■**

2   **tablespoons white or whole wheat bread crumbs (made from toasted or stale bread) ●■**

¼   **teaspoon ground nutmeg**

½   **teaspoon salt ●■**

⅛   **teaspoon freshly ground black pepper**
     Extra flour (about ½ cup)

Topping
2   **tablespoons butter or margarine, melted ●■**

2   **tablespoons grated Parmesan cheese ●■**

2   **tablespoons grated or very finely chopped lowfat or part-skim cheese ●■**

For gnocchi, squeeze as much excess water from the spinach as possible. Place in a bowl with the eggs, ricotta cheese, all the grated or shredded cheese, 2½ tablespoons flour, bread crumbs, nutmeg, salt, and pepper. Mix well until completely combined. With flour-coated fingers, form the spinach-cheese mixture into 1-inch diameter balls, and immediately roll each ball in the extra flour. Shake off any excess. Place the flour-coated balls on a platter, not touching one another.

    Meanwhile, heat about 4 quarts of water to boiling in a 6- to 8-quart pot or Dutch oven. Lower the heat so the water just simmers. Gently drop about a third of the balls into the water. After about 2 to 3 minutes, they will rise to the surface. (Use a spoon to gently dislodge any that happen to stick to the bottom of the pot.) Simmer the gnocchi for 1 minute longer, then remove them with a slotted spoon, and place them in a 9-inch square or 10-inch round or similar baking dish. Repeat with the remaining balls. Do not overcook the gnocchi or they may fall apart.

When all gnocchi are ready, drain off any water in the dish. Then add the topping. Drizzle the melted butter all over the gnocchi; then sprinkle them with grated cheeses.

Just before serving, heat the gnocchi in a preheated 375-degree oven for about 10 minutes, or until the cheese topping is melted and lightly browned. (Or you may place the gnocchi under a preheated broiler for a few minutes.)

Makes about 4 servings (about 48 balls).

VARIATION: Instead of using a butter-cheese topping for the gnocchi, serve them tossed with hot Don't-Tell-'Em-It's-Good-for-'Em Spaghetti Sauce (page 123).

NUTRI-STEP 1

Gnocchi
- Omit the 2 large eggs and USE 1 large egg plus 2 large egg whites.
- Decrease the grated Parmesan cheese to ¼ cup.
- Increase the lowfat or part-skim cheese to ⅓ cup.
- Increase the bread crumbs to 2½ tablespoons.
- Decrease the salt to a generous ¼ teaspoon. *And add* a pinch each of dried thyme leaves and basil leaves to the ricotta mixture.

Topping
- Decrease the melted butter or margarine to 1½ tablespoons.
- Decrease the grated Parmesan cheese to 1 tablespoon.
- Increase the lowfat or part-skim cheese to 3 tablespoons.

NUTRI-STEP 2

- Omit the 2 large eggs and SUBSTITUTE 3 large egg whites.
- Decrease the grated Parmesan cheese to ¼ cup.
- Increase the lowfat or part-skim cheese to ⅓ cup.
- Omit the white flour and SUBSTITUTE 2½ tablespoons whole wheat flour.
- Increase the bread crumbs to 2½ tablespoons. Omit the white bread crumbs and USE whole wheat bread crumbs.
- Decrease the salt to a scant ¼ teaspoon. *And add* ¼ teaspoon each of dried thyme leaves and basil leaves to the ricotta mixture.

Topping
- Decrease the melted butter or margarine to 1½ tablespoons.
- Omit the grated Parmesan cheese.
- Increase the lowfat or part-skim cheese to ¼ cup.

TAMALE BEAN PIE

This very satisfying Tex-Mex main dish is actually a layered casserole rather than a "pie." The combination of spicy beans and cooked cornmeal provides a perfect juxtaposition of flavors and textures, as well as high-quality protein.

Bean Filling
1½   tablespoons vegetable oil ●■
2   medium-sized onions, finely chopped
1   clove garlic, peeled and minced
1   medium-sized green pepper, seeded and diced
1   16-ounce can tomatoes, including juice
1   15- to 16-ounce can plain pinto beans, dark red kidney beans, or soybeans, drained
2   teaspoons chili powder, or to taste ■
½   teaspoon salt ●■

Cornmeal Layers
¾   cup yellow cornmeal (use undegerminated cornmeal, if available; see recipe for Chili Corn Chips on page 272 for more information)
2   cups lowfat milk ●■
1   teaspoon vegetable oil ■
¼   teaspoon salt
2   large eggs (or 1 large egg plus 2 large egg whites), beaten ●■

Topping
½   cup grated Cheddar, Longhorn, or Monterey Jack cheese ●■

For the bean filling, heat the oil in a large skillet. Add the onions, garlic, and green pepper and sauté until tender but not browned. Chop the tomatoes and add them to the skillet along with the beans, chili powder, and salt. Simmer, uncovered, stirring frequently, for about 10 minutes, or until some of the excess liquid has evaporated. Set aside to cool slightly.

For cornmeal layers, mix the cornmeal with ½ cup of the milk, and set aside.

In a medium-sized saucepan, combine the remaining milk, oil, and salt and heat to a simmer. Gradually stir in the moistened cornmeal. Simmer, stirring constantly, for about 5 minutes or until very thick. Remove from the heat, and quickly stir in the beaten eggs until well blended.

To assemble the pie, spread about one third of the cornmeal mixture in the bottom of a lightly greased or nonstick spray-coated 9- to 10-inch square or similar casserole or baking pan. Evenly cover with all the bean filling. Drop the remaining cornmeal mixture in large dollops over the beans. Spread the cornmeal out with a spatula or knife so that it covers the bean filling. Sprinkle the cheese on top. (The casserole may be assembled in advance to this point, and refrigerated.)

Bake in a preheated 375-degree oven for about 25 to 30 minutes, or until hot and bubbly. Serve with a large spoon, including all three layers in each serving. *Makes about 4 main-dish servings.*

NUTRI-STEP 1

Bean Filling
- Decrease the oil to 1 tablespoon. Stir the onions and other vegetables constantly to make sure they don't stick.
- Decrease the salt to ¼ teaspoon.

Cornmeal Layers
- Omit the lowfat milk and SUBSTITUTE 2 cups skim milk or 1⅞ cups water plus ⅔ cup instant nonfat dry milk powder. (Mix the milk powder and ½ cup water with the cornmeal. Heat the remaining water in a saucepan. Then proceed as above.)
- Omit the 2 large eggs and USE 1 large egg plus 2 large egg whites.

Topping
- Omit the regular cheese and SUBSTITUTE ½ cup grated or finely chopped lowfat or part-skim Cheddar-type cheese.

NUTRI-STEP 2

Bean Filling
- Decrease the oil to 1 tablespoon. Stir the onions and other vegetables constantly to make sure they don't stick.
- Increase the chili powder to 2¼ teaspoons, or to taste.
- Decrease the salt to a generous ⅛ teaspoon.

Cornmeal Layers
- Omit the lowfat milk and SUBSTITUTE 2 cups skim milk or 1⅞ cups water plus ⅔ cup instant nonfat dry milk powder. (Mix the milk powder and ½ cup water with the cornmeal. Heat the remaining water in a saucepan. Then proceed as above.)
- Decrease the oil to ½ teaspoon.
- Omit the 2 large eggs and SUBSTITUTE 3 large egg whites.

Topping
- Omit the regular cheese and SUBSTITUTE ⅓ cup grated or finely chopped lowfat or part-skim Cheddar-type cheese.

TACO CASSEROLE

They probably won't even realize this delicious vegetarian dish is meatless!

1	tablespoon vegetable oil
1	large onion, coarsely chopped
1	clove garlic, peeled and minced
1	cup coarsely chopped fresh mushrooms
⅓	cup chopped fresh parsley leaves
¼	cup finely chopped green pepper
2	15-ounce cans kidney beans, well drained
½	cup tomato sauce
2 to 3	tablespoons canned, chopped green chilies (or more for very spicy filling)
2	teaspoons chili powder •
½	teaspoon ground cumin (optional)
⅛	teaspoon celery salt
⅛	teaspoon black pepper, preferably freshly ground
¼	teaspoon salt •
10 to 11	regular-size taco or tostado shells, broken into bite-sized pieces
4	ounces (about 1 cup, lightly packed) part-skim shredded or grated mild Cheddar cheese (if unavailable substitute regular Cheddar) •
2	medium-sized tomatoes, cored and coarsely chopped
1¼	cups shredded Iceberg lettuce
½	cup thinly sliced green onions (scallions), including tops (optional)

Combine the oil, onion, garlic, mushrooms, parsley, and green pepper in a large skillet over medium-high heat. Cook, stirring, for 7 to 8 minutes, or until the vegetables are soft. Coarsely mash the drained kidney beans by pressing them with the bottom of a drinking glass or the back of a large spoon (or by chopping briefly in a food processor fitted with a steel blade). Add the beans to the skillet, along with the tomato sauce, green chilies, and all seasoning ingredients. Lower the heat to medium and continue to cook, stirring frequently, for 15 minutes, or until most of the excess moisture has evaporated from the pan.

Spread half of the taco shell pieces in the bottom of a flat-bottomed 1-quart or similar casserole. Spoon the bean mixture over the taco pieces, and smooth out to form an even layer. Top the bean layer with the remaining taco shell pieces. Sprinkle the cheese over the casserole. Bake in a preheated 250-degree oven 4 to 5 minutes, or until the cheese melts. Sprinkle the tomatoes, lettuce, and chopped green onions over the cheese. Serve immediately.

Makes 4 to 5 servings.

NUTRI-STEP 1

- Increase the chili powder to 2¼ teaspoons.
- Decrease the salt to ⅛ teaspoon.
- Decrease the Cheddar cheese to 3 ounces (¾ cup, lightly packed).

BEANS AND RICE CON QUESO

1 cup uncooked brown rice, rinsed and well drained
2 cups water
2 15- to 16-ounce cans kidney beans, well drained
¼ teaspoon salt •
1 4-ounce can chopped green chilies, drained
¾ cup part-skim ricotta cheese (if unavailable, substitute regular ricotta) •
¼ cup small curd lowfat cottage cheese •
   Pinch of black pepper, preferably freshly ground
4 ounces (about 1 cup) packed shredded mild Cheddar cheese (or part-skim Longhorn), divided •

Combine the brown rice and water in a medium-sized saucepan. Bring to a boil over medium-high heat. Cover, lower the heat to a simmer, and cook for 45 minutes, or until the rice is just tender.

Stir the drained kidney beans, salt, and green chilies into the rice. Transfer half of the rice-bean mixture to a 2½-quart casserole.

In a small bowl, stir together the ricotta, cottage cheese, pepper, and all but 2 tablespoons of the Cheddar cheese. Blend well. Spread the mixture on top of the rice and bean mixture. Top with the remaining rice and beans. Sprinkle the reserved 2 tablespoons of cheese over the top of the casserole.

Bake, covered, in a preheated 350-degree oven for about 35 to 40 minutes, or until the casserole is heated through.

Makes 4 to 5 servings.

NUTRI-STEP 1

- Decrease the salt to ⅛ teaspoon or omit.
- Decrease the ricotta to ½ cup.
- Increase the lowfat cottage cheese to ½ cup.
- Decrease the Cheddar or part-skim Longhorn cheese to 3 ounces (¾ cup). *And add* a generous pinch of garlic powder.

BEAN–RICE–CHEESE PATTIES WITH SAUCE

Patties

1	cup drained, canned garbanzo beans (chick-peas) or other beans
1	cup lowfat small curd cottage cheese
1½	cups *cooked* (warm or cold) white or brown rice •
1¼	cups fresh white or whole wheat bread crumbs •
1	large egg (or 2 large egg whites) •
1	teaspoon dry mustard
1	teaspoon dried thyme leaves
¼	teaspoon dried rubbed sage
¼	teaspoon dried marjoram leaves
¼	teaspoon black pepper, preferably freshly ground
¼	teaspoon salt •
2	tablespoons vegetable oil

Sauce

1	8-ounce can tomato sauce
	Pinch of black pepper, preferably freshly ground
⅛	teaspoon dried thyme leaves
⅛	teaspoon dried basil leaves

For the patties, use a fork to mash the beans with the cottage cheese in a medium-sized bowl. Stir in the cooked rice, bread crumbs, egg, dry mustard, thyme, sage, marjoram, pepper, and salt until very well combined. Form the mixture into patties, using about ¼ cup for each.

Heat the oil in a large skillet and brown the patties on both sides (in batches, if necessary). Drain the patties on paper towels. Discard any oil left in the skillet.

Put all the sauce ingredients in the skillet. Heat to simmering; then return all the browned patties to the skillet. Turn the patties so they are completely coated with the sauce. Serve.

Makes about 12 patties, or 4 servings.

NUTRI-STEP 1

Patties
- Omit the cooked white rice and USE cooked brown rice.
- Omit the white bread crumbs and USE whole wheat bread crumbs.
- Omit the large egg and USE 2 large egg whites.
- Decrease the salt to ⅛ teaspoon.

LAYERED CHEESE BLINTZ CASSEROLE

This slightly sweet casserole is much easier to prepare than traditional-style blintzes, even though it tastes just as delectable. What's more, cheese blintzes are normally laden with eggs, and they are fried in butter; but in this casserole, fat is reduced by cutting down on egg yolks and substituting baking for frying.

Batter
2½   tablespoons butter or margarine, melted •
1   tablespoon sugar
2   large eggs plus 1 large egg white
¾   cup lowfat or skim milk •
¼   cup plain lowfat or regular yogurt •
½   teaspoon vanilla extract
1   teaspoon baking powder
1   cup enriched all-purpose or unbleached white flour

Filling
1   8-ounce package curd-style farmer cheese
1½   cups lowfat small curd cottage cheese
2   tablespoons sugar •
1   large egg (or 2 large egg whites) •
1   tablespoon lemon juice

Topping (optional)
   Ground cinnamon

To Serve (optional)
   Applesauce or Spicy Pearsauce (page 290)

Put all the batter ingredients in a blender, food processor, or mixer, and process or beat until well combined. Grease a 9-inch square pan well or coat it with nonstick vegetable spray, and pour 1 cup of the batter into the bottom to form a thin layer. (Reserve the remaining batter.) Bake in a preheated 350-degree oven for about 10 to 12 minutes or until set. Meanwhile, mix together all the filling ingredients.

When the layer of batter has set, remove the pan from the oven and smoothly spread the filling on top of the baked layer. Stir the reserved batter, and pour it evenly over the filling. If desired, sprinkle the top very lightly with cinnamon for extra color and flavor. Return the pan to the oven, and bake for an additional 35 to 40 minutes, or until the top is puffed and golden and completely set.

Remove the pan from the oven and let it stand for 10 minutes before cutting. Cut into squares to serve. Accompany with applesauce or Spicy Pearsauce, if desired.
Makes 16 squares, about 8 servings.

NUTRI-STEP 1

Batter
- Decrease the butter or margarine to 2 tablespoons.
- Omit the lowfat milk and USE skim milk.
- Omit the regular yogurt and USE lowfat yogurt.

Filling
- Decrease the sugar to 1½ tablespoons.
- Omit the large egg and USE 2 large egg whites.

MIXED VEGETABLE PIE

Some of the most healthful vegetables are used in this tasty quiche-like pie. And the combination of broccoli, cauliflower, and carrots is not only nutritious, it's also quite colorful and appealing. The Nutri-Steps with this recipe eliminate many of the calories and fat by simply replacing the pastry crust with toasted bread.

2	tablespoons vegetable oil ●■
1	medium-sized onion, thinly sliced
1	clove garlic, minced
2	cups very small fresh broccoli flowerets
2	cups very small fresh cauliflower flowerets
1	cup thin carrot slices
¼	cup water
2	large eggs plus 2 large egg whites
½	cup part-skim ricotta cheese (if unavailable, substitute regular ricotta) ■
½	teaspoon dried thyme leaves
½	teaspoon dried marjoram leaves
½	teaspoon dried basil leaves ■
½	teaspoon salt ●■
⅛	teaspoon black pepper, preferably freshly ground
1	prebaked deep-dish 9-inch or 10-inch pie or quiche pastry shell ●■ (page 265)
½	cup grated Swiss cheese ●■

Heat the oil in a large skillet. Add the onion and garlic and sauté until tender but not browned. Add the broccoli, cauliflower, and carrots and stir constantly for about 1 minute. Then add the water, cover tightly, and steam for about 5 minutes, or until the vegetables are crisp-tender.

Meanwhile, beat the eggs and egg whites with the ricotta, thyme, marjoram, basil, salt, and pepper. Remove the vegetables from the skillet with a slotted spoon. Place them in the prebaked pie shell. Stir any juices remaining in the skillet into the egg mixture. Pour the egg mixture evenly over the vegetables. Sprinkle the grated cheese on top. Bake in a preheated 325-degree oven for 25 to 30 minutes, or until set.

Makes 5 to 6 main-dish servings.

NUTRI-STEP 1

- Decrease the oil to 1½ tablespoons. Stir the onion and other vegetables constantly to make sure they don't stick.
- Decrease the salt to a generous ¼ teaspoon.
- Omit the pie shell and SUBSTITUTE 4 or 5 slices of toasted, thinly sliced regular or whole wheat bread. (Remove the crusts if desired.) Cut the bread to fit in the bottom of a deep 9- to 10-inch pie or quiche pan, or use a 9- or 10-inch square baking pan or casserole. Lightly grease the pan, or coat with nonstick vegetable spray; then line the bottom with the bread. Proceed as directed.
- Decrease the Swiss cheese to ⅓ cup.

NUTRI-STEP 2

- Decrease the oil to 1 tablespoon. Stir the onions and other vegetables constantly to make sure they don't stick.
- Omit the ricotta cheese and SUBSTITUTE a generous ½ cup lowfat small curd cottage cheese. Drain the cottage cheese in a sieve while preparing vegetables.
- Increase the basil to ¾ teaspoon.
- Decrease the salt to ¼ teaspoon.
- Omit the pie shell and SUBSTITUTE 4 or 5 slices of toasted, thinly sliced whole wheat bread. (Remove the crusts if desired.) Cut the bread to fit in the bottom of a deep 9- to 10-inch pie or quiche pan, or use a 9- or 10-inch square baking pan or casserole. Lightly grease the pan, or coat with a nonstick vegetable spray; then line the bottom with the bread. Proceed as directed.
- Omit the regular Swiss cheese and SUBSTITUTE ⅓ cup grated or finely chopped lowfat or part-skim Swiss-style cheese.

SPINACH QUICHE

They won't believe it even if you do tell 'em this one is good for 'em! It tastes so rich, they'll swear it's loaded with heavy cream. And they'll never guess it has been nutritionally enriched with one of the extra-healthful cruciferous vegetables, cauliflower.

1   recipe Easy Lowfat Pastry Crust (page 265)
1   10-ounce package frozen chopped spinach, thawed
1   cup part-skim ricotta cheese (if unavailable, substitute regular ricotta) ●■
1   cup lowfat milk ●■
2   tablespoons enriched all-purpose or unbleached white flour
½   teaspoon lemon juice ■
⅛   teaspoon ground nutmeg
¼   teaspoon salt ■
2   large eggs (or 1 large egg plus 2 large egg whites) ●■
1   large onion, finely chopped
1½ tablespoons butter or margarine ●■
1   cup thinly sliced fresh mushrooms
¾   cup finely chopped fresh cauliflower flowerets
1   cup shredded or grated Gruyère or Ementhaler (Swiss) cheese (about 4 ounces) ■

Prepare the pastry dough and press into a 9-inch, deep-dish pie plate. Chill thoroughly, at least 1 hour.

Turn the spinach into a colander and let drain.

In a blender or food processor, combine the ricotta, milk, flour, lemon juice, nutmeg, and salt. Blend on medium speed for 15 seconds; then raise speed to high and purée the mixture for 15 seconds longer, or until smooth. Add the eggs and purée for 10 seconds longer. Set aside.

Combine the onion with the butter in a medium skillet over medium-high heat. Cook the onion, stirring, for 3 to 4 minutes, or until it is limp. Add the mushrooms and cauliflower and continue to cook, stirring, for 5 to 6 minutes longer, or until the mushrooms are softened and most of the excess liquid has evaporated. Remove the skillet from the heat.

Use your hands to press down the spinach in the colander, squeezing out any excess liquid. A handful at a time, squeeze as much more liquid as possible from the spinach. Stir the spinach into the vegetables in the skillet. Return the skillet to medium-high heat and cook, stirring, for 4 to 5 minutes, or until the spinach is warmed through. Spread the mixture evenly in the prepared pie shell. Top the mixture with half of the shredded cheese. Pour the blended ricotta-milk mixture over the vegetable mixture, and gently stir with a fork. Top with the remaining cheese. Bake in a preheated 350-degree oven for 45 to 50 minutes, or until the quiche is

puffy and slightly browned on top. Remove to a rack and cool for 5 minutes before serving. The quiche may also be baked ahead and served reheated, if desired.
Makes 5 to 6 servings.

NUTRI-STEP 1

- Decrease the ricotta cheese to ½ cup. *And add* ½ cup lowfat cottage cheese along with the ricotta.
- Omit the lowfat milk and SUBSTITUTE 1 cup skim milk or ⅓ cup instant nonfat dry milk combined with a scant 1 cup water.
- Omit the 2 large eggs and USE 1 large egg plus 2 large egg whites.
- Decrease the butter or margarine to 1 tablespoon. Stir the onion, mushrooms, and cauliflower constantly and watch carefully to prevent them from sticking.

NUTRI-STEP 2

- Decrease the ricotta cheese to ½ cup. *And add* ½ cup lowfat cottage cheese along with the ricotta.
- Omit the lowfat milk and SUBSTITUTE 1 cup skim milk or ⅓ cup instant nonfat dry milk combined with a scant 1 cup water.
- Increase the lemon juice to ¾ teaspoon.
- Decrease the salt to ⅛ teaspoon.
- Omit the 2 large eggs and USE 1 large egg plus 2 large egg whites.
- Decrease the butter or margarine to 1 tablespoon. Stir the onion, mushrooms, and cauliflower constantly and watch carefully to prevent them from sticking.
- Decrease the shredded or grated Gruyère or Ementhaler cheese to ¾ cup.

Chapter 14

Breads and Quick Breads

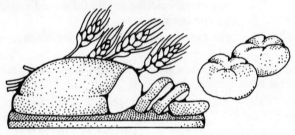

High in fiber and low in fat, whole grain yeast breads and quick breads make a perfect accompaniment to any meal—as well as an ideal snack. Don't think of breads simply as "fillers," though. Keep in mind that when they're made with whole grains and other healthful ingredients, they can make an important nutritional contribution to your diet.

We've tried to keep our bread recipes quick and easy. In fact, many of the quick breads can be mixed up and popped in the oven while your main course is simmering on the stove. Homemade bread with dinner is always a family pleaser at our houses. And we suspect it will be at yours, too.

There's one more point we should mention. For best results, always bake bread with the rack placed in the center of the oven. If either the top or the bottom of the bread is too close to the heat source, it may burn.

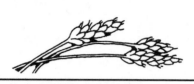

EASY MIXED-GRAINS BREAD

This easy recipe yields delicately flavored, evenly shaped loaves. The bread is particularly good for toast.

3	cups whole wheat flour
¾	cup instant nonfat dry milk powder
¼	cup sugar •
1	teaspoon salt •
2	packets (scant 2 tablespoons) active dry yeast
2¼	cups hot water (120 to 130 degrees F.)
2½	tablespoons vegetable oil •
1	large egg •
1¼	cups quick-cooking or old-fashioned rolled oats
½	cup cornmeal
2¼ to 2⅓	cups enriched all-purpose or unbleached white flour

Combine the whole wheat flour, milk powder, sugar, salt, and yeast in a large mixing bowl. Stir until well mixed.

With the mixer on medium-low speed, gradually beat the water, then the oil and egg into the whole wheat mixture. When the ingredients are well blended, raise the speed to medium and beat for 3 minutes. Stir the oats and cornmeal into the flour mixture by hand. Continuing to stir, gradually add 1⅔ cups white flour to the dough. The mixture will become stiff. A bit at a time, add up to ⅔ cup more white flour to the dough, kneading in the bowl with your hands. The mixture will be slightly soft and sticky, but pliable. Transfer the dough from the mixing bowl to a very large, lightly oiled bowl. Lightly rub the top of the dough with vegetable oil.

Cover the bowl with a clean damp cloth and set in a warm place (75 to 85 degrees). Let the dough rise until doubled in bulk, about 50 to 60 minutes.

Punch the dough down and divide it in half. Shape each portion into a loaf, and place each one in a greased 9- by 5-inch loaf pan. Lightly rub the top of the dough with oil. Cover the pans with a damp cloth and let rise in a warm place for 40 to 45 minutes, or until the loaves are doubled in bulk.

Bake the loaves in a preheated 375-degree oven for 15 minutes. Lower the oven temperature to 350 and bake for 25 to 30 minutes longer, or until the loaves are brown and sound hollow when lightly tapped on top. Remove the pans to racks and cool for 5 minutes. Then lift the loaves from the pans. The bread slices best if allowed to cool thoroughly on the racks first, although it also tastes good served warm. If desired, wrap and freeze the loaves for later use.

Makes 2 loaves.

NO-KNEAD ANADAMA BREAD

Although the proportions often vary, this interesting yeast-raised loaf always contains some cornmeal and molasses. However, it does not taste like corn bread, but rather like a richly flavored whole grain bread. Freshly-baked, it's great with dinner, and leftovers are wonderful toasted for breakfast or a snack. Our version of Anadama Bread is especially quick and easy because it is not kneaded, and has only one short rising right in the pan.

1	packet (scant 1 tablespoon) active dry yeast
¼	cup very warm water (105 to 115 degrees F.) ●
1	cup cornmeal (use undergerminated cornmeal, if available; see note with recipe for Chili Corn Chips, page 272)
1½	teaspoons salt ●
⅓	cup light or dark molasses ●
3	tablespoons vegetable oil ●
¾	cup boiling water
1	large egg (or 2 large egg whites) ●
2¼	cups white bread flour or enriched unbleached white flour ●

Dissolve the yeast in warm water and set aside.

In a large mixing bowl, combine the cornmeal, salt, molasses, and oil. Add the boiling water and stir to combine. Cool to lukewarm. Add the dissolved yeast, egg, and 1 cup of white flour to the cornmeal mixture. Beat for 2 minutes with an electric mixer on medium speed. Add the remaining flour and beat by hand for 1 minute (or use the mixer if it can handle the sticky dough).

Spread the dough evenly in a well-greased or nonstick spray-coated 8½- by 4½-inch loaf pan. If desired, smooth the surface of the loaf with lightly oiled fingertips. Lay a piece of plastic wrap loosely across the top of the pan, and place the pan inside a turned-off, unheated oven. Let the dough rise for about 40 to 45 minutes, or until it is almost to the top of the pan but not touching the plastic wrap. Remove the plastic covering, but leave the loaf in the unheated oven.

Turn on the oven heat to 350 degrees, and bake the loaf for about 45 to 50 minutes, or until the bottom sounds hollow when tapped. (If the top of the loaf appears to be browning too fast, cover it loosely with foil.) Remove the loaf from the pan, and cool it on a wire rack. Serve warm or at room temperature. When completely cool, store at room temperature, wrapped airtight.

Makes 1 loaf.

NUTRI-STEP 1

- Increase the warm water (for yeast) to ⅓ cup.
- Decrease the salt to 1 teaspoon.
- Decrease the molasses to ¼ cup.
- Decrease the oil to 2 tablespoons.
- Omit the large egg and USE 2 large egg whites.
- Decrease the white flour to 1½ cups. *And add* ¾ cup whole wheat flour to the white flour.

POPPY SEED LOAVES

This tasty yeast bread needs no kneading. The dough is beaten with an electric mixer.

2	cups very warm water (105 to 115 degrees F.)
2	tablespoons honey
1½	teaspoons salt •
2	packages (scant 2 tablespoons) active dry yeast
⅔	cup instant nonfat dry milk powder
2 to 4	tablespoons poppy seeds
3¼	cups bread flour or enriched all-purpose or unbleached white flour •
1	cup whole wheat bread flour or all-purpose whole wheat flour •

In a large mixing bowl, combine the water, honey, salt, yeast, milk powder, and poppy seeds. Mix until well blended.

In another bowl, mix the flours together. Add about one third of the combined flours to the yeast mixture. Beat for 2 minutes at medium speed with an electric mixer. Add the next third, and reduce the mixer speed to low. Beat for 2 minutes longer. Stir in the remaining flour by hand until the dough is smooth.

Divide the dough into 2 loaves. Place each in a well-greased or nonstick spray-coated 8½- by 4½-inch loaf pan. Smooth the top of the dough as much as possible. (This may require using an oiled spoon, as the dough is sticky and rubbery.)

Cover pans and let rest in a warm place for 20 minutes. When ready to bake, place the pans in a cold oven and set to 200 to 250 degrees for 10 minutes. Then raise the oven temperature to 350 degrees, and bake for an additional 40 minutes. Test for doneness by slipping the loaves from the pans and thumping your finger on the bottom surface of the bread. The bread should sound hollow. If you hear a "thud" instead, return the loaves to the pans and bake for a few minutes longer. Cool for 5 to 10 minutes on a wire rack before serving.

Makes 2 small loaves.

NUTRI-STEP 1

- Decrease the salt to 1 teaspoon.
- Decrease the white flour to 2¼ cups.
- Increase the whole wheat flour to 2 cups.

COTTAGE CHEESE AND DILL BREAD

No kneading is required for this simple bread.

2 cups enriched all-purpose or unbleached white flour •
2 cups whole wheat flour •
2 packages (scant 2 tablespoons) active dry yeast
1 tablespoon instant minced onions
¾ teaspoon salt •
1 teaspoon dried dillweed
1 cup lowfat cottage cheese, at room temperature
1 cup plus 2 tablespoons hot water (120 to 130 degrees F.)
2 tablespoons honey

Combine the white and whole wheat flours in a medium-sized bowl, and stir until well blended.

In a large bowl, combine 1 cup of this flour mixture with the yeast, onions, salt, and dillweed. Add the cottage cheese, water, and honey to the flour-yeast mixture. Beat for 3 minutes on medium speed with an electric mixer. Add about 1 cup more of the flour mixture, and beat for an additional 2 minutes. (If the dough seems too stiff to beat, add an additional tablespoon of water.)

Use your hands to work in the remaining flour until thoroughly incorporated into the dough. Cover the dough with a clean dish towel and let rise in a warm place until double in bulk (about 1 hour). Punch down the dough. Divide equally and shape with your hands into 2 loaves. Place each loaf in a well-greased 9- by 5-inch loaf pan. Cover with a dish towel and let rise in a warm place until double again (about 30 minutes). Bake in a preheated 375-degree oven for about 30 minutes, or until the bread sounds hollow when thumped on the bottom. If you hear a"thud" instead, bake a few minutes longer. Although the bread is delicious hot, it cuts better when cold.

Makes 2 loaves.

NUTRI-STEP 1

- Decrease the white flour to 1½ cups.
- Increase the whole wheat flour to 2½ cups.
- Decrease the salt to ½ teaspoon.

RUSSIAN BLACK BREAD

As its name suggests, this is a dark, richly colored bread that originated in Russia. It's similar in appearance to pumpernickel, but the flavor is deliciously different and distinctive. Even those who normally prefer pale, refined white flour loaves often get hooked on this wonderfully robust (and incredibly healthful) bread.

First Kneading
1 packet (scant 1 tablespoon) active dry yeast
1½ cups very warm water (110 to 115 degrees F.)
1 cup white bread flour or use enriched unbleached white flour
2½ cups whole wheat flour

Second Kneading
1¼ cups old-fashioned or quick-cooking rolled oats
1 cup rye flour
1 cup whole wheat flour
⅔ cup unprocessed bran (if unavailable, substitute 100-percent bran cereal)
¼ cup wheat germ
1 cup warm water (80 to 90 degrees F.)
1¼ teaspoons salt •
Scant ½ cup dark molasses

⅓ to 1   **cup (approximate) enriched all-purpose or unbleached white flour •**

½ to ⅔   **cup rolled oats (preferably the old-fashioned type) for spreading on the baking sheet**

For the first kneading, sprinkle the yeast over very warm water in a large bowl. Let stand for 5 minutes; then stir until the yeast dissolves. Beat the bread flour and 2 cups whole wheat flour into the yeast mixture with a large spoon until well blended. With your hands, knead in the bowl, gradually working the remaining ½ cup whole wheat flour into the mixture. Vigorously knead in the bowl for 3 to 4 minutes longer, or until the dough seems very elastic and slightly rubbery. Let the dough rest for 5 minutes.

For the second kneading, add rolled oats, rye flour, whole wheat flour, bran, and wheat germ to the bowl with the dough.

Stir together the warm water, salt, and molasses until thoroughly blended. Pour the liquid over the dough and dry ingredients. Stir with a large spoon to mix.

Begin working the liquid and dry ingredients into the dough by kneading in the bowl. The mixture will be sticky at first, but will become more cohesive after several minutes. Continue kneading until the liquid and dry ingredients are thoroughly and evenly incorporated into the dough mass, about 4 to 5 minutes longer.

Gradually knead enough additional white flour into the mixture to produce a firm and cohesive but not dry dough. Cover the bowl with a clean damp cloth and set aside in a warm, draft-free spot. Let the dough rise for 1 hour. Generously sprinkle a large baking sheet with rolled oats. Punch the dough down, divide in half, and shape each portion into a ball. Center each ball on one half of the baking sheet, and place directly on the rolled oats. Set the baking sheet aside in a warm draft-free spot and let the dough balls rise, uncovered, for 50 to 55 minutes, or until they are each about 8 to 8½ inches in diameter.

Bake in a preheated 375-degree oven for 30 minutes. Lower the oven temperature to 350 and bake for 20 to 25 minutes longer, or until the loaves are browned and sound hollow when tapped lightly. Remove the baking sheet from the oven and let stand for 5 minutes. Then loosen the loaves with a spatula and transfer them to racks to cool. Let cool thoroughly before serving. The black bread may be wrapped and frozen for later use, if desired.

Makes 2 large loaves.

NUTRI-STEP 1

Second Kneading
- Decrease the salt to ¾ teaspoon.
- Omit the white flour and SUBSTITUTE ⅓ to 1 cup whole wheat flour in the final stage of kneading. Knead in the whole wheat flour in the same manner described for the white flour.

CHEESY SESAME BUBBLE LOAF

At first glance, this baked bread appears to be a solid, round loaf with an attractive crown of sesame-coated "bubbles." But closer inspection reveals it is actually many small "rolls" which have been baked together. This makes the loaf easy (and fun) to serve at a buffet meal: The rolls can be simply plucked apart from each other.

Although sesame seeds are naturally rich in oil, the tiny whole seeds contribute little fat to the diet because they are not easily broken down and digested. And they do add a delightful flavor and crunch to this bread! In fact, the delicious combination of sesame and Parmesan makes the whole wheat in this loaf hardly noticeable. What's more, you probably won't need to spread it with extra butter because the topping gives it such a wonderfully rich taste.

Dough
2 to 2¾	cups white bread flour or enriched unbleached white flour ●
1½	cups whole wheat flour ●
2	tablespoons sugar ●
1¼	teaspoons salt ●
1	packet (scant 1 tablespoon) active dry yeast
1¼	cups lowfat or skim milk ●
2½	tablespoons butter or margarine ●
1	large egg (or 2 large egg whites) ●

Topping
2	tablespoons butter or margarine, melted ●
2	tablespoons grated Parmesan cheese ●
1½ to 2	tablespoons sesame seeds

In a large mixing bowl, combine 1 cup of the white flour, 1 cup of the whole wheat flour, the sugar, salt, and yeast.

In a small saucepan, heat the milk with the butter until the milk is hot to the touch (120 to 130 degrees F.). The butter does not have to melt. Add the liquid mixture to the flour-yeast mixture, along with the egg. Then beat at medium speed with an electric mixer for 2 minutes.

By hand or with a heavy-duty mixer, mix in the remaining whole wheat flour. Then stir in just enough of the remaining white flour to form a stiff but sticky dough. Cover the bowl loosely, and let the dough rest for 15 minutes (so that the flour can absorb some of the moisture and become less sticky during kneading).

Turn the dough out onto a lightly floured surface, and knead it for 8 to 10 minutes, or until it is smooth and elastic, adding more flour if needed. Place the dough in a lightly oiled bowl, and turn so that all the surfaces are oiled. Cover loosely with plastic wrap topped with a dish towel, and let rise in a warm place (such as a turned-off oven) until doubled in bulk, about 1 hour.

Punch the dough down, and knead it a few times. Use a knife or kitchen shears (or your fingers) to divide the dough into about 40 walnut-sized "balls." Grease (or spray with nonstick vegetable coating) a 9-inch tube pan, a 9-cup Bundt pan, or a 2-quart casserole. Place a layer of balls in the bottom so that they are very loosely packed (to allow room for expansion during rising and baking).

For the "topping," lightly brush the balls in the pan with some of the melted butter. Then sprinkle with some of the grated cheese and seeds. Repeat the layers until all the dough balls and topping ingredients have been used, making sure the top layer is sprinkled with some cheese and seeds.

Cover the pan loosely with plastic wrap topped with a dish towel, and let rise in a warm place until doubled in bulk, about 40 minutes to 1 hour. Bake in a preheated 375-degree oven for about 30 to 40 minutes, or until the bottom or side of the loaf sounds hollow when tapped. (If the top browns too quickly, cover it loosely with a piece of aluminum foil.) Remove the loaf from the pan and cool completely on a wire rack.

Makes 1 very large loaf.

Note: This may be baked in 2 loaf pans, if desired.

NUTRI-STEP 1

Dough
- Decrease the white flour to 1½ to 2¼ cups.
- Increase the whole wheat flour to 2 cups.
- Decrease the sugar to 1½ tablespoons.
- Decrease the salt to 1 teaspoon.
- Omit the lowfat milk and USE skim milk. (If desired, SUBSTITUTE ½ cup instant nonfat dry milk powder plus scant 1¼ cups water. Mix the milk powder with the flour, and heat the water with butter or margarine.)
- Decrease the butter or margarine to 2 tablespoons.
- Omit the large egg and USE 2 large egg whites.

Topping
- Decrease the butter or margarine to 1½ tablespoons.
- Decrease the Parmesan cheese to 1½ tablespoons.

GOLDEN-YELLOW CORN BREAD

1   cup yellow cornmeal •
1   cup enriched all-purpose or unbleached white flour •
3   tablespoons sugar •
1   tablespoon baking powder
⅓   cup nonfat dry milk powder
¼   teaspoon salt •
3   tablespoons soft butter or margarine
1   cup water
2   egg whites, slightly beaten

Combine the cornmeal, flour, sugar, baking powder, milk powder, and salt in a medium-sized bowl. Cut in the butter.

Mix the water and egg whites, and add to the dry ingredients with a few swift strokes. Bake in a greased 9-inch-square pan in a preheated 425-degree oven for 20 to 25 minutes. This tastes best served hot.

Makes 9 squares.

NUTRI-STEP 1

- Increase the cornmeal to 1¼ cups.
- Decrease the white flour to ¾ cup.
- Decrease the sugar to 2 tablespoons.
- Decrease the salt to ⅛ teaspoon.

CHEWY RYE BREAD STICKS

These soft bread sticks are fun to make. They are wonderful on a buffet table or as a highlight for any meal. Coat some with each of the seed toppings suggested below to make them look especially appealing and provide variety. (By the way, dark rye flour is a whole grain flour, just like whole wheat, and thus contains all the nutrients of the rye kernel.)

Bread Sticks
1   packet (scant 1 tablespoon) active dry yeast
1¼   cups very warm water (105 to 115 degrees F.)
1   tablespoon light or dark molasses
2½   tablespoons sugar •

½	teaspoon salt
3	tablespoons butter or margarine, softened •
2	cups rye flour (use "dark," if available)
1½ to 2½	cups white bread flour or enriched unbleached white flour

Glaze and Topping
1	large egg •
½	teaspoon water
	Caraway seeds, poppy seeds, and/or sesame seeds

In a large mixing bowl, combine the yeast, water, and molasses. Stir until the yeast is dissolved; then add the sugar, salt, and butter. Stir in the rye flour and then beat with a mixer or by hand until smooth. By hand (or with a heavy-duty mixer), stir in enough white flour to make a stiff dough. Turn the dough out onto a lightly floured board. Cover loosely with plastic wrap and let rest for about 10 minutes. Then knead until smooth and elastic, about 8 to 10 minutes.

Put the dough in an oiled bowl, turning so that all sides are greased. Cover the bowl loosely with plastic wrap topped with a dish towel, and let the dough rise in a warm place (such as a turned-off oven) until doubled in bulk, about 1 hour.

Punch the dough down, and knead once or twice. Divide the dough into fourths, then divide each fourth into six equal pieces. Roll each piece into a 6-inch-long rope. Place ropes about 2 inches apart on lightly greased or nonstick spray-coated baking sheets. Cover loosely with plastic wrap and let rise until doubled, about 30 minutes.

For the glaze, beat the egg and water together. Brush the glaze gently on top of the dough strips, being careful not to let it puddle on the sides, or the finished bread sticks may stick to the pan. (You will need only part of the glaze mixture; discard any you do not use.) Sprinkle each dough strip lightly with your choice of seeds for a topping.

Bake in a preheated 400-degree oven for 15 to 20 minutes, or until the bottom of a bread stick sounds hollow when tapped. Remove to wire racks to cool completely. Wrap airtight, and store at room temperature. (May be frozen if desired.)

Makes 24 bread sticks.

NUTRI-STEP 1

Bread Sticks
- Decrease the sugar to 2 tablespoons.
- Decrease the butter or margarine to 2 tablespoons.

Glaze and Topping
- Omit the large egg and SUBSTITUTE 1 large egg white. Beat with the water as directed.

BUTTERMILK BISCUITS

These are an old standby of ours. It was gratifying to discover just how much fat we could remove and still produce biscuits with traditional good taste.

2   cups enriched all-purpose or unbleached white flour ●■
2   teaspoons baking powder
1   teaspoon baking soda
¼   teaspoon salt ●■
3   tablespoons cold butter or margarine ●■
     About ⅔ cup commercial buttermilk

Combine the flour, baking powder, soda, and salt in a medium-sized bowl. Stir until well mixed. Cut the butter into the dry ingredients with a fork or pastry blender (or work in with your fingertips), until the mixture resembles coarse meal. Pour a generous three fourths of the buttermilk into the dry mixture and stir with a fork to blend. Stir in enough more buttermilk, a bit at a time, for the particles to hold together, but do not over-moisten. The mixture will seem crumbly at first, but it will become cohesive and smooth. With your hands, knead the dough 9 or 10 times in the bowl.

Place the dough on a sheet of wax paper. Lay another sheet of wax paper on top of the dough, and press or roll out to a thickness of ½ inch. Carefully peel off the top sheet. Cut out the biscuits with a 2-inch or similar round cutter. Transfer the biscuits to an ungreased baking pan.(For soft biscuits, arrange the rounds so they are touching; for crisper biscuits, space about ½ inch apart.) Combine the scraps, re-roll, and cut out additional biscuits. Transfer to the baking pan. Bake in a pre-heated 425-degree oven for 13 to 14 minutes, or until the biscuits are lightly browned and puffy. Biscuits are at their best served hot from the oven.

Makes about 12 (2½-inch) biscuits.

NUTRI-STEP 1

- Decrease the white flour to 1⅔ cups. *And add* ⅓ cup whole wheat flour.
- Decrease the salt to ⅛ teaspoon.
- Decrease the butter or margarine to 2½ tablespoons.

NUTRI-STEP 2

■ Decrease the white flour to 1⅓ cups. *And add* ⅔ cup whole wheat flour.
■ Decrease the salt to ⅛ teaspoon.
■ Decrease the butter or margarine to 2½ tablespoons.

PEAR–BRAN MUFFINS

The combination of naturally sweet, ripe pears, bran, and whole wheat flour makes these muffins a perfect high-fiber addition to a nutritious breakfast or a "brown bag" lunch.

¼   cup butter or margarine, melted ■
⅓   cup packed dark brown sugar ■
1   large egg (or 2 large egg whites) ●■
1   cup commercial buttermilk
1¼ cups enriched all-purpose or unbleached white flour ●■
½   cup whole wheat flour ●■
¼   cup unprocessed bran ●■
¼   teaspoon ground cinnamon ●■
¼   teaspoon ground nutmeg ●■
¼   teaspoon ground ginger
1   teaspoon baking powder
½   teaspoon baking soda
1   large, fully-ripened pear, peeled and finely chopped (about 1 cup) ●■
¼   cup raisins (optional)

In a medium-sized bowl, mix together the melted butter, brown sugar, and egg. Then mix in the buttermilk.

In a separate bowl, mix together the flours, bran, cinnamon, nutmeg, ginger, baking powder, and baking soda. Add to the egg-milk mixture, stirring only until the ingredients are completely moistened. (The batter will be thick.) Stir in the chopped pear and raisins.

Divide the mixture evenly among 12 paper-lined muffin cups. Bake in a pre-heated 375-degree oven for about 18 to 20 minutes, or until golden brown. Cool slightly before serving. Serve warm or at room temperature. (The muffins may stick slightly to the paper.)

Makes 12 muffins.

NUTRI-STEP 1

- Omit the large egg and USE 2 large egg whites.
- Decrease the white flour to 1 cup.
- Increase the whole wheat flour to ⅔ cup.
- Increase the bran to ⅓ cup.
- Increase the cinnamon to a generous ¼ teaspoon.
- Increase the nutmeg to a generous ¼ teaspoon.
- Leave the pear unpeeled.

NUTRI-STEP 2

- Decrease the butter or margarine to 3 tablespoons.
- Decrease the brown sugar to ¼ cup.
- Omit the large egg and USE 2 large egg whites.
- Decrease the white flour to ¾ cup.
- Increase the whole wheat flour to ¾ cup.
- Increase the bran to ½ cup.
- Increase the cinnamon to ½ teaspoon.
- Increase the nutmeg to ½ teaspoon.
- Leave the pear unpeeled.

ORANGE–DATE–CARROT MUFFINS

The orange-carrot combination makes these tasty muffins rich in both vitamins A and C. They are also very low in fat.

1	cup enriched all-purpose or unbleached white flour ●
⅔	cup whole wheat flour ●
¼	cup instant nonfat dry milk powder
1	teaspoon baking soda
1	teaspoon baking powder
⅛	teaspoon ground cinnamon
⅛	teaspoon ground mace
1	small, well-washed thin-skinned juice orange, seeded and cut into eighths
1	medium-sized carrot, cut into 1-inch pieces
	Scant ½ cup sugar ●
1½	tablespoons vegetable oil ●
½	cup water
1	egg white
1	teaspoon vanilla extract
⅓	cup very coarsely chopped pitted dates

Combine the flours, milk powder, baking soda, baking powder, cinnamon, and mace in a medium-sized bowl. Stir until thoroughly mixed and set aside.

Place all the remaining ingredients except the dates in a blender container or food processor bowl. Blend on medium speed or process for 30 seconds. Scrape down the container sides or processor bowl, and blend or process for 1 minute longer, or until the mixture is completely puréed and smooth.

With the blender or processor motor running, add the dates to the puréed mixture. Process for about 15 seconds, or until the dates are finely chopped. Pour the puréed mixture into the dry ingredients and stir lightly to just mix.

Lightly oil 12 medium-sized muffin tins, or fit with paper liners. Divide the mixture evenly among the cups. Bake in a preheated 400-degree oven for 20 to 25 minutes, or until the muffins are nicely browned and the tops are springy to the touch. Serve warm or at room temperature.

Makes 12 muffins.

NUTRI-STEP 1

- Decrease the white flour to ⅔ cup.
- Increase the whole wheat flour to 1 cup.
- Decrease the sugar to ⅓ cup.
- Decrease the vegetable oil to 1 tablespoon.

"BUFFINS"

These quick breads are a cross between a biscuit and a muffin—thus the whimsical name. The batter should be made just before using as it tends to stiffen up on sitting.

1½   cups enriched all-purpose or unbleached white flour ●■
½   cup whole wheat flour ●■
1   tablespoon baking powder
⅛   teaspoon salt ■
3   tablespoons butter or margarine, at room temperature ●■
1   cup lowfat or skim milk ■

In a medium-sized bowl, combine the flours, baking powder, and salt. Cut in the butter with a fork, pastry cutter, or your fingertips. Stir in the milk until just mixed. Drop the batter into greased muffin tins—filling each about three-fourths full. Bake in a preheated 450-degree oven for 10 to 12 minutes.

Makes 12 to 15 buffins.

NUTRI-STEP 1

- Decrease the white flour to 1¼ cups.
- Increase the whole wheat flour to ¾ cup.
- Decrease the butter or margarine to 2 tablespoons.

NUTRI-STEP 2

- Decrease the white flour to 1 cup.
- Increase the whole wheat flour to 1 cup.
- Omit the salt.
- Decrease the butter or margarine to 2 tablespoons.
- Omit the lowfat milk and SUBSTITUTE skim milk or ⅓ cup nonfat dry milk powder and a scant 1 cup water. Add the milk powder with the dry ingredients. Add the water after cutting in the butter or margarine.

BLUEBERRY MUFFINS

1	large egg (or two large egg whites) •
½	cup water
3	tablespoons vegetable oil •
1½	cups enriched all-purpose or unbleached white flour •
⅓	cup sugar •
¼	cup instant nonfat dry milk powder
2	teaspoons baking powder
¼	teaspoon salt •
1	cup fresh or dry packed (unsweetened) frozen blueberries

In a medium-sized bowl, beat the egg with a fork. Stir in the water and oil.

In a separate bowl, stir together the flour, sugar, milk powder, baking powder, and salt until well mixed.

Add the dry ingredients to the egg mixture and stir with a fork just until the flour is moistened. (The batter should be slightly lumpy.) Gently stir in the blueberries. Spoon into lightly greased or nonstick spray-coated muffin cups or use paper liners. Fill the muffin cups about two-thirds full.

Bake in a preheated 400-degree oven for about 20 minutes, or until golden brown. Remove immediately to a wire rack. If muffins are difficult to remove from the tins, loosen with a large spoon. If paper liners have been used, cool slightly before removing.

Makes about 12 muffins.

NUTRI-STEP 1

- Omit the whole egg and USE 2 large egg whites.
- Decrease the vegetable oil to 2 tablespoons.
- Decrease the white flour to 1 cup. *And add* ½ cup whole wheat flour.
- Decrease the sugar to ¼ cup.
- Decrease the salt to ⅛ teaspoon.

NUT-TOPPED COFFEE RING

Cake
5   tablespoons butter or margarine ●■
¾   cup sugar
1   cup plain lowfat yogurt
½   teaspoon vanilla extract ■
1½   cups enriched all-purpose or unbleached white flour ●■
½   cup whole wheat flour ●■
1   teaspoon baking powder
1   teaspoon baking soda
    Pinch of cream of tartar
4   egg whites, at room temperature

Topping
3   tablespoons sugar
¼   cup chopped walnuts ■

In a medium-sized mixing bowl, cream the butter and sugar with an electric mixer on medium speed. Beat in the yogurt and vanilla.

Combine the flours, baking powder, and baking soda in a small bowl, and mix well. Gradually beat them into the creamed mixture.

In a small deep bowl, combine the cream of tartar with the egg whites. Beat on high speed with clean beaters just until soft peaks form.

By hand, gently but thoroughly fold the beaten egg whites into the batter. Spread in a lightly greased, 8-inch tube pan.

In a small bowl, stir the topping ingredients together. Sprinkle the topping mixture over the batter. Bake in a preheated 350-degree oven for 40 to 45 minutes, or until a wooden toothpick inserted in the thickest part of the coffee ring comes out clean. Cool on a wire rack for 10 minutes. Loosen from the pan sides with a knife before removing.

Makes about 8 servings.

NUTRI-STEP 1

- Decrease the butter or margarine to ¼ cup.
- Decrease the white flour to 1 cup.
- Increase the whole wheat flour to 1 cup.

NUTRI-STEP 2

- Decrease the butter or margarine to ¼ cup.
- Increase the vanilla to ¾ teaspoon.
- Decrease the white flour to ¾ cup.
- Increase the whole wheat flour to 1 cup. *And add* ¼ cup soy flour along with the whole wheat flour.

Topping
- Decrease the chopped walnuts to 3 tablespoons.

CRANBERRY–ORANGE BREAD

1   cup enriched all-purpose or unbleached white flour •
1   cup whole wheat flour •
¼   teaspoon salt •
½   teaspoon baking soda
1   cup orange juice
2   tablespoons vegetable oil
¾   cup sugar •
1   large egg (or 2 large egg whites) •
     Grated peel of 1 small orange
1   cup cranberries, washed, sorted, and coarsely ground or finely chopped
¼   cup chopped walnuts or pecans (optional) •

Grease a 9- by 5-inch loaf pan or coat with nonstick vegetable spray. Cut a piece of wax paper to fit the bottom of the pan and press it into place. Set aside.

Combine the flours, salt, and baking soda. Stir to mix well. Set aside.

In a large bowl, combine the orange juice and oil. Beat in the sugar and then the egg with an electric mixer on medium speed. Add the dry ingredients and beat into the batter. By hand, with a large spoon, stir the grated orange peel, cranberries, and chopped nuts into the batter. Pour the batter into the prepared pan. Bake in a preheated 325-degree oven for 60 to 65 minutes, or until a toothpick inserted in the center of the loaf comes out clean. Cool slightly on a wire rack. Loosen the sides

of the loaf with a narrow metal spatula, and turn the pan upside down on a rack to remove the bread. Peel the wax paper from the bottom, then turn the bread right side up. Cool well before slicing. Store well wrapped in the refrigerator.
Makes 1 loaf.

NUTRI-STEP 1

- Decrease the white flour to ¾ cup.
- Increase the whole wheat flour to 1¼ cups.
- Omit the salt.
- Decrease the sugar to ⅔ cup.
- Omit the large egg and USE 2 large egg whites.
- Omit the chopped nuts.

APRICOT BREAD

This makes an attractive, well-flavored, yet not-too-sweet loaf. The recipe includes carrot, which enhances the taste and contributes carotene.

¾ cup coarsely chopped dried apricots
1 large carrot, very finely chopped or grated
½ cup orange juice
1½ cups enriched all-purpose or unbleached white flour ■
1 cup whole wheat flour ■
1½ teaspoons baking powder
½ teaspoon baking soda
3 tablespoons butter or margarine ●■
   Generous ¾ cup packed light brown sugar ●■
1 large egg ●■
1 teaspoon vanilla extract ■
¼ teaspoon almond extract
1¼ cups buttermilk, or 1 cup skim milk soured with 1 tablespoon vinegar

Combine the apricots, carrot, and orange juice in a small saucepan. Stir and bring to a simmer over medium heat. Simmer, stirring constantly, for 5 minutes. Remove from the heat and set aside to cool.

Combine the flours, baking powder, and soda and stir until well mixed. Set aside.

In a medium-sized mixing bowl, with the mixer on medium speed, lightly beat together the butter, brown sugar, egg, and flavorings. Gradually add the dry ingredients, alternating with the buttermilk. Beat after each addition until the mixture is smooth and well blended. Then stir the apricot-carrot mixture into the batter with a large spoon. Pour into a lightly greased 9- by 5-inch loaf pan, spreading the batter out to the pan edges with a spoon.

Bake in a preheated 350-degree oven for 50 to 55 minutes, or until the top springs back when touched and is golden brown. If the top begins to brown too rapidly, lower the oven temperature to 325 degrees for the last 20 minutes of baking time. Remove the pan to a rack, and cool for 10 minutes. Remove the loaf from the pan. Apricot bread can be served warm or cold.

Makes 1 large loaf.

NUTRI-STEP 1

- Decrease the butter or margarine to 2 tablespoons.
- Decrease the brown sugar to a generous ⅔ cup.
- Omit the large egg and SUBSTITUTE 2 large egg whites.

NUTRI-STEP 2

- Decrease the white flour to 1¼ cups.
- Increase the whole wheat flour to 1¼ cups.
- Decrease the butter or margarine to 2 tablespoons.
- Decrease the brown sugar to a generous ⅔ cup.
- Omit the large egg and SUBSTITUTE 2 large egg whites.
- Increase the vanilla extract to 1¼ teaspoons.

PUMPKIN BREAD

¼   cup vegetable oil •
¾   cup sugar •
2   large eggs (or 1 large egg plus two large egg whites), well beaten •
1   teaspoon vanilla extract
1   cup canned solid-pack pumpkin (not pumpkin pie filling) or thawed frozen winter squash purée
1   cup enriched all-purpose or unbleached white flour
⅔   cup whole wheat flour
1   teaspoon baking powder
1   teaspoon baking soda
¼   teaspoon salt •
1   teaspoon ground cinnamon •
½   teaspoon ground nutmeg
½   teaspoon ground allspice
⅔   cup raisins

Lightly grease a 9- by 5-inch loaf pan or coat with nonstick vegetable spray. Cut a piece of wax paper to fit the bottom of the pan and press it into place. Set aside.

Combine the vegetable oil, sugar, eggs, vanilla extract, and pumpkin in a large bowl. Beat with an electric mixer on medium speed until well blended.

Combine the flours, baking powder, baking soda, salt, and spices in a separate medium-sized bowl and stir until blended. Gradually add the dry ingredients to the pumpkin mixture, beating with an electric mixer. Fold the raisins into the batter with a spoon. Spoon the batter into the prepared pan. Bake in a preheated 350-degree oven for 60 to 65 minutes, or until a toothpick inserted in the center comes out clean. Cool slightly on a wire rack. Then loosen the sides of the loaf from the pan with a narrow spatula. Turn the pan upside down on a wire rack to remove the bread. Peel the wax paper from the bottom. Cool completely on a wire rack. Store well wrapped in the refrigerator.

Makes 1 loaf.

Note: This bread slices best when chilled.

NUTRI-STEP 1

- Decrease the vegetable oil to 3 tablespoons.
- Decrease the sugar to ⅔ cup.
- Omit the whole eggs and USE 1 large egg plus 2 large egg whites.
- Decrease the salt to ⅛ teaspoon or omit.
- Increase the cinnamon to 1¼ teaspoons.

FAVORITE BLUEBERRY BUTTERMILK PANCAKES

Although blueberries make these pancakes extra-special, the following recipe can also be used to prepare plain buttermilk pancakes. Just omit the blueberries and proceed with the rest of the directions.

¾   cup Enriched Buttermilk Pancake Mix (page 287)
1   large egg white
1   tablespoon vegetable oil
    Scant 1 cup buttermilk (approximate)
½   cup fresh or fresh-frozen ("dry-pack") unsweetened blueberries

In a small deep bowl, stir together the pancake mix, egg white, oil, and enough buttermilk to yield a fairly thin batter. Add the blueberries and stir until just mixed.

Oil a heavy griddle or skillet and place over medium heat until very hot. Check the griddle for correct temperature by cooking a small test pancake; it should cook to a dark golden brown (but not burn) and lift from the surface neatly after 35 to 40 seconds on the pan.

Form each pancake by spooning about 2½ tablespoons of batter onto the griddle. Cook the pancakes for about 30 seconds. Then, to prevent sticking, with a spatula (pancake turner) loosen from surface, but DO NOT turn over, and continue cooking on the first side about 45 seconds longer. Turn over and cook for about 1½ minutes longer or until lightly puffed and cooked through. (If necessary, re-oil the griddle or skillet by brushing it lightly with a paper towel that has been moistened with oil.)

Makes 12 to 15 medium-sized pancakes.

Note: The Nutri-Step is part of the recipe for Enriched Buttermilk Pancake Mix.

GOOD-AND-HEARTY PANCAKES

1	cup enriched all-purpose or unbleached white flour ∎
½	cup whole wheat flour
½	cup cornmeal
⅛	teaspoon salt ●∎
4	teaspoons baking powder
⅛	teaspoon ground nutmeg
1	tablespoon sugar
½	cup instant nonfat dry milk powder
1	large egg plus 1 large egg white ●∎
3	tablespoons vegetable oil, melted butter, or melted margarine
1¼ to 1¾	cups water

In a large bowl, stir the dry ingredients (including the milk powder) together until well mixed. With a wire whisk or large spoon, beat in the whole egg, egg white, oil, and enough water to yield a smooth creamy batter. (For puffy pancakes, make a thick batter. For crisper pancakes, make the batter thinner.) Ladle the mixture onto a hot, lightly oiled griddle, and cook until bubbles begin to form along the edges and the bottom is browned. Turn and brown on the other side.

Makes 12 to 15 3½- to 4½-inch pancakes.

NUTRI-STEP 1

- Omit the salt.
- Omit the whole egg plus 1 egg white and SUBSTITUTE 3 large egg whites.

NUTRI-STEP 2

- Decrease the white flour to ½ cup. *And add* ½ cup soy flour.
- Omit the salt.
- Omit the whole egg plus 1 egg white and SUBSTITUTE 3 large egg whites.

Chapter 15

Desserts

Even though we are health-conscious cooks, our families still want desserts, at least occasionally. Our solution is to be very selective about the sweet treats offered. We try to make them as wholesome as possible, but still yummy enough to satisfy every sweet tooth in the house.

This chapter features a host of appealing recipes—from frozen lemon mousse, mixed-fruit sherbet, and creamy cheesecake to old-fashioned molasses cookies and apple crisp—that fill the bill. All are designed to meet any dessert-lover's expectations. Yet, we've also kept nutritional considerations in mind. For example, in many recipes we've reduced refined sugar (and increased vitamin and mineral content) by relying primarily on the natural sweetness of fruits. Where appropriate, we've boosted fiber by calling for whole wheat flour, rolled oats, or even bran, and also by suggesting that you leave fruit unpeeled. And in almost all the recipes we've eliminated salt by compensating with spices and other flavor enhancers.

Perhaps even more important, however, are the measures we've taken to cut down fat. For instance, we use cocoa powder in almost all our chocolate desserts, rather than baking chocolate—which has much more fat. We add moistness to our cakes with buttermilk, fruit, or honey, instead of sour cream and extra butter. And in a variety of dishes, we depend on evaporated skimmed milk, whipped nonfat dry milk, or beaten egg whites rather than whipped cream to provide smooth texture and lightness. We've even included several special pie shell recipes which are much lower in fat than conventional versions. One is for a tender pastry crust with only a quarter cup of oil; another is for a meringue crust that's completely fat-free.

FROZEN LEMON MOUSSE

Incredible as it seems, evaporated milk can be whipped to triple its original volume under the right circumstances. (Interestingly, heavy cream only doubles in volume when beaten.) The following light and airy, tangy mousse takes great advantage of whipped evaporated milk. In fact, it's hard to believe this wonderful dessert contains no fat-laden cream at all!

1	13-ounce can regular evaporated milk •
	About 2 tablespoons freshly grated lemon peel (colored part only), divided
½	cup fresh lemon juice (from 3 to 4 lemons)
2	tablespoons water
1	packet unflavored gelatin
¾	cup sugar •

Pour the milk into an ice cube tray or baking pan (or a very large mixing bowl, if it will fit in your freezer), and freeze for a few hours, stirring occasionally, until just crystallized but not frozen solid.

Meanwhile, grate peel from lemons, and then squeeze out the juice. Set aside.

When the milk has partially frozen to the desired consistency, put the water into a small, heatproof metal or glass cup, and sprinkle the gelatin on top. Put the cup in a small skillet or saucepan which contains simmering water about ¾ inch deep. Gently heat the gelatin mixture until it is clear and the gelatin is dissolved. Remove from the heat, and cool to tepid.

If the milk is in a tray or pan, transfer it to a large mixing bowl, breaking up any frozen chunks. (If the milk is already in a mixing bowl, just loosen it from the sides with a spoon.) Beat the milk with an electric mixer at high speed until very frothy and doubled in volume. Slowly add the lemon juice while beating. Then gradually add the sugar, 1½ tablespoons of the grated lemon peel (reserving about ½ tablespoon for garnish), and the dissolved gelatin. Continue beating until the milk triples in volume and is very light and fluffy.

Spoon the mixture into individual cups, parfait glasses, or one large serving bowl. Or, use a 1½-quart soufflé dish that has been fitted with a wax-paper collar to temporarily make the sides about 2 inches higher. (A piece of tape, a paper clip, or a rubber band can be used to secure the collar in place around the perimeter of the dish.) Use the reserved grated lemon peel to garnish the top of the mousse. Freeze the uncovered mousse until it is solid. (If the mousse is stored in the freezer for more than 3 or 4 hours, cover well after it has completely frozen, to prevent crystal formation on the surface.)

Before serving, let the mousse soften slightly in the refrigerator, and remove the wax-paper collar if one was used.

Makes about 8 servings.

NUTRI-STEP 1

- Omit the regular evaporated milk and SUBSTITUTE 1 13-ounce can evaporated skimmed milk.
- Decrease the sugar to ½ cup plus 2 tablespoons.

MAGIC ORANGE–BANANA MOUSSE

This mousse is "magic" for two reasons. First, it takes only five minutes for preparation and is ready to eat in less than half an hour after that. Second, it is so rich and creamy tasting that no one will believe it's really low in fat and calories. When it is garnished with fresh orange slices, and perhaps our Don't-Tell-'Em-It's-Good-for-'Em Whipped Topping, this mousse makes a wonderful company dessert.

2 packets unflavored gelatin
⅔ cup very hot tap water
⅓ cup sugar ●■
1 6-ounce can frozen orange juice concentrate
1 cup plain lowfat or regular yogurt ●■
¾ teaspoon vanilla extract ●■
1 medium-sized ripe banana, cut into chunks
6 standard-sized ice cubes

Garnish
1 orange, peeled and cut horizontally into 6 slices
1 cup Whipped Topping (page 296), optional

Have all the ingredients (except the garnish) ready and handy. Put the gelatin and hot water in a blender container and process until well mixed, about 15 seconds. Add the sugar and process for 30 seconds longer to mix. Add the frozen juice concentrate, yogurt, vanilla extract, and banana chunks, and process until puréed. With the machine running, add the ice cubes one at a time and process until the mixture is completely smooth, about 45 seconds. Immediately pour the mixture into one large serving bowl or about 6 individual serving dishes. Chill until firm (usually less than 30 minutes). Garnish with orange slices and, if desired, small dollops of Whipped Topping.

Makes about 6 servings.

NUTRI-STEP 1

- Decrease the sugar to ¼ cup.
- Omit the regular yogurt and USE lowfat yogurt.
- Increase the vanilla extract to 1 teaspoon.

NUTRI-STEP 2

- Decrease the sugar to 3 tablespoons.
- Omit the regular yogurt and USE lowfat yogurt.
- Increase the vanilla extract to 1 teaspoon.

PLUM SHERBET

With this recipe, it's easy to turn fresh plums into a deliciously refreshing and colorful dessert. Depending on the plum variety selected, your sherbet will range in color from a pretty pink to a radiant rose. We suggest using Red or Black Beaut, or Eldorado plums, although any full-flavored, slightly tart variety will do.

1   **pound fully ripe, tart red or black plums (about 8 medium), pitted and halved**
¼   **cup water**
1   **cup sugar** •
2   **cups well-chilled whole milk** •
    Juice of 1 large lemon

Combine the plum halves, water, and sugar in a medium-sized saucepan over medium-high heat. Bring to a boil, stirring. Then lower the heat and simmer, uncovered, for 8 to 12 minutes, or until the plum pulp and skins are tender. Transfer the cooked plums to a blender container. Blend for 1 minute on medium speed. Scrape down the sides of the container and blend for about 2 minutes longer, or until both the pulp and skins are completely puréed and the mixture is smooth. Refrigerate the puréed plum mixture for 1½ hours, or until thoroughly chilled.

Stir together the plum purée, milk, and lemon juice. Pour into the container of an ice-cream maker and process the mixture according to the manufacturer's directions. Transfer to the freezer and freeze for 1½ hours or longer, or until the sherbet is firm. (If an ice-cream maker is unavailable, divide the mixture between 2 freezer trays and chill in the coldest part of the freezer for 2½ hours, or until the sherbet is frozen but not hard. Transfer the sherbet to a medium-sized mixing bowl. Beat the mixture with an electric mixer on medium speed, until lightened and soft but not mushy. Return the mixture to the trays and freeze for 2 hours longer, or until the sherbet is firm.) The sherbet can be kept in the freezer, tightly covered, for at least a week.

Makes about 1½ quarts sherbet.

NUTRI-STEP 1

- Decrease the sugar to ⅞ cup.
- Omit the whole milk and SUBSTITUTE 2 cups lowfat milk.

MIXED-FRUIT SHERBET

It's hard to believe that this tasty, brightly-colored sherbet has almost no fat and just a small amount of honey. It makes a great company dessert, especially when served in fancy compotes or similar dishes.

1½ cups fresh or fresh-frozen ("dry pack") unsweetened raspberries, blackberries, or blueberries
2   ripe medium-sized bananas, sliced
1   cup juice-packed crushed pineapple, including juice
1   6-ounce can frozen orange juice concentrate
2½ cups commercial buttermilk or plain lowfat yogurt
¼   cup honey •

Combine all the ingredients in a food processor or blender (in batches, if necessary) and process until smooth. (Combine batches.) Pour into metal ice cube trays, which have had the dividers removed, or shallow cake pans. Freeze until firm but not solid. Break into small pieces with a spoon or fork, and return to the food processor, or place in a mixing bowl (in batches, if necessary). Process or beat with the mixer until smooth and creamy.

Spoon the mixture into individual serving dishes or one large dish and freeze, uncovered, until firm, about 4 to 5 hours or longer. (After the sherbet has frozen, it should be covered to help prevent crystal formation on the surface.) Before serving, allow the sherbet to soften slightly in the refrigerator or at room temperature. The sherbet keeps well for at least 1 week.

Makes 6 to 8 servings.

NUTRI-STEP 1

- Decrease the honey to 3 tablespoons.

STUFFED APPLES BAKED WITH HONEY

Very simple to fix, this dessert works well with almost any baking apple (except, perhaps, soft McIntoshes). Some of our personal favorites are Golden Delicious, Granny Smith, and Winesap.

4   **large or 5 medium-sized baking apples** •
2   **tablespoons raisins or dried currants**
2   **tablespoons butter or margarine** •
3   **tablespoons honey** •
¼   **cup orange juice**
1   **cup apple cider, apple juice, or orange juice**
    About ½ cup vanilla ice milk (optional)

Core each apple through the stem end, being careful not to cut all the way through the bottom. The cavity left in each apple should be about 1 inch wide at the top. Peel *only* the top third of each apple, and carefully prick the peeled part in several places with a fork. (The peel on the bottom holds the apple together during baking.) Stand the apples in an 8- to 9-inch-square or similar baking dish or pan.

Divide the raisins and butter among the apple cavities. Drizzle the honey into the cavities and all over the apples. Sprinkle the ¼ cup orange juice over the apples. Finally, pour the cider around the apples.

Bake in a preheated 375-degree oven for 40 to 50 minutes, basting occasionally, until the apples are tender but not mushy. Serve each apple in a small bowl, with some of the basting juice. If desired, place a very small scoop (about 2 tablespoons) of ice milk on top of each apple just before serving.

Makes 4 or 5 servings.

NUTRI-STEP 1

- Save the peel removed from the top part of each apple. Cut into thin strips, and add to the basting liquid before baking. Include a few strips of peel in the juice served with each apple, as a sort of garnish.
- Decrease the butter or margarine to 4 teaspoons. Use about 1 teaspoon for each apple.
- Decrease the honey to 2 tablespoons.

STRAWBERRIES ROMANOFF

This is absolutely wonderful when fresh strawberries are in season. Our version is much lower in fat and calories than the classic one.

Berries
- 4 cups sliced fresh strawberries (hulls removed)
- 3 tablespoons granulated sugar ●■
- 2 to 3 tablespoons compatible liqueur, such as kirsch or amaretto, OR orange juice

Sauce
- 1½ cups part-skim ricotta cheese (if unavailable, use regular ricotta)
- 1 tablespoon regular or lowfat milk ●●
- ½ teaspoon vanilla extract ■
- ¼ cup confectioners' sugar
- 2 tablespoons commercial sour cream ●●
- ⅓ cup regular or lowfat vanilla yogurt ●■

Garnish
About 6 perfect, whole strawberries

About 2 to 3 hours before serving, toss the sliced berries with the granulated sugar and liqueur. Cover and refrigerate, mixing occasionally.

For the sauce, use a food processor or electric mixer to beat the ricotta cheese with the milk, vanilla, and confectioners' sugar until creamy smooth and fluffy. Fold in the sour cream and vanilla yogurt by hand. Refrigerate the sauce in a covered bowl until well chilled.

To serve, divide the sliced strawberries with some of their juices into about 6 dessert cups or stemmed glasses. Top the berries with dollops of the sauce, dividing equally among the servings. Place 1 perfect strawberry on top of each serving.

Makes about 6 servings.

NUTRI-STEP 1

Berries
- Decrease the granulated sugar to 2½ tablespoons.

Sauce
- Omit the milk.
- Omit the sour cream.
- Increase the vanilla yogurt to ½ cup.

NUTRI-STEP 2

Berries
- Decrease the granulated sugar to 2 tablespoons.

Sauce
- Omit the milk.
- Increase the vanilla extract to ¾ teaspoon.
- Omit the sour cream.
- Omit the vanilla yogurt and SUBSTITUTE ½ cup plain lowfat or regular yogurt.

PEACH BROWN BETTY

2	cups cubes cut from slightly stale white bread ●■
1½	cups cubes cut from slightly stale whole wheat bread ●■
2½	cups peeled, pitted, and sliced fresh peaches (6 to 7 large)
2	teaspoons lemon juice
⅔	cup packed light brown sugar
½	teaspoon ground cinnamon
½	teaspoon vanilla extract
2	tablespoons butter or margarine, melted ●■
¼	cup orange juice

To Serve (optional)
   Vanilla lowfat yogurt or vanilla ice milk

Spread the bread cubes in an 8- or 9-inch square (or similar) baking dish. Put the pan in the oven and lightly toast the bread cubes, stirring occasionally, for 8 to 10 minutes.

Meanwhile, toss the sliced peaches together with the lemon juice, brown sugar, cinnamon, and vanilla in a medium-sized bowl. Stir the peach mixture into the bread cubes until well combined. Smooth out in an even layer. Drizzle the melted butter and then the orange juice evenly over the top.

Cover the pan tightly with foil or a lid, and bake in a preheated 375-degree oven for 30 minutes. Remove the foil and bake for 15 minutes longer, or until the mixture is bubbly and slightly crisp on top. Remove the pan to a rack and let stand for 5 minutes before serving. (If desired, peach betty can also be made ahead and rewarmed in a 275-degree oven at serving time.) Serve plain or with dollops of lowfat vanilla yogurt or vanilla ice milk.

Makes 4 to 6 servings.

NUTRI-STEP 1

- Decrease the white bread cubes to 1 cup.
- Increase the whole wheat bread cubes to 2½ cups.
- Decrease the butter or margarine to 1½ tablespoons.

NUTRI-STEP 2

- Omit the white bread cubes.
- Increase the whole wheat bread cubes to 3½ cups.
- Decrease the butter or margarine to 1 tablespoon.

APPLE CRISP

Our version of this old-fashioned dessert is higher in fiber and lower in fat and sugar than most similar recipes.

Filling
7   cups thinly sliced, peeled apples •
1   tablespoon lemon juice
2   tablespoons sugar •
1   teaspoon ground cinnamon

Topping
¾   cup quick-cooking or old-fashioned rolled oats •
¼   cup instant nonfat dry milk powder •
⅓   cup enriched all-purpose or unbleached white flour •
½   cup packed light or dark brown sugar •
1   teaspoon ground cinnamon
⅓   cup butter or margarine, softened •
⅛   teaspoon salt •

To Serve
   Milk, ice milk, or vanilla yogurt

Spread the apple slices in the bottom of a 2-quart casserole or similar baking dish. Add the lemon juice to the slices. Sprinkle the apples with sugar and cinnamon. Stir to coat the apples.

In a medium-sized bowl, combine all the topping ingredients. Blend with a fork until the mixture is crumbly and the butter is incorporated. Spread the topping over the apples. Bake in a preheated 350-degree oven for 30 minutes. Serve warm with milk or a dollop of ice milk or vanilla yogurt.

Makes about 5 servings.

NUTRI-STEP 1

Filling
- Leave the apples unpeeled.
- Decrease the sugar to 1 tablespoon.

Topping
- Increase the rolled oats to 1 cup.
- Increase the milk powder to ⅓ cup.
- Decrease the white flour to ¼ cup.
- Decrease the packed brown sugar to ⅓ cup.
- Decrease the butter or margarine to ¼ cup.
- Omit the salt.

LEMON–BERRY COFFEE CAKE

Batter

⅓ cup butter or margarine ●■
⅔ cup granulated sugar ●■
    Grated peel of 1 lemon (yellow part only)
1 large egg (or 2 large egg whites) ●■
1 cup enriched all-purpose or unbleached white flour ●■
½ cup whole wheat flour ●■
1½ teaspoons baking powder
¼ teaspoon baking soda
½ cup commercial buttermilk, or ⅓ cup skim milk mixed with 1 teaspoon lemon juice
2 cups fresh or fresh-frozen ("dry pack") unsweetened blueberries or raspberries

Lemon Glaze

1½ tablespoons butter or margarine ■
2 tablespoons packed light or dark brown sugar ●■
    Juice of 1 lemon (about 2 to 3 tablespoons) ■

In a medium-sized bowl, cream the butter with the granulated sugar. Beat in the grated lemon peel and egg.

In another bowl or on a large piece of wax paper, mix together the flours, baking powder, and baking soda.

Add the dry ingredients to the batter alternately with the buttermilk, mixing just until the ingredients are combined. (The batter will be very thick.)

Carefully stir the berries into the batter so they are evenly distributed. Then turn out the batter into a greased or nonstick spray-coated 8-inch-square pan. Bake in a preheated 350-degree oven for 40 to 45 minutes, or until a toothpick inserted in the center comes out clean.

When the cake is almost done baking, make Lemon Glaze. In a small saucepan, melt the butter and add the brown sugar. Stir until dissolved. Remove from the heat and stir in the lemon juice. When the cake is done, pour the glaze mixture over the top, spreading it evenly with a spatula. Then place the cake under a preheated broiler for about 1 minute, or until the glaze is bubbly. Cool the cake in the pan on a wire rack. Cut into squares to serve.

Makes 16 squares.

NUTRI-STEP 1

Batter
- Decrease the butter or margarine to ¼ cup.
- Decrease the granulated sugar to a generous ½ cup.
- Omit the large egg and USE 2 large egg whites.
- Decrease the white flour to ½ cup.
- Increase the whole wheat flour to 1 cup.

Lemon Glaze
- Decrease the brown sugar to 1½ tablespoons.

NUTRI-STEP 2

Batter
- Decrease the butter or margarine to ¼ cup.
- Decrease the granulated sugar to ½ cup.
- Omit the large egg and USE 2 large egg whites.
- Omit the white flour.
- Increase the whole wheat flour to 1½ cups.

Lemon Glaze
- Decrease the butter or margarine to 1 tablespoon.
- Decrease the brown sugar to 1 tablespoon.
- Decrease the lemon juice to 1½ tablespoons.

CHOCOLATE SHEET CAKE

Here's an appealing cake that's not only got plenty of chocolate flavor, but is far less fatty than most chocolate desserts. One reason is that it's made with cocoa powder, which is much lower in fat than baking chocolate. Another, of course, is that it contains only a few tablespoons of butter or margarine. (Buttermilk helps keep the cake moist.)

1½ cups white cake flour •
 ½ cup whole wheat flour •
 1 teaspoon baking soda
 ¾ teaspoon baking powder
    Generous ½ cup unsweetened cocoa powder (NOT a drink mix)
 3 egg whites, at room temperature
 ⅛ teaspoon cream of tartar
1¼ cups sugar •
 2 egg yolks
 3 tablespoons butter or margarine •
1⅛ cups commercial buttermilk
1½ teaspoons vanilla extract •
 1 recipe Glossy Chocolate Glaze (page 251), optional

Sift together the flours, baking soda, baking powder, and cocoa powder. Set aside.

Combine the egg whites and cream of tartar in a small, deep, absolutely grease-free mixing bowl. Beat until frothy with a mixer on medium speed. Raise the mixer speed to high and beat for 30 seconds. Continuing to beat the whites, gradually add about ⅓ cup of the sugar, scraping the bowl frequently. Continue beating until the whites are glossy but not dry or stiff. Set aside.

In a large mixing bowl beat the egg yolks, butter, and remaining sugar with the mixer on medium-low speed. Gradually add half the buttermilk, and beat until well blended. Raise the mixer speed to medium and gradually add half the dry ingredients. Scraping the bowl frequently, beat the batter for 1 minute. Gradually add the remaining buttermilk and vanilla, and beat for 30 seconds. Add the remaining dry ingredients and beat, scraping the bowl frequently, for 1 minute longer, or until the batter is completely smooth.

Gently but thoroughly fold the reserved beaten egg whites into the batter. Mix gently until no white streaks remain. Pour the batter into a lightly greased, flat 11 ½- by 8-inch (or slightly larger) baking pan, spreading the mixture out toward the edges with a spoon.

Bake in a preheated 350-degree oven for 35 to 40 minutes, or until the cake top is slightly springy to the touch and a wooden toothpick inserted in the center comes out clean. Transfer the pan to a rack and cool for 25 to 30 minutes. While the cake is still warm but not hot, spread the top with Glossy Chocolate Glaze, if desired. Let the cake stand until completely cold. Cut the cake into squares and serve from the pan.

Makes 12 to 15 servings.

GLOSSY CHOCOLATE GLAZE

This glaze is good on our Chocolate Sheet Cake, and can also be used to ice a Bundt or tube cake. In the latter case, simply drizzle the glaze over the top and sides of the cake.

½ cup sugar
⅓ cup unsweetened cocoa powder (NOT a drink mix)
⅓ cup lowfat or skim milk •
2 teaspoons butter or margarine •
½ teaspoon vanilla extract

Combine the sugar and cocoa powder in a small heavy saucepan and stir until thoroughly blended. Gradually stir the milk into the sugar-cocoa mixture until well mixed.

Place the saucepan over medium heat and bring to a boil, stirring constantly. Boil, stirring, for 1½ minutes. Remove the pan from the heat. Add the butter and stir until completely melted. Stir the vanilla into the glaze. Let the glaze stand for 3 to 4 minutes. Then quickly spread it over the warm but not hot cake with a knife or spatula. Let the cake stand until the glaze is cold.

Makes ½ cup of glaze.

SPICE LAYER CAKE

Remarkably like traditional old-fashioned spice cake in taste, texture, and appearance, this version contains very little fat. It is also lower in sugar than many conventional layer cakes.

2¼   cups white cake flour •
1   teaspoon baking soda
¾   teaspoon baking powder
¾   teaspoon ground cinnamon •
½   teaspoon ground nutmeg
¼   teaspoon ground cloves
¼   teaspoon ground mace
⅛   teaspoon salt
2   large eggs, separated and at room temperature
1   teaspoon lemon juice
⅛   teaspoon cream of tartar
⅓   cup granulated sugar
⅓   cup orange juice
¼   cup butter or margarine, slightly softened •
¾   cup packed light brown sugar •
¾   cup commercial buttermilk
¾   teaspoon vanilla extract •
    Frosting for a 2-layer 8-inch cake, such as Sea Foam Frosting (page 253) or your choice

Lightly grease and flour two 8-inch cake pans. Set aside.

Sift together the flour, baking soda, baking powder, spices, and salt. Set aside.

Combine the egg whites in a small, deep, absolutely grease-free mixing bowl with the lemon juice and cream of tartar. Beat until frothy with a mixer on medium speed. Add the granulated sugar to the whites a tablespoon at a time, scraping the bowl with a rubber spatula after each addition. Raise the mixer speed to high, and continue beating until the whites are glossy and form stiff, but not dry, peaks. Set aside.

In a large mixing bowl lightly beat the egg yolks and orange juice with the mixer on low speed. Add the butter and brown sugar, and continue beating until well mixed. Raise the speed to medium. Beat for 30 seconds, frequently scraping the sides of the bowl with a rubber spatula. Add half the dry ingredients and continue beating for 1 minute, scraping the bowl frequently. Gradually add the buttermilk and vanilla to the batter, and beat for 30 seconds. Add the remaining dry ingredients and beat, scraping the bowl, for 1 minute longer.

With a rubber spatula, gently fold the reserved beaten egg whites into the batter until thoroughly incorporated (but not overmixed). Divide the batter between the cake pans, smoothing out to the edges with a spoon.

Bake in a preheated 350-degree oven for 10 minutes. Lower the oven temperature to 325 degrees. Continue baking for 20 to 25 minutes, or until the cake edges are just tinged with brown and a toothpick inserted in the center comes out clean. Transfer the pans to racks and let cool 15 minutes. Loosen the cake layers with a spatula, then remove from the pans and transfer to racks to cool. Let stand until completely cooled.

Ice the cake with a favorite frosting or with our Sea Foam Frosting. Cover the iced cake and let stand until the frosting is cooled and set before serving.

Makes about 12 servings.

NUTRI-STEP 1

- Decrease the white cake flour to 1¾ cups. *And add* ½ cup whole wheat flour or whole wheat pastry flour.
- Increase the cinnamon to 1 teaspoon.
- Decrease the butter or margarine to 3 tablespoons.
- Decrease the brown sugar to ⅔ cup.
- Increase the vanilla to 1 teaspoon.

SEA FOAM FROSTING

Unlike most frostings, Sea Foam contains absolutely no fat. Nevertheless, it's silky-smooth, fluffy, and good tasting.

Our Sea Foam Frosting is much easier to make than the old-fashioned versions. The egg whites are beaten in a mixing bowl instead of in a double boiler on top of the stove.

Note: Begin preparing this icing after the cake layers are cooled. The frosting needs to be used as soon as it is prepared, and should only be placed on a cooled cake.

2	large egg whites, at room temperature
	Pinch of cream of tartar
⅔	cup packed light brown sugar •
⅓	cup light corn syrup •
3	tablespoons water
1	teaspoon vanilla extract

Put the egg whites in an absolutely grease-free small, deep mixing bowl. Beat with a mixer on medium speed until the whites are frothy. Add cream of tartar, raise the mixer speed to high, and continue to beat until firm, but not dry, peaks form. Turn off the mixer and set the egg whites aside.

In a small, heavy saucepan combine the brown sugar, corn syrup, and water. Place over medium heat and bring to a simmer, stirring. Remove the spoon, cover the pan, and cook, without stirring, for 4 minutes. Remove the lid and insert a candy thermometer into the pan. Continue cooking, uncovered and without stirring, a few minutes longer until the mixture registers 235 or 236 degrees F. on the thermometer. (Alternately, if a candy thermometer is unavailable, cook the mixture until a drop of syrup dropped into cold water forms a soft, pliable ball that loses its shape on removal.) Immediately remove the saucepan containing the syrup from the heat.

Turn the mixer on high speed and beat the reserved beaten egg whites for 30 seconds. In a slow, very thin stream, beat the cooked syrup and then the vanilla into the egg whites. Continue beating until the frosting is glossy and stiff enough to form firm peaks. Ice the cake immediately.

Makes enough frosting to generously cover 2 8-inch layers and adequately cover 2 9-inch layers.

NUTRI-STEP 1

- Decrease the brown sugar to a packed ½ cup.
- Decrease the corn syrup to ¼ cup.

LIGHT AND EASY CHEESECAKE

This remarkable cheesecake tastes wonderfully rich and creamy. Yet it contains only a third as much fat as most conventional cheesecake recipes.

Crust
⅔	cup graham cracker crumbs
1½	tablespoons slightly softened butter or margarine
1	tablespoon sugar
⅛	teaspoon freshly grated lemon peel (yellow part only)

Filling
2	cups part-skim ricotta cheese (or use regular ricotta if unavailable)
1	cup plain lowfat yogurt (drained of any liquid) ●■
	Grated peel (yellow part only) and juice of 1 small lemon
1	cup sugar ●■
2½	tablespoons enriched all-purpose or unbleached white flour ●■

1   package (8 ounces) cream cheese, at room temperature ●■
2   large eggs plus 2 large egg whites
2½ teaspoons vanilla extract ■

To prepare the crust, combine all the crust ingredients in a small deep bowl or in a food processor fitted with a chopping blade. Mix with a fork, or with on/off processor bursts, until the mixture is well blended and crumbly. Turn the mixture into an 8½- or 9-inch springform pan. Spread out evenly, extending the crumbs to the edges of the pan bottom. Press down firmly to form a smooth, well-packed bottom layer. Bake in a 350-degree oven for 15 minutes, or until the crust is crisp and lightly browned. Set aside on a rack to cool.

In a blender, or a food processor fitted with a chopping blade, combine the ricotta cheese, yogurt, lemon peel and juice, sugar, and flour. Blend on medium-high speed or process for 1½ to 2 minutes, or until the mixture is liquefied and completely smooth.

If a blender is used, set the blended ricotta mixture aside. Place the cream cheese in a medium-sized bowl. With the mixer on medium speed, beat the cream cheese until it is smooth. Then beat in whole eggs, egg whites, and vanilla. Gradually add the reserved mixture from the blender container, beating until it is thoroughly incorporated and smooth.

If a food processor is used, leave the ricotta mixture in the bowl. Cut the cream cheese into 8 pieces and, with the processor running, add them one at a time through the feed tube. Process on medium speed for 1½ minutes longer, or until thoroughly incorporated. Add the eggs and egg whites along with the vanilla, and process for 10 to 15 seconds longer, or until just blended.

Pour the cheesecake batter over the prepared graham cracker crust. Bake in a preheated 350-degree oven for 15 minutes. Lower the oven temperature to 325 degrees. Bake for 1 hour and 15 to 20 minutes longer, or until the cheesecake center is slightly puffed and seems "set" when the surface is lightly tapped. Remove to a rack and cool. Refrigerate the cake until thoroughly chilled (preferably overnight) before serving.

Makes 8 to 10 servings.

NUTRI-STEP 1

Filling
- Increase the yogurt to 1¼ cups. (Drain off any excess liquid before using.)
- Decrease the sugar to ⅞ cup.
- Increase the flour to 3 tablespoons.
- Decrease the cream cheese to 6 ounces (2 3-ounce packages).

Filling
- Increase the yogurt to 1½ cups. (Drain off any excess liquid before using.)
- Decrease the sugar to ⅞ cup.
- Increase the flour to 3½ tablespoons.
- Decrease the cream cheese to 3 ounces (1 3-ounce package).
- Increase the vanilla to 1 tablespoon.

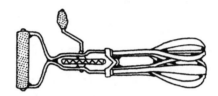

SPICY CARROT CAKE

½ cup enriched all-purpose or unbleached white flour ●■
½ cup whole wheat flour ●■
1 teaspoon baking powder
½ teaspoon baking soda
1 teaspoon ground cinnamon ■
½ cup sugar ●■
⅓ cup vegetable oil
2 large eggs (or 1 large egg plus 2 large egg whites), lightly beaten ●■
1½ cups grated carrots
½ cup juice-packed crushed pineapple, well drained
¼ cup raisins
   Confectioners' sugar for topping (optional)

Lightly grease and flour a 9-inch-square pan.

In a medium-sized bowl combine the flours, baking powder, baking soda, and cinnamon. Stir well. Add the sugar, oil, and eggs and stir vigorously until the batter is smooth. Stir in the carrots, pineapple, and raisins.

Bake in a preheated 350-degree oven for about 30 minutes, or until the top is nicely browned and a toothpick inserted in the center comes out clean. Cool thoroughly in the pan before dusting lightly with confectioners' sugar. Cut in squares to serve.

Makes 8 to 9 servings.

NUTRI-STEP 1

- Decrease the white flour to ⅓ cup.
- Increase the whole wheat flour to ⅔ cup.
- Decrease the sugar to ⅓ cup.
- Omit the 2 large eggs and USE 1 large egg plus 2 large egg whites.

NUTRI-STEP 2

- Decrease the white flour to 3 tablespoons.
- Increase the whole wheat flour to ⅔ cup. *And add* 3 tablespoons soy flour to the other flours.
- Increase the cinnamon to 1¼ teaspoons.
- Decrease the sugar to ⅓ cup.
- Omit the 2 large eggs and SUBSTITUTE 4 egg whites.

CHOCOLATE CHIPPERS

Although even we can't make good-tasting chocolate chip cookies that are really healthful, our version comes a lot closer to it than most!

- ¾ cup enriched all-purpose or unbleached white flour ■
- ¾ cup whole wheat flour ■
- ¼ teaspoon baking soda
- 6 tablespoons butter or margarine, slightly softened
- ⅓ cup light brown sugar, packed
- ¼ cup granulated sugar ●■
- 1 large egg ●■
- 1¾ teaspoons vanilla extract
- 1 tablespoon water
- 1 6-ounce package semisweet chocolate chips ●■
- ½ cup quick-cooking rolled oats

Combine the flours and baking soda in a small bowl. Stir well and set aside.

In a small deep mixing bowl, lightly beat the butter with an electric mixer on medium speed. Continuing to beat, add the sugars, creaming the mixture well. Then beat in the egg, vanilla extract, and water. Gradually add the dry ingredients to the creamed mixture, beating until the dough is well blended and smooth. Stir the chocolate chips and rolled oats into the dough with a spoon.

Drop the dough by small rounded teaspoonfuls about 2 inches apart on lightly greased or nonstick spray-coated baking sheets. Bake in a preheated 375-degree oven for about 9 minutes, or until the edges are just barely tinged with brown. (For very tender cookies, be careful not to overbake.) Immediately remove the baking sheets from the oven. Loosen the cookies with a spatula and transfer them to racks to cool. Let the cookies stand until cold. Pack in airtight containers.

Makes about 3 dozen (2½-inch diameter) cookies.

NUTRI-STEP 1

- Decrease the granulated sugar to 3 tablespoons.
- Omit the large egg and SUBSTITUTE 2 large egg whites.
- Decrease the chocolate chips to 4 ounces (¾ cup).

NUTRI-STEP 2

- Decrease the white flour to ½ cup.
- Increase the whole wheat flour to 1 cup.
- Decrease the granulated sugar to 2½ tablespoons.
- Omit the large egg and SUBSTITUTE 2 large egg whites.
- Omit the semisweet chocolate chips and SUBSTITUTE 4 ounces (¾ cup) carob chips.

CHEWY MOLASSES COOKIES

½   cup butter or margarine ●■
¾   cup sugar ●■
¼   cup light or dark molasses
1   large egg (or 2 large egg whites) ●■
1   cup enriched all-purpose or unbleached white flour ■
1   cup whole wheat flour
2   teaspoons baking soda
1   teaspoon ground cinnamon ●■
½   teaspoon ground cloves
½   teaspoon ground ginger ●■
¼   teaspoon salt ●■

In a medium-sized bowl, cream the butter and sugar with an electric mixer on medium speed. Add the molasses and egg and beat well.

In a small bowl, combine the flours, baking soda, spices, and salt. Stir to combine well. Add to the creamed mixture, and completely combine. Cover and chill.

With your hands, form the dough into 1-inch balls, and place on greased cookie sheets about 2 inches apart. Bake in a preheated 375-degree oven for 10 to 11 minutes, or until lightly browned. The cookies will puff up and then flatten during baking. For chewy cookies, do not overbake. Cool on a wire rack.

Makes about 3 dozen cookies.

NUTRI-STEP 1

- Decrease the butter or margarine to ⅓ cup.
- Decrease the sugar to ⅔ cup.
- Omit 1 large egg and USE 2 large egg whites.
- Increase the ground cinnamon to a generous 1 teaspoon.
- Increase the ground ginger to a generous ½ teaspoon.
- Decrease the salt to ⅛ teaspoon.

NUTRI-STEP 2

- Decrease the butter or margarine to ¼ cup. Combine the butter, sugar, and molasses. Cream the mixture well, then beat in the egg whites.
- Decrease the sugar to ⅔ cup.
- Omit 1 large egg and USE 2 large egg whites.
- Decrease the white flour to ½ cup. *And add* ¼ cup soy flour (if unavailable, use white flour). *And add* ¼ cup whole wheat flour.
- Increase the ground cinnamon to a generous 1 teaspoon.
- Increase the ground ginger to a generous ½ teaspoon.
- Omit the salt.

OATMEAL–RAISIN COOKIES

These are light, crispy, high-fiber cookies. Just like Grandma used to make!

½   cup enriched all-purpose or unbleached white flour •
⅓   cup whole wheat flour •
¼   teaspoon ground cinnamon
⅛   teaspoon ground mace
½   teaspoon baking soda
⅓   cup butter or margarine
⅔   cup packed light brown sugar •
¼   cup lowfat or skim milk
1   teaspoon vanilla extract
½   cup coarsely chopped raisins
2   cups quick-cooking oats

Combine the flours, spices, and baking soda in a small bowl, stirring until well blended. Set aside.

In a small deep mixing bowl combine the butter and brown sugar. Beat on medium speed with an electric mixer for 1 minute, or until blended. Gradually add the milk, then the vanilla and beat for 2 minutes longer, or until the mixture is smooth and light. Gradually beat in the flour and spice mixture until well blended. Stir in the raisins and oats by hand. (The dough will be stiff.)

Dampen your hands very lightly with water, and shape the dough into 1-inch balls. (Moisten your hands again, as needed, to prevent the dough from sticking to them.) Space the balls about 3 inches apart on lightly greased baking sheets. Flatten the balls by pressing down firmly with the bottom of a drinking glass. Dip the glass bottom in cold water to prevent the dough from sticking to the surface.

Bake the cookies in a preheated 375-degree oven for about 10 minutes, or until the edges of the cookies are just tinged with brown. Remove from the oven and immediately loosen the cookies with a metal spatula. Transfer to racks to cool.

Makes 30 to 35 (2½-inch) cookies.

NUTRI-STEP 1

- Decrease the white flour to ⅓ cup.
- Increase the whole wheat flour to ½ cup.
- Decrease the brown sugar to ½ cup.

CHOCOLATE CHIFFON DESSERT OR PIE FILLING

This tastes quite luxurious, almost like a chocolate mousse; however, it is very low in calories and fat. Carob powder (which is available at most health food stores and by mail order) is substituted for cocoa in Nutri-Step 2 because carob has much less fat than cocoa. In addition, it does not contain caffeine as does cocoa, and it is naturally sweeter (requiring the addition of less sugar). It's also perfect for anyone who is allergic to chocolate. For a "chocolate-like" flavor and color, be sure to use the "dark"-style carob powder, if this is available.

1	packet unflavored gelatin (plus 1 teaspoon from a second packet, if dessert will be used as a pie filling)
½	cup sugar ▪
2	tablespoons cool water
¾	cup boiling water
½	cup unsweetened plain cocoa powder (NOT a drink mix) ▪

¾   cup ice-cold lowfat milk •■
1   cup instant nonfat dry milk powder •■
2   teaspoons vanilla extract
1   large egg white
    Prepared "Meringue Pie Crust," (page 264) (optional)

Garnish
½   ounce semisweet chocolate, grated, or 2 tablespoons chocolate chips or chocolate sprinkles ■

Have ready and handy all the ingredients except the egg white, meringue crust (if used), and grated chocolate, chips, or sprinkles. Put the gelatin and sugar in a blender container. Add 2 tablespoons cool water, and blend for 15 seconds, or until mixed. Add the boiling water and blend for 1 minute to completely dissolve the gelatin. Add the cocoa, ice-cold milk, milk powder, and vanilla extract. Blend for 1 minute longer to make sure the ingredients are thoroughly mixed. (During the blending, stop the blender once, and scrape down the sides of the container with a rubber spatula.)

Pour the mixture into a large mixing bowl and refrigerate until it jells enough to mound on a spoon. (*Note:* It does not matter if the mixture jells completely. In fact, the dessert can be prepared to this point, refrigerated overnight, and then finished the next day.) Loosen the jelled mixture from the sides of bowl with a rubber scraper, then beat with an electric mixer until soft. Beat in the egg white and continue beating several minutes at high speed until the mixture doubles in volume and becomes very light. Immediately spoon into individual serving cups, one large bowl, or the prepared Meringue Pie Crust, heaping the mixture on top. Sprinkle the surface lightly with grated chocolate, chips, or sprinkles. Chill until completely firm (about 1 hour).

Makes about 6 to 8 servings.

NUTRI-STEP 1

- Omit the lowfat milk and SUBSTITUTE ¾ cup ice-cold water.
- Increase the milk powder to 1¼ cups.

NUTRI-STEP 2

■ Decrease the sugar to ⅓ cup.
■ Omit the cocoa and SUBSTITUTE ½ cup carob powder, preferably the "dark" style.
■ Omit the lowfat milk and SUBSTITUTE ¾ cup ice-cold water.
■ Increase the milk powder to 1¼ cups.
■ Omit the grated chocolate, chocolate chips, or sprinkles and SUBSTITUTE ½ ounce grated bar carob or 2 tablespoons carob chips.

BANANA CREAM PIE

Crust
1   9-inch graham cracker crust, or 1 prebaked 9-inch pie shell (page 265)

Filling
2   large eggs
3   cups whole milk •
½   cup plus 2 tablespoons sugar •
¼   cup cornstarch
½   cup instant nonfat dry milk powder
    Scant ¼ teaspoon salt •
2   teaspoons vanilla extract •
1   tablespoon butter or margarine
2   bananas, sliced

Topping
2   bananas, sliced
    Lemon juice

Prepare the crust and set it aside.

For the cream filling, beat the eggs in a small bowl with a fork or wire whisk until they are smooth, frothy, and lemon-colored. Set aside.

In a medium-sized saucepan, over medium-high heat, cook the milk until it is very hot but not boiling. Remove the milk from the heat and set it aside.

In a large saucepan, combine the sugar, cornstarch, milk powder, and salt. Gradually stir in the hot milk. Cook over medium to medium-high heat, stirring constantly, for about 14 to 18 minutes, or until the mixture thickens and boils. (Cooking time will be at the lower range if medium-high heat is used, but you must stir very carefully, making sure the milk mixture doesn't stick to the bottom of the pan and burn. At the first sign of sticking and burning—that is, brown flecks in the mixture or on the spoon—lift the pot from the burner; stir vigorously, and reduce the heat before replacing it.)

Boil for 1 minute, stirring. Remove from the heat. Very gradually stir about half of the hot mixture into the eggs. Then blend back into the hot mixture in the saucepan. Cook for 1 minute longer, stirring constantly to prevent the mixture from boiling. Remove the pan from the heat and stir in the vanilla and butter. Cover and cool them in the refrigerator for about ½ hour, stirring frequently.

When the custard mixture has cooled to lukewarm, slice 2 bananas and arrange them in concentric circles in the bottom of the prepared pie shell. Spoon the custard mixture over the banana slices, cover the pie, and refrigerate.

Shortly before serving, thinly slice the 2 bananas for the topping, and sprinkle with a small amount of lemon juice to prevent them from browning. Arrange the slices attractively on the pie top and serve.

Makes 6 to 7 servings.

Filling
- Omit the whole milk and SUBSTITUTE 3 cups lowfat milk.
- Decrease the sugar to ½ cup.
- Decrease the salt to ⅛ teaspoon.
- Increase the vanilla extract to 2½ teaspoons.

PUMPKIN PIE

Because pumpkin is a member of the orange-yellow plant group, this traditional dessert provides a wonderfully effective and painless way of boosting carotene consumption. Our pie filling recipe cuts fat to a minimum, yet is well flavored and creamy-smooth.

1	recipe Easy Lowfat Pastry Crust (page 265)
3	tablespoons granulated sugar •
½	cup packed light brown sugar
1½	tablespoons enriched all-purpose white or whole wheat flour
1¼	teaspoons ground cinnamon •
¾	teaspoon ground ginger
½	teaspoon ground mace
¼	teaspoon ground cloves
1	large egg, lightly beaten •
1	16-ounce can solid-pack pumpkin (NOT pie filling)
1	13-ounce can evaporated skimmed milk
¾	teaspoon vanilla extract •

Prepare the pastry and press it into the bottom and sides of a 9-inch deep-dish pie pan. Chill thoroughly.

Combine the sugars, flour, and spices in a medium-sized bowl. Stir with a fork until well mixed. Add the beaten egg and pumpkin, and continue stirring until the ingredients are thoroughly blended. Add the evaporated milk and vanilla to the mixture a bit at a time, stirring until the filling is completely smooth. Pour the filling into the prepared pie shell, smoothing it out to the edges of the plate. Bake in a preheated 375-degree oven for 55 to 60 minutes, or until the crust is lightly browned and the center of the filling appears "set" when the pan is jiggled slightly. Transfer the pie to a rack and let it cool. Refrigerate until cold before serving.

Makes 6 to 8 servings.

- Decrease the granulated sugar to 2 tablespoons.
- Increase the cinnamon to 1½ teaspoons.
- Omit the large egg and SUBSTITUTE 2 large egg whites.
- Increase the vanilla extract to 1 teaspoon.

MERINGUE PIE CRUST

Much lower in calories than conventional pie crusts, this one contains almost no fat, to boot! It tastes great with Chocolate Chiffon Pie Filling (page 260) or any other similar filling of your choosing.

3   large egg whites
¼   teaspoon cream of tartar
½   teaspoon vanilla extract
⅔   cup sugar •

In a very clean bowl (preferably not plastic), beat the egg whites with the cream of tartar and vanilla until foamy. Gradually beat in the sugar. Then continue beating at high speed until the whites form very stiff, shiny peaks. Use the back of a spoon to spread the meringue in a greased or nonstick spray-coated 9-inch pie plate, so that the bottom and sides of the plate are coated in an even layer. Build up the meringue around the perimeter of the plate so it is about ½ inch higher than the plate rim.

Bake the meringue crust in a preheated 275-degree oven for about 1½ hours, or until firm to the touch and pale beige in color. Turn off the heat, but leave the pie crust in the closed oven for at least 1 to 2 hours so it can continue to dry as the oven cools. (*Note:* The crust can be left in the turned-off oven overnight, if this is convenient.) Cool the crust completely before filling. An unfilled meringue crust will keep for 1 week or longer at room temperature if wrapped airtight (or it may be frozen).

Makes 1 9-inch pie crust.

Note: Once this meringue crust has been filled, the bottom of it tends to "melt away" on standing. So it is best not to fill the crust more than a few hours before serving.

NUTRI-STEP 1

- Decrease the sugar to ½ cup.

GRAHAM CRACKER PIE CRUST

1   cup graham cracker crumbs
1   tablespoon sugar •
3   tablespoons butter or margarine, melted

Combine the graham cracker crumbs and sugar in a small, deep bowl, stirring with a fork until blended. Add the butter and stir until evenly distributed throughout the crumb mixture. Turn the crumb mixture into an 8- or 9-inch pie pan. Use your fingers to press the mixture to form a thin, even layer over the bottom and sides of the pan to within ½ inch of the rim. The crust is now ready to be filled and baked according to individual pie recipe directions, or it may be baked unfilled.

To bake the crust unfilled, put it in a preheated 375-degree oven and bake for 8 to 9 minutes, or until lightly tinged with brown. Remove the pan to a rack, and let stand until the crust is cool. Fill with prepared pie filling as desired.

NUTRI-STEP 1

• Omit the sugar.

EASY LOWFAT PASTRY CRUST

This convenient and tasty pastry is mixed right in the pie pan and pressed into place with the hands. Besides being easier to prepare than most pastry recipes, this pie crust contains far less fat—only ¼ cup of oil.

1¼   cups enriched all-purpose or unbleached white flour •■
¼   teaspoon salt •■
¼   cup corn or vegetable oil
2   tablespoons plus 1 teaspoon skim or lowfat milk (or a little more, if necessary)

Stir the flour and salt together in the bottom of an 8- or 9-inch pie plate. (A regular or deep-dish pie plate may be used; crust will be thin in a deep-dish plate.) Measure the oil into a cup; then beat in the milk with a fork until the completely incorporated. Add the oil-milk mixture to the flour and salt in a thin stream, stirring vigorously with a fork. Continue adding until the flour mixture is moistened and holds together. (If all the oil-milk mixture is incorporated and the dough is still a bit dry, add a few extra drops of milk until the dough holds together. However, be careful not to over-moisten the pastry.) Stir the dough for about 15 seconds, or until the ingredients are well blended. With your fingers, press the mixture into place in the pie plate, working it out thinly and evenly over the bottom and up the sides. Press the dough up to the pan rim all the way around. Crimp the pastry rim with your fingers, or decorate with the tines of a fork. Cover and refrigerate for at least 1 hour or, preferably, 2 or 3 hours, before using. (This storage time allows the dough to "relax" and yields a tenderer crust.)

To bake the pastry shell along with a filling, follow the directions given in a specific pie (filling) recipe. To bake the pastry unfilled, carefully press a large piece of aluminum foil (shiny side up) into the shell. Fill the shell with dried beans or rice to weight down the foil and hold it in place.

Bake the shell in a preheated 400-degree oven for 15 minutes. Gently lift out the aluminum foil along with the beans or rice, and discard. Return the shell to the oven and continue baking for about 5 to 6 minutes longer, or until lightly browned. Remove the pie plate from the oven and let stand on a rack until the shell is cool. Fill the shell as desired.

NUTRI-STEP 1

- Decrease the white flour to 1 cup. *And add* ¼ cup whole wheat flour or whole wheat pastry flour to the white flour.
- Decrease the salt to ⅛ teaspoon.

NUTRI-STEP 2

- Decrease the white flour to ¾ cup. *And add* ½ cup whole wheat flour or whole wheat pastry flour to the white flour.
- Decrease the salt to ⅛ teaspoon.

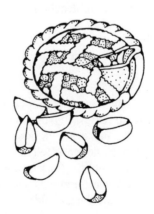

Chapter 16

Snacks, Appetizers, and Beverages

T here's no doubt about it—snacking is a favorite American pastime. The challenge is to satisfy between-meal appetites with appetizers, snacks, and beverages that are both tasty and nutritious.

In this chapter, you will find an appealing variety of dips, spreads, hors d'oeuvres, frothy drinks, and even crackers and mini-pizzas that are right on target. Best of all, your family and guests will never guess these delicious snacks are "good for 'em," unless you reveal that the "goodies" are actually packed with an assortment of healthful fruits and vegetables, as well as whole grains and legumes.

With these recipes, you can relax, knowing that your snacks are just as wholesome as your meals.

MINI-PIZZA SNACKS

Kids of all ages like these individual mini-pizzas. Offer them as tasty, nourishing snacks, or serve two or three together as a light main dish. (For convenience, mini-pizzas can be made ahead and frozen, then popped into the oven and reheated as needed.)

Although most pizzas call for mozzarella, you'll notice that our recipe specifies Cheddar. We find this lends a fuller and richer flavor with a smaller amount of cheese.

Notice, too, that the mini-pizza dough is made using our recipe for Buttermilk Biscuits. When preparing this biscuit dough for mini-pizzas, we suggest you jump right to Nutri-Step 2.

Note: If you're really in a hurry, regular or whole wheat mini-pita breads (about 5 inches in diameter) may be substituted for the biscuit dough. In this case, divide the sauce and garnishes among about 8 pita breads. Then continue to assemble the pizzas as directed in the recipe. Heat pita pizzas in a preheated 400-degree oven for 5 to 6 minutes, or until the cheese melts.

Sauce

1   6-ounce can tomato paste
1   teaspoon instant minced onions
2   tablespoons finely chopped fresh parsley leaves
2   tablespoons finely chopped green pepper or celery
1   teaspoon dried oregano leaves
⅛   teaspoon salt •
    Pinch of garlic powder (optional)
    Pinch of dried (hot) red pepper flakes (optional)

Dough and Garnishes

1   recipe Buttermilk Biscuits, prepared using Nutri-Step 2 (page 228)
⅔   cup shredded part-skim mild Cheddar or Longhorn cheese (if un-available, substitute regular Cheddar or Longhorn) •
2   tablespoons grated Parmesan cheese •
2   tablespoons finely chopped fresh parsley leaves and/or green pepper

Combine all the sauce ingredients in a small bowl. Stir until well mixed; then set aside.

Prepare Buttermilk Biscuits, rolling and cutting them out as directed in the recipe. Transfer the biscuits to two very lightly greased baking sheets, placing them about 4 inches apart. Press each biscuit out flat with the palm of your hand, until the biscuits are about 3½ inches in diameter.

Top each dough round with a portion of the reserved sauce. Spread the sauce out to the edges of the rounds with a knife or spoon. Sprinkle the pizza rounds with the cheeses and then with the chopped parsley and/or green pepper.

Bake in a preheated 400-degree oven for about 9 minutes, or until the mini-pizzas are puffy and cooked through and the cheese is melted. Immediately remove the pizzas from the baking sheets with a spatula.h diameter)

If desired, mini-pizzas may be made ahead and frozen for later use. In this case, lay the baked and cooled pizzas on a baking sheet and put in the freezer until frozen. Then pack in an airtight container or bag and store in the freezer for up to 3 weeks. Transfer the frozen pizzas directly to baking sheets. Reheat in a preheated 350-degree oven for about 6 to 8 minutes before serving.

Makes 11 to 12 (4½-inch diameter) biscuit-dough mini-pizzas (or 8 pita bread pizzas).

NUTRI-STEP 1

Sauce
- Omit the salt.

Dough and Garnishes
- Decrease the Cheddar or Longhorn cheese to ½ cup.
- Decrease the Parmesan cheese to 1 tablespoon.

BUTTERY OAT THINS

Even though these tasty crackers do not take very much time to prepare, they seem to impress guests immensely—especially those who never knew crackers could be made at home.

1	cup enriched all-purpose or unbleached white flour ●
½	cup whole wheat flour ●
1½	cups old-fashioned or quick-cooking rolled oats
½	teaspoon salt ●
¼	cup butter or margarine, melted and cooled to lukewarm
2	tablespoons vegetable oil ●
1	tablespoon honey
⅓	cup lowfat or skim milk ●

In a medium-sized bowl, combine the flours, oats, and salt. Add the melted butter and oil and mix until crumbly. Add the honey and milk and mix well to make a slightly sticky dough that comes away from the sides of the bowl. (If the dough is too dry, add a drop or two more milk; if it is too wet, add a sprinkle of flour.)

Grease well (or coat with nonstick vegetable spray) a large, flat baking sheet which has at least two rimless edges. (Or, use the inverted bottom of a large baking pan.) Roll out the dough to a 12- by 16-inch rectangle *directly on the baking sheet or pan bottom.* (If necessary, you may use *two* medium-sized baking sheets, and roll half of the dough to an 8- by 12-inch rectangle on each.) Try to keep the thickness of the dough as even as possible.

Prick the dough all over with a fork. Then use a sharp knife, pizza cutter, or pastry wheel to cut the rolled-out dough into 1½- by 2-inch rectangles, *leaving the dough in place* on the baking sheet or pan bottom. (An easy way to evenly cut the dough is to divide it into 16 equal rectangles, then cut each rectangle into four smaller ones.)

Bake the crackers right on the baking sheet or inverted baking pan (do not turn it over) in a preheated 350-degree oven for about 25 minutes, or until crisp. (They will crisp even more as they cool.) Carefully remove the crackers from the baking sheet with a metal spatula (pancake turner), separating any that are stuck together. Cool the crackers on a wire rack. When cool, store in an airtight container.

Makes 64 (1½- by 2-inch) crackers.

NUTRI-STEP 1

- Decrease the white flour to ½ cup.
- Increase the whole wheat flour to 1 cup.
- Decrease the salt to a generous ¼ teaspoon.
- Decrease the oil to 1 tablespoon.
- Omit the lowfat milk and USE skim milk. Increase the amount to 6 tablespoons.

HOMEMADE HONEY GRAHAM CRACKERS

Though these look remarkably like store-bought graham crackers, they taste even better. Also, they use less sweetener and include whole wheat flour, which many commercial brands lack. That's actually quite ironic, as the terms "Graham flour" and "Graham crackers" used to be synonymous with "whole wheat flour" and "whole wheat crackers." They were named for nineteenth-century physician Sylvester Graham, who was ahead of his time in proclaiming the nutritional deficiencies of unenriched white bread and encouraging the use of whole wheat flour.

The following crackers use a particularly quick and easy technique that we developed, in which the dough is thinly rolled out right on a baking sheet.

1   cup whole wheat flour •
½   cup enriched all-purpose or unbleached white flour •
½   teaspoon baking powder

½ teaspoon baking soda
¼ teaspoon salt •
3 tablespoons sugar •
¼ cup vegetable oil
2 tablespoons honey
1 tablespoon light or dark molasses
3 tablespoons water

Put the flours, baking powder, baking soda, salt, and sugar in a mixing bowl. Add the oil, honey, and molasses and mix until crumbly. Add the water and mix well to make a soft dough that comes away from the sides of the bowl. (If the dough is too dry, add a drop or two more water; if it is too wet, add a sprinkle of flour.)

Grease well (or coat with nonstick vegetable spray) a large, flat baking sheet which has at least 2 rimless edges. (Or, use the inverted bottom of a large baking pan.) Roll out the dough to a 10- by 15-inch rectangle *directly on the baking sheet* or pan bottom. (If necessary, you may use *two* medium-sized baking sheets, and roll half of the dough to a 7½- by 10-inch rectangle on each one.) Try to keep the thickness of the dough as even as possible.

Prick the dough all over with a fork. Then use a sharp knife, pizza cutter, or pastry wheel to cut the rolled-out dough into 2½-inch squares, *leaving the dough in place* on the baking sheet or pan bottom. Use the edge of a ruler to press a line down the center of each square, dividing it into two even rectangles. (Graham crackers always come in pairs which stay together.)

Bake the crackers right on the baking sheet or inverted baking pan (do not turn it over) in a preheated 350-degree oven for about 20 minutes, or until crisp. (They will crisp even more as they cool.) Carefully remove the crackers from the baking sheet with a metal spatula (pancake turner), separating any squares that are stuck together. Cool the crackers on a wire rack. When cool, store in an airtight container.

Makes 24 double crackers.

NUTRI-STEP 1

- Increase the whole wheat flour to 1½ cups.
- Omit the white flour.
- Decrease the salt to ⅛ teaspoon or omit.
- Decrease the sugar to 2 tablespoons.

CHILI CORN CHIPS

These crackers are very easy to make, and will undoubtedly delight and impress family and friends. What's more, they are neither deep-fried nor laden with salt, as are many store-bought corn chips. The nutritional value of these chips can be boosted by using "undegerminated" cornmeal (sometimes referred to as "stone ground" cornmeal) in the recipe.

The "germ" of the corn kernel (just like wheat germ) contains many valuable nutrients; however, much commercial cornmeal is degerminated to increase its shelf life. (The cornmeal package should indicate if the "germ" of the corn has been removed during processing.) As with any whole grain product, the nutrients in undegerminated cornmeal will keep best if it is stored in the refrigerator or freezer.

1	cup yellow cornmeal (use "undegerminated" cornmeal, if available)
½	cup enriched all-purpose or unbleached white flour ●■
¾	teaspoon salt ●■
½	teaspoon baking soda
¾	teaspoon chili powder ●■
⅛	teaspoon cayenne pepper, or to taste
½	cup commercial buttermilk
3	tablespoons vegetable oil
	Paprika

In a medium-sized bowl, mix together the cornmeal, flour, salt, baking soda, chili powder, and cayenne pepper. Add the buttermilk and oil, and mix until the dough is completely moistened. Use a mixing spoon or your fingers to knead dough a few times until smooth.

Grease well (or coat with nonstick vegetable spray) a large, flat baking sheet which has at least 2 rimless edges. (Or, use the inverted bottom of a large baking pan.) Roll out the dough to a 12- by 16-inch rectangle *directly on the baking sheet* or pan bottom. (If necessary, you may use TWO medium-sized baking sheets, and roll half the dough to an 8- by 12-inch rectangle on each.) Try to keep the thickness of the dough as even as possible. Sprinkle the dough lightly with paprika.

Prick the dough all over with a fork. Then use a sharp knife, pizza cutter, or fluted pastry wheel to cut the rolled-out dough into small squares about 1¼ to 1½ inches on a side, *leaving the dough in place* on the baking sheet or pan bottom.

Bake the crackers right on the baking sheet or inverted baking pan (do not turn it over) in a preheated 350-degree oven for about 25 minutes, or until crisp. (They will crisp even more as they cool.) Carefully remove the crackers from the baking sheet with a metal spatula (pancake turner), separating any that are stuck together. Cool the crackers on a wire rack. When cool, store in an airtight container.

Makes about 125 chips.

NUTRI-STEP 1

- Decrease the white flour to ¼ cup. *And add* ¼ cup whole wheat flour to the dry ingredients.
- Decrease the salt to ½ teaspoon.
- Increase the chili powder to a generous ¾ teaspoon.

NUTRI-STEP 2

- Omit the white flour and SUBSTITUTE ½ cup whole wheat flour.
- Decrease the salt to ½ teaspoon.
- Increase the chili powder to a generous ¾ teaspoon.

POPCORN BALLS

Here's an old-fashioned treat that's fun for kids and adults to make together. However, molasses syrup is very hot and should be handled with care.

2	quarts unsalted freshly popped corn ●■
½	cup dark molasses
½	cup light corn syrup
½	teaspoon apple cider vinegar
1	tablespoon butter or margarine ●■
⅛	teaspoon salt ●■

Check the popcorn for any unpopped kernels and discard as these are hard on the teeth when incorporated into popcorn balls. Put the popped corn into a large ceramic bowl. (Do not use metal since this holds the heat of the candy mixture too readily and can cause burned fingers.) Set aside.

In a medium-sized saucepan, combine the molasses, syrup, and vinegar. Cook over medium-high heat. The syrup will boil up and thicken quickly. This is normal. Continue cooking until the mixture reaches 255 degrees F. when tested with a candy thermometer. (This will take about 12 to 15 minutes.) If a candy thermometer is not available, occasionally test for doneness by dropping a small amount of syrup into a cup of very cold water; it should form a hard ball. Stir the syrup occasionally with a wooden spoon during the early stages of cooking. Then as it nears the desired temperature, stir continually to prevent burning.

Remove the pan from the heat. Stir the butter and salt into the syrup, and pour the syrup slowly over the popped corn, stirring with a large wooden spoon. Be very careful to keep the hot mixture away from your hands. Try to distribute the syrup as evenly as possible.

Continue stirring to coat the popcorn evenly. Very lightly and carefully, test the syrup with your fingers to see if it is cool enough to handle. *Wait until the syrup has cooled to the touch, as hot syrup can stick and burn your hands.* Then begin shaping the popcorn into balls about 2 inches in diameter. (The mixture will hold together well with very gentle pressure.) Let the popcorn balls cool before eating. Store in an airtight container or plastic bag.

Makes 15 to 18 balls.

NUTRI-STEP 1

- Increase the popped corn to 2½ quarts. Press the balls firmly to shape.
- Decrease the butter or margarine to ½ tablespoon.
- Omit the salt.

NUTRI-STEP 2

- Increase the popped corn to 2½ quarts. Press the balls firmly to shape.
- Omit the butter or margarine.
- Omit the salt.

WALDORF CHEESE BALL

Although this cheese ball is typically served on crackers, it is also perfect as a stuffing for celery.

Cheese Ball
5 ounces (1¼ cups, packed) shredded sharp Cheddar cheese or Cheddar-style lowfat or part-skim cheese
2 tablespoons mayonnaise ●■
¼ cup finely chopped peeled apple ●■
¼ cup finely chopped walnuts ●■
¼ cup finely chopped celery
¼ cup dried currants or raisins
¼ cup finely chopped pitted dates
2 teaspoons lemon juice
½ teaspoon Worcestershire sauce (optional)

Coating
2 tablespoons finely chopped walnuts ●■

To Serve
Regular, whole wheat, or rye crackers ●■

Using a wooden spoon, mix together all the cheese ball ingredients until well combined and evenly distributed. Shape into a ball or log, and lightly coat the outside surface with the 2 tablespoons finely chopped walnuts. Wrap the ball or log in plastic or foil, and refrigerate until chilled. Serve with crackers.
Makes 1 ball or log.

NUTRI-STEP 1

Cheese Ball
- Omit the mayonnaise and SUBSTITUTE 2 tablespoons sour cream.
- Leave the chopped apple unpeeled.
- Decrease the walnuts to 3 tablespoons.

Coating
- Decrease the walnuts to 1 tablespoon. *And add* 2 to 3 tablespoons fresh whole wheat or pumpernickel crumbs, and mix with the walnuts to coat the outside of the cheese ball or log.

To Serve
- Omit the regular crackers and USE whole wheat or rye crackers.

NUTRI-STEP 2

Cheese Ball
- Omit the mayonnaise and SUBSTITUTE plain regular or lowfat yogurt.
- Leave the chopped apple unpeeled.
- Decrease the walnuts to 2 tablespoons. *And add* ¼ cup finely shredded or very finely chopped carrot. *And add* 2 tablespoons unprocessed bran.

Coating
- Omit the walnuts. *And add* 3 to 4 tablespoons fresh whole wheat or pumpernickel crumbs and use to coat the outside of the cheese ball or log.

To Serve
- Omit the regular crackers and USE whole wheat or rye crackers.

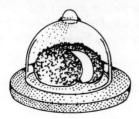

MIDDLE EASTERN DIP PIQUANT

Yes, it's made with eggplant, but this spicy dip is good! Just serve the dip without mentioning the unusual ingredient.

2   medium-sized, firm eggplants (about 2 pounds)
1   tablespoon olive oil or corn oil •
1   medium-sized onion, finely chopped
1   large clove garlic, peeled and minced
3   tablespoons chopped fresh parsley leaves
1   large tomato (preferably vine-ripened), peeled, cored, and chopped
3   tablespoons red bell pepper, chopped (if unavailable, substitute 3 tablespoons canned, well-drained, chopped pimiento)
1   teaspoon lemon juice •
¾   teaspoon paprika
¾   teaspoon salt •
⅛   teaspoon freshly ground black pepper
⅛   teaspoon cayenne pepper, or to taste

To Serve
1   large tomato, cored
1   tablespoon chopped fresh parsley leaves
    Pita bread triangles, stoned wheat thins, and/or thin slices of Italian bread

Put the whole, unpeeled eggplants in a small roasting pan in a preheated 450-degree oven. Roast, turning occasionally, for about 50 minutes, or until the skin wrinkles and the eggplants are soft. Remove from the oven and let stand until cool enough to handle. Cut the eggplants open and scoop the pulp into a colander. Drain well.

Combine the oil, onion, garlic, and parsley in a large, heavy skillet over medium-high heat. Cook, stirring, 4 to 5 minutes, or until the vegetables are soft.

Meanwhile, press down the eggplant pulp with the back of a spoon to remove any excess moisture. Turn the eggplant onto a cutting board and chop coarsely. Add the chopped eggplant to the onion mixture, stirring. Stir the tomato, red bell pepper, lemon juice, and all the seasonings into the eggplant mixture. Lower the heat to medium and simmer the mixture, uncovered, for 20 to 25 minutes, or until most of the excess liquid has evaporated. Stir frequently. Remove the skillet from the heat and let the mixture stand until cool.

Cut the garnishing tomato into 8 wedges, leaving them attached at the bottom. Place the tomato in a serving bowl and spread the wedges apart, petal-style. Stuff the tomato with the eggplant mixture. Sprinkle the top of the dip with the chopped parsley. Chill the dip, covered, until cold. Serve with pita bread triangles, stoned wheat thins, or thin slices of Italian bread.

Makes about 1½ cups of dip.

DILL AND ONION DIP

Dip
⅓   cup plain lowfat yogurt ●
½   cup commercial sour cream ●
3   tablespoons mayonnaise ●
¾   teaspoon dried dillweed
1   teaspoon instant minced onion
    Pinch of garlic powder
¼   teaspoon celery salt
¼   teaspoon salt ●
2   drops hot pepper sauce
2   tablespoons finely chopped fresh parsley leaves

To Serve
    Raw vegetables, such as carrot and celery sticks, cucumber rounds, broccoli and cauliflower flowerets, green pepper slices, and peeled turnip slices

Combine all the dip ingredients except the parsley in a small bowl. Stir with a spoon to mix well. Stir in the parsley. Cover and chill for several hours to allow the flavors to blend. Serve with an assortment of raw vegetables for dipping.
Makes about 1 cup.

HUMMUS

This tasty Middle Eastern dip, made from garbanzo beans (chick-peas) and sesame seeds, is a favorite of ours.

Dip

1	tablespoon olive oil
1½	tablespoons vegetable oil •
1	tablespoon hulled, raw sesame seeds
1	15- to 16-ounce can garbanzo beans (chick-peas), well drained
	Scant ¼ teaspoon salt •
1 to 2	cloves garlic, peeled and chopped
1½	teaspoons lemon juice, or more to taste •
¼	cup water (or possibly more if blender is used)
⅛	teaspoon black pepper, preferably freshly ground

To Serve

5 or 6	small white or whole wheat pita breads •

Put all the dip ingredients in a blender or food processor container. Process until smooth. (If a blender is used, more water may be needed. Add it, a tablespoon at a time, through the opening in the top of the lid, until the mixture will just blend.)

Hummus should be made several hours ahead and refrigerated so that the flavors will mingle. The dip will become stiffer as it chills. (It keeps several days in the refrigerator and also freezes quite well for longer storage.) Serve with pita bread cut into triangles for dipping.

Makes about 1½ cups.

NUTRI-STEP 1

- Decrease the vegetable oil to 1 tablespoon.
- Decrease the salt to a generous ⅛ teaspoon.
- Increase the lemon juice to 2 teaspoons, or more to taste.

To Serve
- Omit the white pita bread and USE whole wheat pita bread.

TABOULLI

This Middle Eastern appetizer salad is made with nutritious bulgur wheat and fresh summer vegetables. Taboulli involves no cooking: The bulgur—which has a mild, nutty taste—is softened by soaking it in water first, and then oil and vinegar. Taboulli is usually eaten inside triangles of pita (pocket) bread, on crackers, or on leaves of lettuce. While it is traditionally served as an appetizer, it makes a nice side dish as well. Mint gives taboulli a wonderfully cool flavor; however, if you are unable to obtain mint, it may be left out. (For more information on bulgur wheat, see our recipe for Plain-cooked Bulgur, page 100.)

1¼	cups bulgur wheat
	Warm water
3	medium-sized, vine-ripened tomatoes, cored and finely chopped
1	cup finely chopped fresh parsley leaves
1	cup thinly sliced green onions (scallions), including tops
¼	cup olive (or vegetable) oil •
⅓	cup lemon juice •
1	teaspoon salt •
¼	cup finely chopped fresh spearmint leaves, or 2 tablespoons dried mint leaves, crumbled (optional)

To Serve (your choice)
   White or whole wheat pita bread, cut into triangles •
   Regular or whole wheat crackers •
   Lettuce leaves

Put the bulgur into a large sieve; then lower the sieve into enough warm water so that the bulgur is covered. Let the bulgur soak for about 20 minutes. Then remove the sieve from the water, and drain the bulgur for about 5 minutes. (Or put the bulgur in a bowl, and cover with water. Soak as directed, then carefully drain off as much water as possible.)

Put the soaked and drained bulgur in a medium-sized bowl and add the tomatoes, parsley, green onions, oil, lemon juice, salt, and mint leaves. Mix very well, cover, and refrigerate for at least 2 hours (or overnight), to allow the bulgur to absorb the dressing and soften, and for the flavors to mingle. Mix again before serving.

Serve in an attractive bowl. Accompany with pita bread triangles, crackers, and/or lettuce leaves.

Makes about 8 to 10 appetizer, or 4 to 6 salad servings.

- Decrease the oil to 3 tablespoons.
- Decrease the lemon juice to ¼ cup.
- Decrease the salt to ¾ teaspoon, or less to taste.

To Serve
- Omit the white pita bread and USE whole wheat pita bread.
- Omit the regular crackers and USE whole wheat crackers.

TERRIFIC TUNA MOUSSE

Unlike many other mousses, this low-cal version has no cream or eggs, yet it is creamy and light—perfect on slices of cucumber or green pepper, or with whole wheat crackers. If you use a "fish"-shaped mold, and garnish the mousse with greens, tomatoes, etc., it can be a truly elegant appetizer or luncheon main course.

1   packet unflavored gelatin
2   tablespoons lemon juice
½   cup boiling chicken broth
½   cup mayonnaise ●■
¼   cup lowfat or skim milk ●■
2   tablespoons chopped fresh parsley leaves
1   teaspoon dried dillweed
1   tablespoon minced fresh onion or green onion (scallion), or 1 teaspoon instant minced onions ■
1   teaspoon prepared mustard ●■
¼   teaspoon freshly ground black pepper
1   6½-ounce can water-packed tuna, drained
1   cup peeled and cubed cucumber

Soften the gelatin in the lemon juice. Add the boiling broth and stir to dissolve the gelatin completely.

Put the remaining ingredients in a blender or food processor, and add the dissolved gelatin. Then process everything until almost, but not completely, smooth.

Pour into a nonstick spray-coated (or very lightly oiled) 3-cup mold. Chill until firm, at least 3 hours. To unmold, run the tip of a small knife around the edge of the mousse. Cover the mold with a serving platter and invert. Hold the platter and mold together, and shake if necessary to loosen the mousse.

Makes 6 to 8 servings.

NUTRI-STEP 1

- Decrease the mayonnaise to ⅓ cup.
- Decrease the milk to 2 tablespoons. *And add* ⅓ cup plain yogurt; put in the blender or food processor with the other ingredients.
- Increase the prepared mustard to 1¼ teaspoons.

NUTRI-STEP 2

- Decrease the mayonnaise to ¼ cup.
- Omit the milk. *And add* ½ cup plain lowfat yogurt; put in the blender or food processor with the other ingredients.
- Increase the onion to 2 tablespoons fresh or 1½ teaspoons instant.
- Increase the mustard to 1½ teaspoons.

COCKTAIL CHICKEN NUGGETS

These tidbits are served warm in a very light sauce, and can be eaten on toothpicks, along with their accompanying vegetables. They can also be made larger, and served as a first course for a dinner.

4   large chicken breast halves, skinned and boned (about 1¼ pounds skinned and boned chicken meat)

1   large egg plus 1 large egg white

½   cup fresh white or whole wheat bread crumbs (from about 1 slice bread) •

3   tablespoons finely chopped fresh parsley leaves

½   teaspoon dried marjoram leaves

¼   teaspoon dried thyme leaves •

¼   teaspoon paprika

½   teaspoon salt •

⅛   teaspoon black pepper, preferably freshly ground

1   medium-sized celery stalk, cut in half lengthwise and then into 1½-inch-long pieces •

1   carrot, cut into quarters lengthwise and then into 1½-inch-long pieces •

1   clove garlic, finely minced

2   cups chicken broth or bouillon

1½   tablespoons cornstarch

1½   tablespoons water

Use a meat grinder or a food processor fitted with a steel blade to chop the chicken very fine. Put the chopped chicken in a bowl, and add the egg plus egg white, bread crumbs, parsley, marjoram, thyme, paprika, salt, and pepper. Then mix until very well combined.

(*Note:* If using a food processor, you may mix everything using the steel blade.)

In a large deep skillet, combine the celery, carrot, garlic, and chicken broth. Cover and heat to boiling. Lower the heat and simmer for about 5 minutes.

Meanwhile, use WET hands to form the chicken mixture into small balls, about 1 inch in diameter. When all balls are shaped, gently place them in the hot broth with the vegetables. Cover the skillet and simmer for about 10 minutes, or until the balls are cooked through. Turn the balls once or twice to make sure they cook evenly. When the balls are done, use a slotted spoon to remove them and the vegetable pieces from the skillet to a serving dish. Reserve the broth.

Mix the cornstarch with the water, then stir the mixture into the hot broth remaining in the skillet. Stir over medium heat until the sauce thickens slightly and boils. Pour as much sauce as desired over the balls and vegetables, and discard the remainder. (The balls and vegetables should be lightly coated with sauce, and not swimming in it.) Serve warm, with toothpicks or small forks.

Makes about 35 chicken nuggets with vegetables.

NUTRI-STEP 1

- Omit the white bread crumbs and USE whole wheat bread crumbs.
- Increase the thyme to ½ teaspoon.
- Decrease the salt to a generous ¼ teaspoon.
- Increase the celery to 2 stalks.
- Increase the carrots to 2.

SWEET AND SOUR COCKTAIL MEATBALLS

A wonderful party recipe, this is quick and easy to make, and can be prepared in advance. In fact, the meatballs and sauce can be frozen in separate containers. The sauce is reheated first, and then the meatballs are reheated in the sauce.

The meatballs in this recipe are lower in fat than most because they are baked rather than fried. Not only does this eliminate the need for extra fat for frying, but the excess fat in the meat cooks out during baking and can be discarded.

Meatballs
- 2   pounds lean ground beef •
- 2   large eggs (or 1 large egg plus 2 large egg whites) •

½   teaspoon dried oregano leaves
½   teaspoon dried basil leaves
¾   teaspoon salt •
¼   teaspoon black pepper, preferably freshly ground
1   clove garlic, peeled and finely minced
1   medium-sized onion, grated
1   cup fresh white or whole wheat bread crumbs •
½   cup lowfat milk, skim milk, or water •

Sauce
1   16-ounce can tomato paste
1¼ cups water
2   tablespoons packed light or dark brown sugar •
2   tablespoons apple cider vinegar •
1   8-ounce can juice-packed pineapple chunks, undrained

For the meatballs, mix all the ingredients together and blend well with a fork, food processor, or your hands until very smooth. Form into 1-inch diameter balls and place in very lightly greased or nonstick spray-coated jelly roll pans (or similar shallow baking pans) about ½ inch apart.

Bake in a preheated 350-degree oven for about 20 to 25 minutes, or until browned. Carefully remove the meatballs from the pans with a flat metal spatula, leaving the fat behind. Set aside. (The meatballs may be frozen at this point, if desired.)

For the sauce, combine all the sauce ingredients in a saucepan (or in a slow-cooker or chafing dish to be used for serving), and simmer for about 20 minutes. Gently stir in the meatballs and heat for about 20 minutes more. Serve with toothpicks or a large spoon.

Makes about 4 to 5 dozen meatballs.

NUTRI-STEP 1

Meatballs
- Decrease the ground beef to 1¾ pounds.
- Omit the 2 large eggs and USE 1 large egg plus 2 large egg whites.
- Decrease the salt to ½ teaspoon.
- Increase the bread crumbs to 1¼ cups and USE whole wheat bread crumbs.
- Omit the lowfat milk and USE skim milk or water.

Sauce
- Decrease the brown sugar to 1½ tablespoons.
- Decrease the vinegar to 1½ tablespoons.

APRICOT OR PEACH SMOOTHIE

Although this drink is very thick and rich tasting, it's low in fat and calories. And it takes only seconds to prepare.

1	16-ounce can juice-packed apricots or peaches •
½	cup lowfat milk •
1	cup orange juice •
2	teaspoons lemon juice
1	tablespoon honey •
1	medium-sized ripe banana, cut into chunks
¼	teaspoon vanilla extract
4 or 5	sprigs of fresh mint (optional)

In a blender container or food processor (in batches, if necessary), combine the apricots including their can juice, milk, orange juice, lemon juice, honey, banana, and vanilla. Blend or process until very smooth, then refrigerate until cold. Shake well before pouring into glasses to serve. If desired, float a sprig of mint on each serving.

Makes 4 to 5 servings.

NUTRI-STEP 1

- If available, SUBSTITUTE 3 unpeeled, juicy-ripe, fresh peaches or 6 unpeeled, ripe, fresh apricots for the canned ones.
- Omit the lowfat milk and SUBSTITUTE skim milk.
- If using fresh fruit, increase the orange juice to 1¼ cups.
- Decrease the honey to 1 to 2 teaspoons (to taste) or omit.

STRAWBERRY–PINEAPPLE DELIGHT

This refreshing and nourishing drink is a magnificent, natural pink color—a perfect way to use some strawberries when they are in season.

2	cups sliced, hulled strawberries
1½	cups unsweetened pineapple juice
2	cups commercial buttermilk, as fresh as possible
1½	tablespoons sugar (or less to taste, if strawberries are sweet) •
½	teaspoon vanilla extract
	Extra sliced strawberries, for garnish

In a blender container or food processor (in batches, if necessary), combine the 2 cups sliced strawberries, pineapple juice, buttermilk, sugar, and vanilla. Blend or process until almost smooth; a few tiny pieces of strawberry will remain. Refrigerate until very cold. Shake well before pouring into tall, clear glasses to serve. Garnish each serving with a few extra strawberry slices floating on top.

Makes 4 to 5 servings.

NUTRI-STEP 1

- Decrease the sugar to 1 tablespoon or less. If the strawberries are very sweet, omit the sugar.

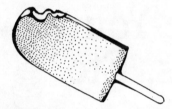

ORANGE-YOGURT POPS

- 1   **cup plain lowfat yogurt**
- 1   **6-ounce can frozen orange juice concentrate**
- 1   **medium-sized banana, cut into chunks**
- ½   **teaspoon vanilla extract**
- 1   **tablespoon sugar •**
- 5 or 6   **ice cubes**

Combine all the ingredients except the ice cubes in a blender container and process until puréed. With the blender on, add the ice cubes one at a time through the opening in the container top, blending well after each cube is added. Continue blending until the ice cubes are completely puréed.

Pour the mixture into popsicle forms or small paper cups, and freeze for 3 or 4 hours before serving. If desired, popsicle sticks can be inserted in the paper cups when mixture is partially frozen. If popsicle sticks have been used, peel off the paper cup before eating. If popsicle sticks are unavailable, thaw treats slightly and serve with spoons.

Makes 5 to 6 pops or slushes.

NUTRI-STEP 1

- Omit the sugar.

Chapter 17

Make-Your-Own Mixes, Etc.

By preparing the foods and condiments in this chapter, rather than purchasing ready-made products, you'll have more control over the amount of fat, salt, sugar, and potentially harmful additives your family consumes. And you can even increase their intake of nutrients.

For instance, our homemade sausage has no nitrate or nitrite, and the fat and salt are cut down considerably. Our tasty condiments are lower in salt than most pre-packaged ones; our whipped topping has almost no fat, though it is high in protein and calcium. Our convenient buttermilk pancake mix is free of chemical additives, yet much higher in protein and fiber than comparable commercial versions.

Also, some innovative recipes in this chapter enable you to try nutritious spreads such as pear butter and yogurt cheese (a lowfat substitute for cream cheese), which you can't find on most supermarket shelves.

ITALIAN-STYLE COATING MIX

This easy-to-make coating mix is handy for "oven-frying" both fish and chicken. (See our Crusty Italian-seasoned Oven-fried Chicken and Oven-fried Fish.)

1½ cups coarsely cubed, slightly stale white bread (preferably crusty French- or Italian-style bread)
1½ cups coarsely cubed, slightly stale whole wheat bread
3   tablespoons grated Parmesan cheese •
1½ tablespoons instant minced onions
1   tablespoon dried parsley flakes
2   teaspoons dried oregano leaves
½   teaspoon dried marjoram leaves
¼   teaspoon black pepper, preferably freshly ground
¼   teaspoon dry mustard
    Scant ⅛ teaspoon cayenne pepper
½   teaspoon salt •

Combine all the ingredients in a blender or a food processor fitted with a steel blade. Process until the bread is finely crumbed. Store the coating mix in the refrigerator, in an airtight container, for up to 2 weeks. The coating mix may also be frozen for up to 3 months.

Makes enough crumb mix to coat about 3 pounds of chicken or fish.

NUTRI-STEP 1

- Decrease the Parmesan cheese to 2 tablespoons.
- Decrease the salt to ¼ teaspoon.

ENRICHED BUTTERMILK PANCAKE MIX

Use this mixture to prepare the pancakes on page 237.

2¾ cups enriched all-purpose white or unbleached flour •
1   cup quick-cooking rolled oats
¾   cup whole wheat flour •
¼   cup soy flour (if unavailable, substitute ¼ cup whole wheat flour)
3   tablespoons baking soda
1   teaspoon baking powder
1   tablespoon sugar •
½   teaspoon ground cinnamon
1   teaspoon salt •

Combine all the ingredients in a container with a tight-fitting lid. Shake until blended. Store in the refrigerator or freezer.

Makes about 5 cups of mix, or 70 to 80 medium-sized pancakes.

NUTRI-STEP 1

- Decrease the white flour to 2½ cups.
- Increase the whole wheat flour to 1 cup.
- Decrease the sugar to 1½ teaspoons.
- Decrease the salt to ¾ teaspoon.

ALL-PURPOSE LOW-SALT SEASONING MIX

The following low-salt seasoning mix makes a good substitute for plain salt. It takes only a few minutes to make ahead and can be kept on hand to season eggs, meat, or chicken. You can even combine it with oil and vinegar for a tangy salad dressing.

2	teaspoons onion powder
¼	teaspoon black pepper, preferably freshly ground
½	teaspoon garlic powder
1	teaspoon dry mustard
1	teaspoon paprika
½	teaspoon dried thyme leaves
½	teaspoon celery seed
2	teaspoons dried basil leaves
½	teaspoon parsley flakes
½	teaspoon ground marjoram
½	teaspoon curry powder (optional)
¾	teaspoon salt ●■▲

Combine all the ingredients in a small jar. Cover the jar tightly and shake to mix well.

NUTRI-STEP 1

- Decrease the salt to ½ teaspoon.

- Decrease the salt to ¼ teaspoon.

NUTRI-STEP 3

▲ Omit the salt.

GINGER–PEAR BUTTER

  8   **cups, peeled, cored, and sliced ripe pears** ●■
  4   **cups water**
1⅓ **cups sugar** ●■
  1   **teaspoon ground ginger**

Coarsely chop the sliced pears in a food processor or by hand. Combine the chopped pears, water, sugar, and ginger in a medium-sized saucepan. Bring to a boil over high heat. Cover, lower the heat, and simmer gently for about 3 hours. Stir the mixture occasionally to prevent sticking and burning. Remove the pot cover, raise the heat slightly, and, stirring frequently, allow the mixture to cook down to a thick consistency, about 45 minutes. (As the pear butter thickens, the heat may have to be lowered to prevent splattering.) To check for proper consistency, place a half teaspoonful of the butter on a plate. Only a small amount of liquid should run out of the butter. (The butter will thicken slightly after it cools.) Ladle the thickened butter into sterilized jars, leaving ½ inch of headroom at the top. Cover loosely with sterilized lids. When the butter has cooled, tighten the lids. Store the cooled jars in the freezer until needed. The butter will keep well in the freezer for up to 2 years. Opened jars will keep in the refrigerator for 3 to 4 weeks.
   Makes about 5½ cups.

NUTRI-STEP 1

- Leave the pears unpeeled.
- Decrease the sugar to 1¼ cups.

NUTRI-STEP 2

- Leave the pears unpeeled.
- Decrease the sugar to 1 cup.

SPICY PEARSAUCE

Naturally sweet and high in fiber, pears make a delicious sauce.

⅔   cup water
3   tablespoons sugar •
¾   teaspoon ground ginger
4   cups peeled, cored, and coarsely chopped or ground fully ripe pears
     (about 7 or 8 medium) •

Combine all the ingredients in a medium-sized saucepan over medium heat. Bring to a boil, stirring. Lower the heat, cover, and simmer for 25 to 30 minutes. Cool slightly. For chopped pears, purée in a blender for about 5 seconds, or until smooth. With ground pears, the sauce should be fairly smooth. Store, covered, in the refrigerator for up to 1 week. Serve at room temperature or chilled.
     Makes 4 cups.

NUTRI-STEP 1

- Decrease the sugar to 2 tablespoons.
- Leave the pears unpeeled. (Peel will be virtually undetectable if pears are very finely ground before cooking or puréed well after cooking.)

CHUNKY APPLE BUTTER

This tangy apple butter has far less sugar than conventional jam or jelly, yet it's wonderfully satisfying on biscuits or toast. Because the sugar content is low, we keep it in the freezer for long-term storage and remove individual jars as needed.

8   cups cooking apples, peeled, cored, and sliced •■
4   cups water
1⅓   cups sugar •■
1   teaspoon ground cinnamon
½   teaspoon ground cloves
¼   teaspoon ground allspice

Combine the apples, water, sugar, and spices in a large saucepan. Bring to a boil over high heat. Cover, lower the heat, and simmer gently for about 3 hours. Stir the mixture occasionally to prevent sticking and burning. Remove the pot cover, raise the heat slightly, and, stirring frequently, allow the mixture to cook down to a thick consistency, about 45 minutes. (As the apple butter thickens, the heat may have to be lowered to prevent splattering.) To check for correct consistency, place a half teaspoonful of apple butter on a plate. Only a small amount of liquid should run out of the butter. (The butter will thicken slightly after it cools.) Ladle the thickened butter into sterilized jars, leaving ½ inch of headroom at the top. Cover loosely with sterilized lids. When the butter has cooled, tighten the lids. The butter will keep well in the freezer for up to 2 years. Opened jars will keep in the refrigerator for about a month.

Makes 5½ cups.

NUTRI-STEP 1

- Leave the apples unpeeled. Chop the apples in a food processor or by hand before cooking.
- Decrease the sugar to 1¼ cups.

NUTRI-STEP 2

- Leave the apples unpeeled. Chop the apples in a food processor or by hand before cooking.
- Decrease the sugar to 1 cup.

COCKTAIL SAUCE

½	cup tomato sauce
¼	teaspoon chili powder, or to taste
1	teaspoon prepared horseradish
	Scant ½ teaspoon sugar ●
⅛	teaspoon salt ●
1 or 2	drops hot pepper sauce (optional)

In a small bowl, combine all the ingredients and mix to blend well. Chill for several hours before serving so that the flavors can blend. The cocktail sauce will keep for about 2 weeks in the refrigerator.

Makes about ½ cup.

NUTRI-STEP 1

- Decrease the sugar to ¼ teaspoon.
- Omit the salt.

TARTAR SAUCE

Our homemade tartar sauce still has savory flavor and zip and goes well with our Oven-fried Fish (page 182).

¼ cup mayonnaise •
2½ tablespoons plain lowfat yogurt
3 tablespoons finely chopped sweet gherkin pickle
3 tablespoons finely chopped dill pickle •
2 teaspoons apple cider vinegar
½ teaspoon instant minced onions
¼ teaspoon dry mustard
Generous ⅛ teaspoon dried dillweed
Generous ⅛ teaspoon black pepper, preferably freshly ground

Stir all the ingredients together in a small bowl or glass jar until well blended. Cover and refrigerate for 30 minutes or, preferably, 1 hour to allow flavors to blend. Stir before serving. Tartar sauce will keep, refrigerated, for 4 or 5 days.
Makes about ¾ cup.

NUTRI-STEP 1

- Decrease the mayonnaise to 3 tablespoons.
- Decrease the chopped dill pickle to 2 tablespoons. *And add* 1½ tablespoons finely chopped celery to the sauce along with the other ingredients.

BARBECUE SAUCE

Make your own tangy barbecue sauce, and avoid the high salt, sugar, and fat of commercial preparations. This delicious all-purpose sauce is excellent on chicken, hamburgers, or pork.

1 15-ounce can tomato sauce
2 tablespoons packed light or dark brown sugar •■
1 tablespoon plus 1 teaspoon apple cider vinegar •■
1 teaspoon lemon juice
½ teaspoon dry mustard
⅛ teaspoon garlic powder
2 teaspoons instant minced onions

¼   teaspoon salt ●■
3 or 4 drops hot pepper sauce (or to taste)
⅛   teaspoon ground cloves
      Generous pinch of black pepper, preferably freshly ground

Combine all the ingredients in a small bowl or glass jar. Stir to combine thoroughly. May be stored in the refrigerator for up to 2 weeks or the freezer for longer storage.
Makes about 2 cups.

NUTRI-STEP 1
• Decrease the brown sugar to 5 teaspoons. • Decrease the vinegar to 1 tablespoon. • Decrease the salt to ⅛ teaspoon.
NUTRI-STEP 2
■ Decrease the brown sugar to 4 teaspoons. ■ Decrease the vinegar to 2 teaspoons. ■ Omit the salt.

BLENDED HERB VINEGAR

This recipe and the one that follows have no Nutri-Steps since they're already completely free of salt, sugar, and fat.

1   16-ounce bottle apple cider vinegar
1   clove garlic, peeled and coarsely chopped
4 or 5 whole black peppercorns
3 or 4 sprigs fresh parsley, each about 4 inches long
1   bay leaf
½   teaspoon dried thyme leaves

Combine all the ingredients in a medium-sized enamel, glass, or stainless steel pot over medium heat. (Iron or aluminum will affect the taste of the final product.) Stir to make sure all herbs and seasonings are immersed in vinegar.

Heat until very warm, but DO NOT boil. Remove the pan from the heat and allow the mixture to cool. When cool, ladle or funnel the vinegar and all the herbs and seasonings into the original vinegar bottle. Cap the bottle, label, and date. Set aside at room temperature. The herbs should remain in the vinegar for at least 2 weeks to allow the flavors to blend. After that, they can be strained out, if desired. Vinegar keeps well for at least 1 year at room temperature.
Makes 1 pint.

MILD HERB VINEGAR

        1   16-ounce bottle apple cider vinegar or red wine vinegar
        4   pieces of fresh green onion (scallion) top, each about 4 inches long,
             or 10 fresh chive sprigs, each about 5 inches long
        1   teaspoon dried basil leaves
   3 or 4   sprigs fresh parsley, each about 4 inches long

Follow the directions for Blended Herb Vinegar above.
   Makes 1 pint.

HOMEMADE SAUSAGE PATTIES

There are several good reasons for preparing these easy sausage patties at home. For one thing, you can season them with plain table salt and avoid nitrate/nitrite compounds. Also, you can use lean meat cuts, and thus control the fat content. In addition, it's often possible to save money with homemade patties; commercial ones generally cost much more per pound.

   1½   pounds moderately lean, coarsely ground pork, preferably from fresh
        shoulder
    ¼   cup water
   1¾   teaspoons salt •
   1½   teaspoons dried sage leaves, crumbled
    ½   teaspoon dried thyme leaves
    ¼   teaspoon black pepper, preferably freshly ground
    ⅛   teaspoon dried (hot) red pepper flakes

Combine all the sausage ingredients in a medium-sized bowl. Mix with your hands or a fork until the seasonings are evenly distributed throughout the meat. (If you wish to sample a bit of sausage and correct the seasonings during preparation, remember that the meat MUST BE thoroughly cooked first. Also keep in mind that the flavors will intensify slightly as the sausage is stored.) Divide and roll the sausage mixture into 16 or 17 balls. Flatten the balls to form 3½-inch-diameter patties. Patties may now be cooked immediately, wrapped and refrigerated up to 12 hours, or frozen up to 2 months.

   To freeze the sausage patties, lay, slightly separated, on wax paper-lined baking sheets. Cover the baking sheets lightly with plastic wrap or foil, and place in the freezer. When the patties are frozen solid, remove them from the baking sheets and store, frozen, in heavy plastic bags. Before cooking, thaw the desired number of patties for several hours at room temperature or overnight in the refrigerator.

To cook the patties, put them in a heavy skillet over medium-high heat. Cook, without turning, about 5 minutes, until browned on one side; adjust the heat as necessary to prevent burning. Carefully loosen the patties from the pan bottom with a spatula (pancake turner), turn over, and cook for 5 minutes more. Lower the heat to medium. Loosen the patties from the pan bottom and continue cooking, turning occasionally to ensure even browning, about 15 minutes longer, or until the meat is cooked completely through. Transfer the patties to paper towels, and let drain for 3 to 4 minutes before serving.

Makes 16 or 17 3-inch-diameter (cooked) sausage patties.

NUTRI-STEP 1

- Decrease the salt to 1½ teaspoons.

CREAMY YOGURT CHEESE

This can be substituted for cream cheese as a spread and as an ingredient in many recipes. It has a texture similar to whipped cream cheese, although it is a bit tangier. It has only about a third of the calories of cream cheese and about a tenth of the fat.

2   **cups plain lowfat or regular yogurt ●**
    Pinch of salt (optional)
    Your choice of finely minced fresh herbs to taste, such as parsley, dillweed, tarragon, or chervil (optional)

Rinse several layers of clean cheesecloth (about 12 inches square) in running water; then squeeze dry. Line a large sieve or strainer (or the bottom of a colander) with the layers of cheesecloth. Spoon the yogurt into the center of the cheesecloth; then tie the corners together to form a pouch, or secure them together with a rubber band. Set the strainer over a bowl, and let the yogurt drain in the refrigerator overnight or until it is the consistency of whipped cream cheese. (Do not squeeze the cheesecloth bag; just let it drip undisturbed.) The longer the yogurt drains, the drier and sharper the yogurt cheese will taste.

Plain, unseasoned yogurt cheese may be eaten as is or seasoned for spreading on sandwiches, crackers, etc. To season, mix in salt (if desired) and herbs.

Makes about 1 cup.

NUTRI-STEP 1

- Omit the regular yogurt and USE lowfat yogurt.

"DON'T-TELL-'EM-IT'S-GOOD-FOR-'EM" WHIPPED TOPPING

Here is a whipped "cream" to be enjoyed without any pangs of guilt since it has almost no fat, compared to the approximately 45 grams of fat per cup of real whipped cream. And it is high in protein. It can be used as a topping for desserts, or as an ingredient in mousses and similar cold concoctions.

½   cup instant nonfat dry milk powder
½   cup ice-cold water
2   tablespoons water
1   teaspoon plain gelatin (about half the contents of 1 packet of gelatin)
1   teaspoon lemon juice
2   tablespoons plain lowfat or regular yogurt (or commercial buttermilk) •
½   teaspoon vanilla extract
2½ tablespoons sugar •

Sprinkle the milk powder over the ice-cold water; then stir to mix well. Place in the freezer for a short while, just until crystals begin to form around the edges of the milk mixture.

Meanwhile, put the 2 tablespoons of water in a small, heatproof metal or glass cup, and sprinkle the gelatin on top. Place cup in a small skillet or saucepan which contains simmering water about ¾ inch deep. Gently heat the gelatin mixture until it is clear and the gelatin is dissolved. Remove from the heat and cool to tepid.

Remove the milk mixture from the freezer and transfer it to a large mixing bowl. Beat at high speed with an electric mixer until soft peaks form (about 5 minutes or longer). Then gradually beat in the lemon juice, yogurt, and dissolved gelatin. Continue beating until very stiff peaks form. Beat in the vanilla extract and sugar until completely combined. Use the topping immediately, or chill until serving time.

Chilled topping will keep for several hours, up to overnight; however, it should be handled gently, as it tends to "deflate" if stirred vigorously after chilling. (For the very best texture, rebeat the chilled topping to stiff peaks shortly before serving. When the topping is re-beaten after chilling, its final volume decreases but the texture becomes more dense and whipped cream-like than after just one beating.)

Makes about 2 to 3 cups.

NUTRI-STEP 1

- Omit the regular yogurt and USE lowfat yogurt or buttermilk.
- Decrease the sugar to 2 tablespoons.

Appendix

H ere are some easy substitutions to help you quickly improve the nutritional value of the food you prepare. Simply replace less healthful ingredients in the LEFT column with more healthful ones from the RIGHT column. Use equivalent amounts unless otherwise indicated.

REPLACE:

WITH:

1 cup whole milk	1 cup lowfat milk
	1 cup skim milk
	$\frac{1}{3}$ cup instant nonfat dry milk powder plus scant 1 cup water
part of the mayonnaise in salads or dressings	sour cream
sour cream in baked goods	plain yogurt

REPLACE:	WITH:
part of the sour cream in salads or dressings	plain yogurt
regular yogurt	lowfat yogurt
regular creamed cottage cheese	lowfat cottage cheese
powdered coffee whitener	instant nonfat dry milk powder
part of the white flour in baked goods	whole wheat flour
part of the sugar in baked goods	fruit juice concentrate
	puréed fruit
cooked white rice	cooked brown rice (follow package directions)
	cooked bulgur (page 100)
	cooked millet (page 100)
	cooked buckwheat groats (page 100)
1 whole egg	2 egg whites (except for custards)
2 whole eggs	3 egg whites (except for custards)
salt as a seasoning	lemon juice (to taste)
	herb and spice mixture (to taste)
	extra ground black pepper (to taste)
about a fourth to a third of the ground beef in a recipe	ground up (or very finely chopped) fresh vegetables, such as broccoli (including stems) and carrots
flour and butter as a soup thickener	shredded raw potatoes cooked with soup
white bread crumbs	whole wheat bread crumbs made in the blender or food processor
regular croutons	whole wheat croutons made from cubed and toasted whole wheat bread
jam on a sandwich or as a flavoring for yogurt	low-sugar Apple Butter (page 290)
	low-sugar Pear Butter (page 289)
whipped cream	Whipped Topping (page 296)
	whipped evaporated milk
cream cheese as a spread	Yogurt Cheese (page 295)
plain unsweetened cocoa powder	"dark-style" carob powder
grated hard or semi-soft cheese	grated, shredded, or very finely chopped, lowfat or part-skim (hard or semi-soft) cheese
butter, margarine, or oil for greasing a baking pan or casserole	nonstick vegetable spray, preferably in a pump-style (not aerosol) bottle
fatty cuts of beef	lean cuts of beef, such as round, sirloin tip, chuck arm, standing rump, flank, lean ground beef
fatty cuts of lamb	lean cuts of lamb, such as leg, shank, loin

REPLACE:	WITH:
fatty cuts of pork	lean cuts of pork, such as loin, fresh ham, fresh shoulder (picnic), tenderloin
thinly sliced veal scallops	thinly sliced raw turkey breast
canned vegetables (especially those packed in salted water)	fresh or frozen vegetables
high-salt commercial bouillon or broth	low-salt homemade broth highly seasoned with herbs
	low-salt (or unsalted) commercial bouillon
commercial potato chips, salted nuts, and similar high-salt, high-fat snacks	unbuttered, unsalted (or very lightly salted) popcorn
	homemade crackers (pages 269–272)
	cut-up raw vegetables, such as carrots, green peppers, and celery
	fresh fruit

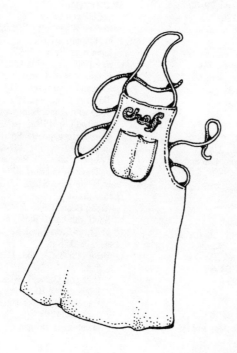

Index